D1235840

War and Peace

in the 20th Century and Beyond

Proceedings of the Nobel Centennial Symposium

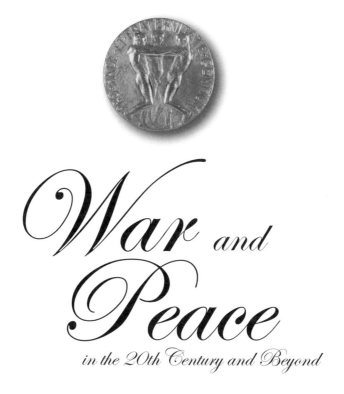

War and Peace

in the 20th Century and Beyond

editors

Geir Lundestad and Olav Njølstad

World Scientific
New Jersey • London • Singapore • Hong Kong

Published in 2002 by

World Scientific Publishing Co. Pte. Ltd.

5 Toh Tuck Link, Singapore 596224

USA office: Suite 202, 1060 Main Street, River Edge, NJ 07661

UK office: 57 Shelton Street, Covent Garden, London WC2H 9HE

British Library Cataloguing-in-Publication Data
A catalogue record for this book is available from the British Library.

WAR AND PEACE IN THE 20TH CENTURY AND BEYOND
Proceedings of the Nobel Centennial Symposium

ISBN 981-238-196-1
ISBN 981-238-197-X (pbk)

Printed in Singapore by Mainland Press

Contents

Notes on Contributors

Dr. Michael W. Doyle
*Edward S. Sanford Professor of Politics and International Affairs,
Princeton University*

Dr. Louise Fawcett
*Wilfred Knapp Fellow and Tutor in Politics at St. Catherine's College,
Oxford University*

Dr. Eric Hobsbawm
*Fellow of the British Academy and Professor (Emeritus) of History
at Birkbeck College, University of London*

Dr. Akira Iriye
*Charles Warren Professor of American History at Harvard
University*

Dr. Mary H. Kaldor
*Principal Research Fellow and Programme Director, Centre for the
Study of Global Governance, London School of Economics*

Kim Dae-jung
President, the Republic of Korea

Dr. Mahmood Mamdani
Herbert Lehman Professor of Government and Director, Institute of African Studies, Columbia University

Dr. Geir Lundestad
Director, the Norwegian Nobel Institute and Associate Professor of History, University of Oslo

Dr. Joseph S. Nye
Professor of Political Science and Dean, John F. Kennedy School of Government, Harvard University

Dr. Olav Njølstad
Research Director, the Norwegian Nobel Institute

Dr. Amartya Sen
Professor of Economics at Trinity College, University of Cambridge (UK), and the 1998 Nobel Prize winner in Economic Sciences

War and Peace

in the 20th Century and Beyond

Geir Lundestad & Olav Njølstad

Introduction: The Conflicts of the 20th Century and the Solutions for the 21st Century

In December 2001 the Nobel prizes celebrated their 100th anniversary. When Alfred Nobel, the Swedish inventor of dynamite among many other things, died in 1896 he left a will stating that most of his great wealth should go to the prizes in physics, chemistry, medicine, literature, and peace that were to bear his name. The first four prizes were to be awarded by Swedish institutions while the peace prize was to be awarded by "a committee of five persons to be elected by the Norwegian Storting". The peace prize was to go to the person "who shall have done the most or the best work for fraternity between nations, for the abolition or reduction of standing armies and for the holding or promotion of peace congresses".

The Nobel Peace Prize has been called "the most prestigious prize in the world". Its announcement in October of each year leads to comments from presidents, prime ministers and leading newspapers in many different parts of the world. Representatives of many of the other more than 300 peace prizes come to the Nobel Institute in Oslo to try to find out what the secrets of the success of the Nobel Peace Prize are.

There is no single secret behind the Nobel Peace Prize. Its prestige probably flows from its long history, it belonging to the Nobel family of prizes where all members of the family gain from the relationship, the respectable, but far from perfect record the Norwegian Nobel Committee has compiled in selecting the peace laureates, the flexibility of the Committee in adapting to new concerns and interests, and possibly the substantial monetary amount of the Nobel prizes. (10 million Swedish kronor in 2001, or almost one million dollars.)

For the 100th anniversary the Norwegian Nobel Committee invited all living Peace Prize laureates to come to Oslo for almost a week of celebration during December 6–11th. The first part of the week was taken up by the Committee's Centennial Symposium under the heading "The Conflicts of the 20th Century and the Solutions for the 21st Century". The celebration of the Peace Prize laureates of 2001, the United Nations and its Secretary General Kofi Annan, constituted the second part of the week.

About 30 out of a possible 39 Peace Prize laureates came to Oslo for the entire week or for parts of it. 36 of the laureates had actually accepted the Nobel Committee's invitation to attend, but illnesses and the difficult situation in the Middle East made for some unfortunate last-minute cancellations. For the symposium the Nobel laureates were joined by a group of distinguished academics. The division of labor was that the academics would be responsible primarily for the analysis of the past while the Nobel laureates would present their views and recommendations for the future.

The Centennial Symposium was divided into nine main sessions, with one academic and several laureates speaking during each session. Then there was free and even spirited debate among the participants. The symposium attracted a great deal of media attention. The entire symposium was webcast by the Nobel Electronic Museum (NeM) and the tapes are available on the Nobel website nobelprize.org (previously nobel.se). On the television side CNN had a 90 minute program where all the laureates participated. Many other television stations also presented extensive reports from the symposium, including interviews with many of the laureates.

Naturally, the media's primary interest was on the Nobel laureates. The laureates have their strength in speaking forcefully on their respective matters of concern. In this sense their contributions were best enjoyed there and then. Many of them also spoke without extensive written manuscripts. Most of their presentations are nevertheless available from the Norwegian Nobel Institute in their written form or electronically on www.nobel.no. In this book, therefore, we have decided to focus on the papers of the group of academics. The analyses of such a distinguished group clearly deserved a much wider audience than simply those who were invited to take part in the symposium. After the symposium all the academics had the chance to revise their papers in the light of the discussion there. What is published here, then, are these revised contributions.

We have, however, in addition chosen to include the contribution of the Nobel laureate of 2000, Kim Dae-jung, the President of South Korea. Kim was the introductory speaker at the symposium and his wide-ranging remarks set the tone for the discussions that followed. The remarks also provide insight into the thinking of a truly remarkable individual, able to combine long-range perspectives with concrete political attitudes and initiatives.

Kim Dae-jung was awarded the Nobel Peace Prize for the year 2000 for his human rights policies and for his Sunshine Policy towards North Korea. In his contribution "Dialogue and Cooperation to Achieve World Peace" he sees two main reasons for the many bloody conflicts of the 20th century, nationalism and ideology. The ethnic-national dimension is still with us, and is most dramatically expressed in the Middle East. The ideological dimension, particularly in the form of the Cold War, has almost disappeared, although a last remnant is found on the Korean peninsula in the still difficult relationship between North and South Korea, a relationship Kim has worked so hard to improve. He also discusses the background of his Sunshine Policy and, despite recent setbacks, expresses his hope that the policy will continue to bring positive results for the people of Korea.

Kim sketches the tremendous economic and technological progress that the world has enjoyed from the birth of human species and the emergence of agrarian civilizations some 10,000 years ago and culminating in the information revolution of the 21st century, called the sixth epochal event in Kim's scheme of history. Globalization has the potential to improve the material situation for so many of the world's citizens, but it also presents a huge challenge in the form of the digital divide, a divide that threatens to widen the gap between the rich and poor. Kim argues that "We cannot guarantee world peace in the 21st century unless there is a resolution of the gap between rich and poor". Terrorism should not be seen as an isolated phenomenon, but related to this gap. At the same time he reaffirms his belief in the universality of democracy and human rights. The laureate is convinced that "when the problems of the poor are resolved and democracy is put into practice, world peace in the 21st century will be possible, and all mankind will be safe and happy. More than anyone, we, the Nobel Peace laureates, must take the lead in such efforts".

In his chapter "War and Peace in the 20th Century", Eric Hobsbawm comes to rather bleak conclusions. The 20th century was the most murderous century in recorded history. The total deaths caused by or associated with its wars have been estimated at 187 million. (Kim Dae-jung set this number at 110 million. No one will of course be able to estimate this number with any degree of certainty.) Although some regions have been peaceful for very long periods of time, a war has been going on somewhere in the world in virtually every year of the 20th century. The thirty years of the First and the Second World War, then we add in the inter-war years, and the forty years of the Cold War dominated most of the century. Civilian casualties have been rising rapidly both in terms of direct casualties and in the form of refugees, civil wars are becoming increasingly numerous, and the use of force is no longer a monopoly for the government. Separatist tendencies exist within many nation-states with attendant risks of destabilization.

To improve this rather miserable record, the world needs some form of global authority, but no such effective authority is in sight, argues Hobsbawm. Some progress has been made in international law, but the world is clearly a long way from such law limiting the freedom of action of the Great Powers. No new world order can be seen on the horizon to provide for greater stability. Unilateral interventions can be (more or less) helpful, but Hobsbawm thinks that it remains unclear whether a general model for the future control of armed conflict can emerge from such improvizations. The dramatic growth of social and economic inequality within as well as between countries is definitely an element undermining peace.

The comments during the symposium on Hobsbawm's contribution indicated that some felt that his analysis of the 20th century might have been overly pessimistic. While possibly the most murderous century in history in absolute numbers, in relative terms there have probably been even more terrible ones, particularly the 17th century. Even in the relatively peaceful 19th century there were bigger or smaller conflicts virtually every year, even inside the British empire. Despite the many conflicts, certain underlying factors pointed in the direction of greater optimism as far as peace and stability were concerned. Democracy was spreading, particularly towards the end of the century; economic conditions were improving in great parts of the world.

Hobsbawm offers the only marginally optimistic forecast that "War in the 21st century is not likely to be as murderous as in the 20th". Since his task was to analyze the past, not to make predictions about the future, he does not offer any reasons for his rather tempered optimism. It appears, however, that Great Power wars have become increasingly unlikely. They are simply too dangerous and too costly. Still, China could become involved in a war over Taiwan and India and Pakistan have gone to war three times already. With the Cold War over, the Great Powers should also be less tempted to intervene in all kinds of local conflicts around the world. Along the same lines, the number of interstate conflicts has become quite low. On the other hand, civil wars have taken on added prominence and the number of failed states would seem to be increasing, in part because the Great Powers are no longer so interested in keeping their partners in power, particularly not in Africa, but primarily because of difficult political, economic, and cultural conditions in many parts of the world.

Michael W. Doyle has been in the very forefront of the growing international debate on the peaceful effects of democracy. In his contribution "Ideologies and Policies: Liberal Democracy and National Dictatorship in Peace and War", he starts off by repeating the general argument that liberty and democracy make for peace while nationalism and dictatorship make for war. Then, however, he goes on to discuss when and how liberty and democracy can bring about war and nationalism and dictatorship stimulate peace. Some realist and even other theorists of world politics claim that domestic regimes make little difference for the foreign policy of states. Properties of the international system, the offensive versus defensive nature of weapons, etc. are the determining factors. Dictators may also be reluctant to go to war exactly because of the domestic fragility of their countries; wars may be lost or coups encouraged. On the democracy side, Doyle reminds us that from Thucydides to Machiavelli, popular government, rather than being a force for peace, was seen as the ideal foundation for imperial power. A free society allows for an "adventurous spirit" to rule, producing a popular willingness to take risks. Democracies can also be tempted in various ways to intervene against dictatorships.

Still, Doyle reverts to the general conclusion that democracies are indeed peaceful towards other democracies. Towards non-liberal states democracies have much more of a mixed record. Liberal states have been attacked by non-liberal states, but they have also gone on the attack themselves. The best examples are the many colonial wars initiated by various more of less democratic, but still imperial powers. Doyle discusses the qualifications that Kant attached to the peaceful nature of liberal states and finds that they are still valid. While majority rule may be a necessary condition of a state of peace, it is not a sufficient condition. Autarky and nationalism can undermine democratic liberal peace. The liberal peace, far from being automatic, will require both moral politics and prudent statesmanship. Thus, Doyle, who initially did more than anyone to resurrect Kant's claims about the peaceful nature of liberal states, has been surpassed by a whole array of scholars in being rather absolutist about the peaceful nature of democracies.

As so often, much depends on how we define the key terms. If "democracy" is defined very stringently, it is indeed difficult to find examples of a democracy going to war against another democracy. At the same time it is easy to find examples of change in a more democratic direction leading to greater, not more limited conflict. One thinks of the situation in the former Yugoslavia and even in the

Caucasus. No doubt the regimes in power in these regions are more democratic than their predecessors, but there has definitely been more conflict that there was during the Cold War when Tito and the Soviet leaders ruled with a dictatorial hand.

To the extent that there is a connection between democracy and peace, and there certainly seems to be, although probably not so simple and straightforward as sometimes alleged, the spread of democracy after 1945 should give reason to optimism about the state of the world in the 21st century. So should freer trade between nations in that this too appears to strengthen peace. With the collapse of Communism in Russia and Eastern and Central Europe, for the first time in history more than half the world's population lives under some form of democratic rule. Democracy has also made great progress in virtually all of Latin America, in the most rapidly developing countries in Asia, and, much more modestly, even in a few countries in Africa. China and most of the Muslim world constitute most of the non-democratic parts of the world. Compared to the tenuous state of democracy in the period up to the Second World War this is dramatic progress indeed.

In his contribution "Making Sense of Violence in Postcolonial Africa" Mahmood Mamdani distinguishes between, on the one hand, revolutionary and counter-revolutionary violence which arises from market-based identities such as class and non-revolutionary random violence on the other. On the local level we often refer to the latter type as communal or ethnic, on the world scale we call them clashes of civilization. Revolutionary violence appears to make sense and is apparently easily explained by historians, the non-revolutionary types seem to stand "outside historical time". It is the latter that provides the focus for Mamdani's essay.

The two examples of such violence seemingly devoid of meaning that Mamdani deals with are the Holocaust and the Rwandan genocide. He follows Hannah Arendt in insisting on locating the Holocaust in the history of genocide. Imperialism provided many such examples: The natives of Tasmania, the Maoris of New Zealand, the Native Americans, the Hareros of Southwest Africa, etc. Hitler was acutely aware of such examples of settlers killing natives. "The

Holocaust was the imperial chickens coming home". Rwanda was the counter-tendency, the natives annihilating the settlers' servants.

Mamdani contends that the colonial powers were fundamentalist in that they tagged non-natives as races, governed by civil law, and natives as tribes, governed by customary law. While ethnic differences existed in Africa prior to colonialism, such differences were cultural and consensual. The colonial powers made these differences political and enforced them by law. They became frozen and thereby produced conflict. This provides the setting for Mamdani's analysis of the genocide in Rwanda, where roughly 800,000 Tutsis were killed in 100 days. Again, Tutsi privilege existed before colonialism, but the Belgians provided a justification for this that made Tutsis racially and legally superior. After independence this distinction was taken over by the two groups and provided the rationale for the Rwandan Revolution of 1959 where the majority Hutu took over power and thus reversed the master-servant relationship. 1959 was actually the first time where the battle lines were drawn sharply between Hutu on one side and Tutsi on the other. The Tutsi exiles of 1959 found refuge in many countries, particularly in Uganda. The civil war of 1990–94 and the ensuing genocide was thus the result of Belgian colonialism and the racialization of the state, of the 1959 Revolution and the reinforced racialized identities, and of post-colonial crisis between Rwanda and its neighbors.

At the symposium it was argued that Mamdani might be overdoing the effects of colonialism both on the Holocaust and on the history of Rwanda. Colonialism came late in Africa's long history and it ended several decades ago. The distinction between revolutionary and non-revolutionary violence is often far from clear. They often overlap. Seeing the Hutu as simply reversing the settler-native relationship also leaves a taste of the Rwandan genocide being primarily their pursuit of political justice.

Mamdani closes his paper by arguing that "The challenge is to create a single political community and citizenship from diverse cultural and historical groups and identities". In a world that is becoming increasingly globalized the question of identity seems to become only more important. On the international level this is reflected in the debate about Samuel Huntington's provocative *The Clash of Civilizations and the Remaking of World Order*. On the local level we see this in the high number of ethnic, religious, and political conflicts in many different parts of the world. While many lose their identity in the process of globalization, others have their identities strengthened, probably in part as a direct response to the very pressures of globalization. The world is becoming increasingly complex. While many examples can be found of Huntington's clashes of civilization, many argue that some norms, for instance human rights, cut across such divides and that differences within civilizations might be so big that the term civilization itself becomes questionable.

Indeed, in his chapter "Global Inequality and Persistent Conflicts" Amartya Sen takes issue with the whole idea of civilizations. The concept is too grandiose; there is no such thing as a civilization. This is to reduce people into one dimension only, most frequently religion. We all have a plurality of identities "which cut across each other and work against sharp divisions around one uniquely hardened line of impenetrable division". Yet, in his contribution the Nobel laureate in economics focuses on what he calls "economic reductionism", i.e. the basic presumption that political conflict and economic inequality and poverty have firm causal links. While conflict frequently occurs in poor areas, Sen sees several reasons for caution before jumping into explaining hostility and carnage through poverty and privation. First, conflict does not occur in all poor countries, suggesting that other factors may also be important for the outcome. Sen sees the famine years in Ireland in the 1840s as having been among the most peaceful in modern Ireland. He also tells the story of the sight from his childhood in Calcutta of "starving people dying in front of sweet shops with various layers of luscious food displayed behind glass windows, without a single glass being broken, or law and order disrupted".

Second, Sen stresses the need to go beyond empirical observation into causal analysis. Thus, destitution can be accompanied not only by economic debility, but also by political helplessness. Suffering and inequity have often been accompanied by peace and quiet. Third, there is the question of the direction of the causality in those cases where there would appear to be a cause and effect relationship. Sen argues that "there is at least as strong a causal linkage going from war and violence to famines and destitution, than from the latter to the former". He discusses various reasons why the relationship might be rather the reverse of what is frequently assumed.

Sen takes great care to explain that poverty and massive inequality are terrible enough in themselves to provide reasons for placing priority on their removal, without any indirect causal presumption about the relationship between poverty and conflict. He also comes out strongly against the involvement of the Great Powers in the globalized trade in arms.

To bear out Sen's analysis the major conflicts of the 20th century would seem to have had little to do with poverty as such. The First World War had much more to do with the rivalry of the Great Powers, the rise of Germany, and the nationality question than with economics and poverty. The same would apply to the Second World War, although here the rise of Hitler in Germany was certainly related to Germany's *relative* economic problems during the Great Depression. Similarly the Cold War was an ideological Great Power conflict where the economic dimension was primarily tied to the question of which system could provide the greatest benefit for the greatest number. After September 11 the presumption has again been that poverty is the breeding ground of terrorism. That might certainly be the case, for instance in the Palestinian areas, but most of the Saudi Arabians that provided the core of the al Qaeda network were rather wealthy, educated, religious fanatics.

Of course all this does not mean that one should overlook the connections that may undoubtedly lead from poverty to conflict. In fact, it was argued that Sen made matters too easy for himself by concentrating on what could be seen as exceptions to this general connection. Looking at the vast number of conflicts in poor African countries, countries that were poor well before the conflicts broke out, and the lack of such armed conflicts in most rich countries it is difficult not to believe that strong connections exist. Yet, Sen's contribution makes it evident that we should definitely get away from the tendency to automatically assume that this is the only, or even the main dimension involved.

Joseph S. Nye analyzes "The Rise and Fall of Great Powers". He sees the "declinists" who in the 1970s and 1980s predicted the fall of the United States, as wrong. Clearly today the United States is the leading power in the world. Although nothing lasts forever, it is likely to remain so for some time to come. In analyzing power, Nye argues that it resembles a complex three-dimensional chess game. On the military chessboard, with the fall of the Soviet Union, power is largely unipolar. No power can rival the military strength of the United States. But on the middle economic chess board, power is multipolar with the United States and the European Union having economies of about the same size, Japan being quite important, and China's dramatic growth likely to make it reemerge as a major player early in this century. The bottom chessboard is the realm of transnational relations that cross borders outside of government control. On this bottom board, power is widely dispersed.

While many political science realists have extolled the virtues of the balance of power and see this as the most stable order, Nye argues that "a good case can be made that inequality of power can be a source of peace and stability". The balance of power was frequently unstable and shifts in power were often associated with tension and conflict. Thus, the two world wars can be related to the rise of Germany and the Cold War can be seen as the effort of the West to balance against a rising Soviet threat. The *Pax Americana*, like the *Pax Romana* and the *Pax Britannica*, on the other hand, provided relative peace and security.

It has often been assumed that the hegemony of one country leads to balancing against this hegemon. This balancing can then provide for conflict. Today there seems to be very little balancing against the United States. The reasons for this might be many: the United States is so superior to others that it would be very difficult to balance against it; the potential challengers are so diverse that it would be virtually impossible for them to form a common front against the United States; the geographical position of the U.S. is such that territorial expansion, the most threatening form of hegemony, becomes much less likely outside the Western Hemisphere; the position of the United States is founded also on soft power, a form of power that makes America attractive to other countries and often leads to other countries supporting American goals. In fact "bandwagoning", that is, joining the seemingly stronger rather than the weaker side, may follow instead of the expected balancing against the United States.

Nye assumes that the fact that the United States will continue as Number One will provide for greater stability in a complex world. This might well be so at the Great Power level. It is difficult to see that any Great Power would want to enter into an armed conflict with the United States, either directly or by promoting objectives that more indirectly could lead to a war with the United States. On the other hand, we should not assume that the U.S. will be able to guarantee peace at the regional level, for instance between, India and Pakistan. Even more important, we have witnessed time and again how limited the influence of the United States is on the myriad of local conflicts around the world. In some cases the supreme power of the United States becomes a source of conflict in itself. The terrorist attacks on New York and Washington on September 11, 2001 provide only the most recent example of this.

In her chapter "Beyond Militarism, Arms Races and Arms Control", Mary Kaldor is definitely less upbeat about the peaceful effects of American supremacy than is Joseph Nye. In the 20th century there have been two major arms races, the first before the First World War and the second after the Second World War. The first centered on the naval competition, particularly in battleships, and was an expression of growing militarism and nationalism. It was also a competition among arms companies. The arms race after 1945 focused on nuclear weapons, missiles, aircraft, and tanks. Kaldor sees this race too as to a large extent internally driven, by pressure from laboratories and defense companies. At the same time pressure from the peace movement was growing and even without the dramatic events of 1989 the West would therefore have had to reduce its nuclear arsenals.

In the aftermath of the Cold War Kaldor sees three main challenges to a peaceful world. One is the new phenomenon of armed networks of non-state and state actors that she terms Netforce (paramilitary groups, warlords, terrorist cells, fanatical volunteers, mercenaries, etc.). They could also be described as organized crime (illegal and private violence) or as massive violations of human rights (violence against civilians.) "The New American Militarism" represents the second challenge to peace and stability. Here Kaldor argues that "if September 11 had not happened, the American military-industrial complex might have had to invent it". The new threat scenarios have made it possible for the United States to increase defense spending again, with added emphasis on the research and development that is so important for the military-industrial complex. National missile defense (NMD) and the Revolution in Military Affairs (RMA) should be seen as the search for a casualty-free war, as high-tech warfare against "rogue states" sponsoring terrorists. The third challenge is represented by "neo-modern militarism", by which Kaldor means the evolution of classical military forces in large states moving towards a more open market-oriented system. Typical examples are Russia, India, and China. The type of warfare that is associated with neo-modern militarism is either limited inter-state warfare (India-Pakistan) or counter-insurgency (Chechnya, Palestine).

Peace-keeping (defined as separating sides) and peace-enforcement (taking sides) is one way to control war, although Kaldor argues that this has not lived up to expectations, partly due to the lack of resources put into such efforts. The end of the Cold War has also led to a reduction in the number of nuclear weapons and the danger of nuclear annihilation receding. Kaldor holds the largest hopes for the extension and application of international humanitarian law and human rights law (the ban on land mines, the Biological Weapons Convention, the efforts to control small arms). In line with this she argues that September 11 should have been interpreted not as a direct attack on the United States, but rather as a crime against humanity to be punished by international bodies. She ends on the pessimistic note that the world is "on the brink of a global new war, something like the wars in the Balkans or the Israel-Palestine war, on a global scale with no outsiders to constrain its course".

Needless to say, Kaldor's contribution provoked many comments. Some felt that in her historical analysis she had paid too much attention to the domestic sources of arms races and too little to international factors. This goes back to the old debate about whether arms races are actually two or more races between states or separate "autistic" races driven by domestic factors. Most likely it is not a question of either-or. Kaldor's analysis of the role of the United States clashed dramatically with the views of Joseph Nye and others and this led to spirited exchanges during the symposium. So did her pessimism about the future.

In her contribution "Rivalry over Territory and Resources and the Balance of War and Peace: The Twentieth Century", Louise Fawcett analyzes another set of important factors for peace and stability in the world. She contends that "if the nature and purpose of war has changed for some states, conflict and competition over territory and resources continue to dominate the balance of war and peace". In this perspective she sees the First and the Second World Wars as well as the Cold War to a large extent as conflicts over territory and resources. Similarly, the decolonization process was about new entities gaining control over their own territory and resources. The wars that took place outside the Cold War framework both during and after the Cold War have virtually all been related to the same dimensions. India-Pakistan, the Middle East, the Persian Gulf, the former Yugoslavia, and Central Africa are some of the geographical areas that spring to mind.

It has been argued by some, particularly by Richard Rosecrance, that conflicts over territory and resources are outdated, in that these two dimensions matter less and less for the welfare of countries integrated in a globalized economy. Countries with a very limited resource and even territorial base, such as Luxembourg, Switzerland and Japan, have become very wealthy indeed. In a global economy increasingly dominated by services and information technology, territorial and physical resources mean less and less, as opposed to human resources. Many poor countries in the South have rather strong resource bases, but this has not brought much prosperity to their citizens. (Indonesia, Nigeria, and Zimbabwe would seem to provide some examples.) Similarly there seems to be very little correlation between the size of a country's territory and its wealth.

Yet, these arguments would appear to closely resemble the arguments before the First World War about the economic interdependence of the world acting as a barrier to war. Since the various countries' economies were so closely tied together, this would make the leaders realize all they had to lose by going to war. Thus, both analyses represent examples of how leaders ought to think, unfortunately much less so of how they actually think. Although there has not been a case of *successful* territorial aggrandizement since the mid-1970s (Morocco's control over Western Sahara, Turkish control over part of Cyprus, and Indonesia's over East Timor, the last now ended), this has not prevented several new attempts to change the status quo. (Efforts to break up states have been much more successful as seen from the Soviet and the Yugoslav experiences.)

As Michael Doyle and others have pointed out, in some countries, however, conflicts over territory and resources are solved by other means than war. Among the democratic states a zone of peace has developed. One should not conclude from this that democratic states will not fight for their territories or their resources. The United States fought for the oil from the Persian Gulf, Britain for the Falklands, and Russia is mired in wars in Chechnya, although the democratic peace theory is allegedly saved by the fact that their opponents — Iraq, Argentina, and Chechnyan "separatists" — were not democracies. (In Chechnya this is doubtful in that elections were actually held there, resulting in a clear victory for the separatists.)

Finally, when Fawcett argues that "... very few conflicts have *no* territorial or resource components", it might be replied that in analyzing the causes of war territory and resources represent too much of a catch-all. The fact that territories and resources might be involved does not automatically mean that these dimensions *caused* the war in question. In some cases they may provide camouflage for more important reasons related to ideology, religion, security, or even personal factors. In virtually all major conflicts, the historical jury is still out, and will probably always be out on what caused the war in question, i.e. how all the relevant factors were related.

Akira Iriye analyzes "Misperception, Mistrust, Fear" as factors that have caused war and conflict. He takes globalization as his starting point. Globalization promoted the internationalization of certain norms, but Iriye focuses on "the persistent, even increasing, gap between material modernization and mental traditionalism (one could even call it tribalism)...." On the cultural side globalization promoted new fears. Thus, the West feared the rest of the world both when it was not modernizing and remained in a state of alleged pre-modern barbarism and when it modernized, as in the concept of the "yellow peril". While the First World War had started as a civil war among European states, the Second World War, in Iriye's analysis, began when two Asian neighbors, Japan and China, collided and when Italy, a European state, attacked Ethiopia, an African state. In Germany's conceptions of the world the distinction between Aryans and non-Aryans, especially the "floating" Jews and Roma, was basic; in the view of the Japanese they were fighting against the white rulers of Asia on behalf of the colored peoples of the world.

Efforts were certainly made to promote variants of cultural internationalism, but these had rather limited effect. In 1919 a group of European and American intellectuals issued a manifesto declaring that they would honor only one truth, "free, without frontiers, without limits, without prejudices of race or caste". After the Second World War these ideas were most eloquently expressed by the United Nations in 1948 in the Universal Declaration of Human Rights. In joining the United Nations almost 200 countries have formally committed themselves to the ideals of the Universal Declaration of Human Rights.

At the end of the 20th century more than 30,000 international non-governmental organizations existed, a truly spectacular expansion compared to the situation 100 years earlier when the number appears to have been around 100. Many of the most prominent among these organizations have received the Nobel Peace Prize: the Red Cross, Amnesty International, the Pugwash Conferences, the International Campaign to Ban Landmines, and Médecins Sans Frontières. For their efforts to generate a sense of common humanity, it is to many individuals and to such organizations "we need to pay tribute even as we recount innumerable instances of misunderstanding and hostility among nations and people. For ultimately it is the individual heart that counts". Thus, despite the many wars and tragedies of the

20th century, it can still be maintained that the world has made progress in certain areas.

Again, it is virtually impossible to separate misperception, mistrust, and fear from all the other factors discussed at the symposium. Mistrust comes from somewhere; it does not exist in a vacuum. Tribalism appears in many ways to be increasing even in today's modern world, as can be seen for instance in the growth of fundamentalism within major religions. Maybe globalization encourages us to define our tribal identities anew. Then, Sigmund Freud reminded us of the "narcissism of the small difference". Sometimes the differences that helped produce conflict did not seem to be that significant. Thus, to most outsiders differences between Serbs and Croats were not dramatic; those between Hutus and Tutsis appeared to be even smaller; differences between the clans of Somalia smaller still. If even such small differences produce conflict, what then of the future?

In the final contribution from the Nobel symposium one of the editors, Geir Lundestad, offers his reflection on "The Nobel Peace Prize in its Next Century: Old and New Dimensions". Despite the standing of the Nobel Peace Prize, very few of the issues the Prize has tried to address have been solved. Therefore the work of the Norwegian Nobel Committee will probably continue much along the same lines as in the first century of the history of the Prize. Despite the advances made in creating a better organized and more peaceful world, the world has walked only a few steps on a very long road indeed. Despite the tremendous advances democracy and human rights have made in the 20th century, substantial parts of the world still live under more or less totalitarian rule, particularly in Africa and in parts of Asia. Despite the almost incredible improvements in material conditions for most of the world's population, 1.2 billion still live on less than one dollar a day. As far as "the reduction in standing armies" in Alfred Nobel's testament is concerned, it is indeed arguable how much progress the world has seen in the 20th century. New and more dreadful weapons have been produced more or less continuously. The agreements to control these weapons have been relatively few and weak. The most notable "success" would have to be that nuclear weapons have not been used after Hiroshima and Nagasaki, despite their great number.

Thus, it seems a rather safe bet that the Norwegian Nobel Committee will continue to select laureates very much within the categories already established. The link between the environment and peace would seem to represent the best candidate for a new field. Other possible fields could include the importance of accurate news reporting, the work of various types of science, including even peace research, and possibly even the work done by various kinds of celebrities for peace. The safest conclusion would appear to be that the Nobel Peace Prize will be considerably more pluralistic, both in the fields selected and even more in the geographical basis of the laureates, than in the first century of the Prize.

At the symposium there was some debate about what influence the Nobel Peace Prize can realistically be said to have had. Clearly it is no magic wand. If the definition of success is that the Prize has produced peace in a certain region, then clearly it has often failed. The effects were seen as more limited. The Nobel Peace Prize can act as an effective loudspeaker for the lesser known laureates; many were the laureates who told stories about how virtually all doors were suddenly opened to them; some had even been given physical protection by it. In a few cases, though, the Nobel Peace Prize was also seen as having helped transform events. The best example was probably how the Prize of 1996 to Bishop Carlos Belo and José Ramos-Horta had been instrumental in changing East Timor from a harshly suppressed part of Indonesia into an independent country. These were no small achievements for a committee of five internationally rather unknown Norwegians.

Kim Dae-jung

Dialogue and Cooperation to Achieve World Peace

The Honorable Gunnar Berge, chairman of the Norwegian Nobel Committee, members of the Committee, fellow Nobel laureates and distinguished guests.

First, I am very pleased to be able to join you in congratulating the centennial anniversary of the Nobel Peace Prize. I also applaud the Norwegian Nobel Committee that has done great work over the past 100 years. I have profound respect for it.

Above all, it is an incomparable honor for me to have this opportunity to speak to you from this privileged podium.

Distinguished Guests,

In the wake of the terrorist attacks on the United States, we cannot help worrying about peace. On the occasion of the centennial of the Nobel Peace Prize, it is most significant and timely for us to look back on the issue of war and peace in the past century and ponder about welfare and peace of humanity in the 21st century.

There were more than 250 wars of various sizes worldwide in the 20th century. As a result, an astounding 110 million people lost their lives, of which about 60%, or 63 million people, were civilians.

There were two main causes for war in the 20th century: One was nationalism, the other ideology. The confrontation caused by nationalism swept the world in the first half of the 20th century. Humanity experienced it through two world wars. Even today, world peace is threatened by the ethnic confrontation continuing in some parts of the Middle East.

The confrontation caused by ideology, too, brought the East-West Cold War for more than 40 years, including the Korean War in 1950. The remnants of the Cold War still remain on the Korean Peninsula. Aside from nationalism and ideology, conflicts between races, religions and cultures are occurring in various places around the world. Terrorists are trying to justify their attacks against the United States on religious grounds.

Ladies and Gentlemen,

We ardently hope that the 21st century will be a century of peace. World peace is the noblest goal of all humanity, the supreme task that must be accomplished at any cost. If we are to forge the 21st century into a peaceful era, we must first correctly grasp what menaces peace. Then, the international community must make common efforts to address it. I would like to express my ideas briefly on these issues.

In the history of the world, there have been five epochal events until now. First was the birth of the human species. Second was the emergence of agrarian civilizations some 10,000 years ago. Third was the birth of four great civilizations along the Nile, the Tigris-Euphrates, the Indus and the Yellow Rivers some 5,000 to 6,000 years ago. Fourth was the revolution of thought that took place in China, India, Greece and Israel 2,500 years ago. And fifth was the industrial revolution that began at the end of the 18th century in the United Kingdom.

The industrial revolution laid the economic foundation for the emergence of modern nations. At the same time, it prepared the way for full-fledged nationalism. Stronger peoples did not hesitate to proceed on the path toward "aggressive nationalism", namely, imperialism, while weaker peoples resorted to a strategy of "defensive nationalism". Confrontation between them resulted in the tragedy of two world wars in the 20th century.

The industrial revolution surely brought development and great affluence to civilization. But behind it were the dark shadows of the miserable sacrifices of weaker peoples and the wars of imperialism of stronger nations.

Ladies and gentlemen, what then will be the bright areas and shadows of the age of information and globalization in the 21st century — the age of the sixth epochal event?

The information revolution, known as the "Third Wave", opens the door to the new possibilities of knowledge-based economies. Knowledge and information have emerged as the core elements creating wealth. Poor nations and the underprivileged people are now able to take part in the creation of new wealth if they are able to make good use of computers. This is the new paradigm that will help us overcome the limitations of industrial societies that were dependent on the tangible elements of land, capital and labor. At the same time, because the flow of enormous amounts of information overcomes restrictions of time and space, the process of globalization is accelerated further.

In particular, the establishment of the World Trade Organization in 1995 heralded the opening of full-fledged globalization. Goods and services as well as capital now flow freely across national borders within what has now become the global village. All mankind are able to come closer to each other and greater wealth can be created.

All these things are the bright sides of the age of information and globalization. Behind this light, however, is a dark shadow. It is none other than the digital divide. The nations that have economic power derived from information capabilities are overwhelming the economies of developing countries.

In the age of knowledge-based economies, the digital divide among nations created a rapidly widening gulf between the rich and poor. If we ignore this phenomenon, the gap between the advanced and developing nations will be widened further. Behind the destructive fundamentalism that is occurring in various places in the world today or the anti-globalization movement is anger over the gap between the rich and poor. Moreover, worldwide environmental degradation will be accelerated if the digital divide triggers excessive development by developing nations as a means of survival.

Whenever there have been international conferences of various kinds, we have witnessed violent demonstrations by those who were angered by the gap between the rich and poor and the social inequality, which is a side effect of globalization.

We cannot guarantee world peace in the 21st century unless there is a resolution of the gap between the rich and poor. Nuclear weapons or missiles will not be completely effective because how war is waged is changing. War against terrorism is the problem now.

The terrorist attacks on the United States last September have fundamentally changed the concept of war. Terrorism is a war without a declaration. It is a faceless adversary. We do not know when or where it will occur. We do not know what kind of weapon will be used. It kills civilians indiscriminately. International law or treaties are useless. Private life cannot be maintained. We cannot make air travel with peace of mind. We cannot go up a high-rise building or open our mail without anxiety.

We must root out such cowardly, cruel and barbaric terrorist acts. But we must solve the root cause of terrorism in the long run while imposing immediate punishment against terrorists. The gap between the rich and poor is the foundation of religious, cultural, racial and ideological conflicts.

All humanity must share the benefits from enhanced information capabilities and globalization. The interests and diversity of all nations and all peoples must be respected. We must not expect poor nations and the underprivileged people to be patient forever. I urge the international community to hold serious and active discussions on these issues.

At the same time, human rights and democracy must be respected and realized as universal values. I am convinced that when the problems of the poor are resolved and democracy is put into practice, world peace in the 21st century will be possible, and all mankind will be safe and happy. More than anyone, we, the Nobel Peace laureates, must take the lead in such efforts.

Distinguished Guests,

Finally, I would like to touch on the issue of the Korean Peninsula, the last legacy of the Cold War of the 20th century. Peace on the Korean Peninsula is not only the ardent wish of the 70 million Korean people but also directly linked to peace in East Asia and the World. Since I was inaugurated President of the Republic of Korea in 1998, I have consistently pursued the Sunshine Policy. It aims at preparing for eventual peaceful unification by accomplishing coexistence and peaceful exchange between South and North Korea. All nations and all peace-loving organizations, including the United Nations, support this policy.

I visited Pyongyang in June last year and held a historic inter-Korean summit with Chairman Kim Jong-il of North Korea's National Defense Commission. We agreed not to repeat the tragedy of war but to make joint efforts for exchanges and cooperation. Since then, tensions have eased greatly and a lot of positive changes have occurred on the Korean Peninsula. Exchanges and cooperation between the South and North have proceeded rapidly at times and slowly at other times.

On September 15, only four days after the terrorist attacks on the United States, inter-Korean ministerial talks were held in Seoul, and ten agreements were reached such as reunions of separated families, the relinking of a railway and several other projects. In view of the international developments at the time, they were a great achievement, indeed. Although inter-Korean relations are in a stalemate now, I, along with the people of Korea, am convinced that the path toward success will open again without fail, if we make our utmost efforts with patience and consistency. There is no alternative to the Sunshine Policy; it is a win-win policy that contributes to peace and stability not only of South and North Korea but also of the entire world. I hope that you will give it your continuing support.

Distinguished Guests,

In conclusion, the 20th century was an age of world wars, the Cold War and various armed conflicts. Amid such conditions, however, we have not given up hope for peace. After the First World War, the League of Nations was formed, after the Second World War, the United Nations that could be described as an amalgamation of the wishes and efforts of humanity. The role of the Norwegian Nobel Committee over the past 100 years in spreading the message of peace throughout the world through the awarding of the prize was also great, indeed.

Our advancement toward peace will continue in the 21st century. The driving force of such progress will be dialogue and cooperation. I have no doubt that humankind will be able to cope wisely with the new issues of the 21st century, including the problem of poverty.

We must keep forging cooperative relations between nations, cultures, religions and races through dialogue. Where there is dialogue, there is understanding; where there is understanding, there is cooperation. Where there is cooperation, we can expect a resolution of the problem of poverty. When these things are realized, the threat of war will disappear.

The preamble of the UNESCO Constitution reads, "…wars begin in the minds of men…." Let us wipe the thought of war from our mind. Let us proceed on the path of dialogue and cooperation. Thus, let us leave a proud record in history that will define the 21st century as an age of peace and the common prosperity of all humanity.

Thank you.

Eric Hobsbawm

War and Peace in the 20th Century

Let me begin with the basic facts about war and peace in the 20th century, which, for the purposes of this paper, begins in 1914.

- It was the most murderous century in recorded history. The total deaths caused by, or associated with its wars have been estimated at 187 millions, which is the equivalent of over 10% of the world population in 1913.[1]
- It has been a century of almost unbroken war, with few and brief periods without organized armed conflict somewhere or other. However for most of its length it was dominated by world wars, that is to say by wars between territorial states or alliances of such states across the entire globe. We may regard the period from 1914 to 1945 as a single "Thirty Years' War" broken only by a short pause in the 1920s — between the final withdrawal of the Japanese from the Soviet Far East in 1922 and the beginning of the Japanese attack on Manchuria in 1931. This was followed, almost immediately, by some forty years of "Cold War", which conforms to the great

---

[1]Estimate from Z. Brzezinski, *Out of Control: Global Turmoil on the Eve of the 21st Century* (New York, 1993), population estimate from Angus Maddison, *The World Economy: A Millennial Perspective* (OECD, Paris, 2001), p. 241.

philosopher Thomas Hobbes' definition of war, of which I may remind you. "War", he wrote, "consisteth not in battle only or the act of fighting, but in a tract of time wherein the will to contend by battle is sufficiently known".[2] How far the actions in which the armed forces of the USA have been involved since the end of the Cold War in various parts of the globe constitute a continuation of the era of world war, is a matter for debate. However, there can be no doubt that the 1990s were filled with formal and informal military conflict, in Europe, Africa, and the western and central parts of Asia. The world as a whole has not been effectively at peace since 1914 and is not at peace now.

• Nevertheless, and in spite of increasing globalisation, the century cannot be treated as a single block, either chronologically or geographically. Chronologically, it falls into three parts which can be loosely called: the era of world war centred on Germany (1914–1945), the era of confrontation between the two super-powers (1945–1989) and the era since the end of the classic international power system. We are today confronting a different problem of war and peace from any in the past three hundred years. I shall call these periods I, II and III. Geographically the impact of military operations and other repercussions of war have been highly unequal. With one exception (the Chaco war of 1932–35 between Paraguay and Bolivia) there were no significant inter-state wars (as distinct from civil wars) within the western hemisphere at all in the 20th century, enemy military operations have barely touched these territories — hence the shock of the bombing of the World Trade Center and the Pentagon on September 11 — and the world wars of period I, so far from being an era of economic, political and human disruption were creators of prosperity. Since 1945 inter-state wars have also disappeared from Europe, which had previously been the main battlefield region. Although in period III war returned to Southeastern Europe, it seems very unlikely in

---

[2]Thomas Hobbes, "LEVIATHAN or the matter, forme and power of a COMMONWEALTH ecclesiastical and civil", Part I Chapter 13 cited from the edition by M. Oakeshott (Oxford, 1946), p. 82.

the rest of the continent. On the other hand, during period II inter-state wars, not necessarily unconnected with the global confrontation, remained endemic in the Middle East and South Asia, and major wars directly springing from the global confrontation occurred in East and Southeast Asia (Korea, Indochina). At the same time parts of the world like sub-Saharan Africa, which had been comparatively unaffected by war in period I (apart from the belated colonial conquest of Ethiopia by Italy in 1935–36) came to be theatre of armed conflict during period II, and became at times perhaps the major scene of carnage and suffering in period III.

2

However, two other characteristics of the development of war in the 20th century must be briefly considered. The first is less obvious than the second. At the start of the 21st century we find ourselves in a world where armed operations are no longer essentially in the hands of the governments of territorial states or of their authorized agents, and where the contending parties have no common characteristics, status or objectives, except the willingness to use violence. At the end of the last century almost all violent conflicts took place within the frontiers of states. Inter-state wars (including the armed interventions of states outside their borders) dominated the image of war so much in periods I and II that civil or other armed conflicts *within* the territories of existing states or empires have been somewhat obscured. Even the civil wars in the territories of the Russian empire after the October Revolution, and in those of the Chinese empire after its collapse, have been fitted into the framework of international conflicts, and they were indeed inseparable from them. Latin America may have been almost immune to armies crossing the frontiers of states in the twentieth century, but it has been the scene of major civil conflicts, for instance in Mexico after 1911, in Colombia since 1948, and in various countries of central America during period II. It has not been noticed that the absolute number of violent conflicts across frontiers (international) has tended to decline fairly continuously since the middle 1960s, when the number of violent conflicts within state frontiers (internal) passed the number of international conflicts and continued to rise steeply until levelling off in the 1990s.[3] We shall consider the significance of this trend later.

3

A more familiar transformation in the nature of war during the 20th century was the erosion of the distinction between combatants and non-combatants. The two world wars of the first half of the century being *total* wars, both mobilised and involved the entire populations of belligerent countries, though, obviously, more so in the regions of immediate military operations. Both combatants and non-combatants suffered. However, in the course of the century the burden of war shifted increasingly from armed forces to civilians, who were not only its victims, but increasingly the essential object of military or military-political operations. The contrast between the first and second world wars is dramatic. Civilian suffering is not as exactly quantifiable as military casualties, but an estimate by the Swiss Federal Office for Civilian Protection holds that the casualties directly imputable to World War I were 1 civilian death per 200 military deaths, but that in World War II they were approximately equal — most people would put civilian deaths higher — and in the Vietnam War 20 civilians were killed for every military person.[4] It is generally supposed that 80–90% of those suffering in war today are civilians. Their share of casualties has increased since the end of the Cold War by the fact that military operations since then have only rarely been conducted by armies based on universal military service, but mainly by generally quite small bodies, regular or irregular, of those who actually fight or operate the high-technology instruments of fighting. The British military forces in the Falklands War of 1982 between Britain and Argentina amounted to 9500 persons, of whom 256 (2.7%)

---

[3]See Stiftung Entwicklung und Frieden, *Globale Trends 2000: Fakten, Analysen, Prognosen* (Frankfurt a/M, 1999), p. 420 Schaubild 1.

[4]M. Sassoli and R. Bouvier, *How Does Law Protect in War?* ICRC Geneva, 1999, p. 145.

were killed and 777 (8.2%) wounded.[5] Moreover, these are often deliberately protected against the risks of incurring casualties, which ,it has been correctly observed, "tends to increase the danger to civilians".[6] If we look at the armed violence that has taken place in the world since the last international war readily classifiable as such (the Gulf War of 1991), they have led to immeasurably more suffering among civilians than among armed combatants. While it is true that the precision of modern high-tech weaponry has made it possible in some cases to re-establish a distinction between military and civilian targets, and therefore between combatants and non-combatants, there is no reason to doubt that the main victims of wars will continue to be civilians.

What is more, it has become increasingly evident in the past thirty or forty years that the suffering of civilians is not proportionate to the scale or intensity of military operations. In strictly military terms, the 1971 two-week war between India and Pakistan over the independence of Bangladesh was a modest affair, but it produced a total number of ten million refugees. The fighting between armed units in Africa during the 1990s can hardly have involved more than a few thousands of mostly ill-armed combatants in all — and yet it produced, at its peak, almost seven millions of refugees — a far greater number than at any time during the Cold War when the continent had been the scene of the proxy wars between the superpowers.[7] In the new century the armed operations in Israel, the Palestinian territories and Lebanon, as well as recent operations in Afghanistan, have only confirmed this unhappy disproportion in areas where actual fighting is taking place. Fortunately for them, this does not apply to civilians living in states intervening in such conflicts from afar.

Nevertheless this phenomenon is not necessarily confined to poor and remote areas. In some ways the effect of war on civilian life

---

[5]*British Army Review*, August 1996, p. 80.

[6]A. P. V. Rogers, "Zero Casualty Warfare" (*International Review of the Red Cross* No. 837, 31 March 2000, pp. 165–81.

[7]Data from UNHCR, *The State of the World's Refugees 2000: Fifty years of humanitarian action* (Oxford, 2000).

is magnified by the process of globalisation and the increasing reliance of the world's operations on a constant, unbroken flow of communications, technical services, deliveries and supplies. Even a comparatively brief interruption of this flow — as, for instance, by a few days' closing of US airspace after September 11, 2001 — must have considerable, and perhaps lasting, effects on the global economy.

4

Let me now turn from war to peace. It would be easier to write about the subject of war and peace in the 20th century if the difference between the two were as clear-cut as it was supposed to be at the beginning of the century, in the days when the Hague Conventions of 1899 and 1907 codified its rules. It was supposed to take place primarily among sovereign states or, if occurring within the territory of any of them ("civil war"), between parties sufficiently organized as to be accorded belligerent status by other sovereign states. It was supposed to be sharply distinguished from "peace", normally by a declaration of war at one end, a treaty of peace at the other. Military operations were supposed to distinguish clearly between combatants, marked as such by wearing uniform, or other signs of belonging to an organized armed force, and non-combatant civilians. War was supposed to be between combatants. Non-combatants were not the object of military operations, but should be protected so far as possible in wartime. It was always clear that these conventions did not cover all civil and international armed conflicts, and very notably not those arising out of the imperial expansion of western states in regions not covered by internationally recognized sovereign states, although some of these (but by no means all) were known as "wars". Nor did it cover even large rebellions against established states such as the so-called "Indian Mutiny". Nor did it cover the normal armed activities in regions beyond the effective control of the state or imperial authorities nominally ruling them, such as the raiding and blood-feuding in the mountains of Afghanistan or Morocco. Nevertheless, it still served as a guideline in the First World War. In the course of the 20th century this relative clarity was replaced by confusion.

- *First*, the line between conflicts between and conflicts within states, international and civil wars, became hazy, because the 20th century was characteristically a century not only of wars, but of revolutions and the break-up of empires. Revolutions or liberation struggles within one state had implications for the international situation, particularly during the Cold War. Conversely, since the Russian Revolution intervention by states in the internal affairs of other states of which they disapproved, has become common, at least where it seems comparatively risk-free, this remains the case.
- *Second*, the clear distinction between war and peace tended to disappear. Except here and there, the Second World War neither began with declarations of war nor ended with treaties of peace. It was followed by a period so hard to classify as either war or peace in the old sense that the neologism "Cold War" had to be invented to describe it. The sheer obscurity of the situation since the Cold War may be illustrated by the current state of affairs in the Middle East. Neither "peace" nor "war" can exactly describe the situation in Iraq since the formal end of the Gulf War, still bombed almost daily by foreign powers, or the relations between Palestinians and Israelis, nor between Israel and its neighbours Lebanon and Syria. Neither word seems to fit the bill. All this is an unfortunate heritage of the era of twentieth century world wars, but perhaps also of an era when wars increasingly mobilised the whole population by means of the increasingly powerful machinery of mass propaganda, and of an era of confrontation between incompatible and passion-laden ideologies which brought a crusading element comparable to the religious conflicts of the past into its wars.

Unlike the traditional wars of the international power system, they were increasingly waged for infinite and non-negotiable objects such as "unconditional surrender" or regarded as conflicts between contestants between whom no compromise was possible. Since both wars and victories were seen as total, any limitation on the belligerent's capacity to win, as by the accepted conventions of 18th and 19th century warfare, or even by formal declarations of war, was rejected. So was any limitation of the victors' power to assert their will subsequent to victory, as by the formal provisions of treaties. In any case experience had shown that agreements could be as easily broken and denounced as signed.

- In recent years the situation has been further complicated by the tendency in public rhetoric to extend the use of the term "war" to the use of organized force against various national or international activities regarded as antisocial, as in phrases like "the war against the Mafia" or "the war against the drug traffic". This metaphorical use of the term "war" confuses the situation in two ways.

- First, it obscures the nature of the adversary group and the nature of the operations needed to oppose, control or, if possible, to eliminate it. Consider the phrase "War against terrorism". "Terrorism" (insofar as it is more than a term indicating disapproval) is not a potential belligerent, but a type of armed or violent action, generally by small groups, employed by movements and organizations in the pursuit of, usually, political ends. It is an instrument, not an end. The objectives pursued by the various movements, groups or networks which can or could be described as "terrorist" may be similar, but need have no common interests. The political party now governing Israel was (correctly) described as "terrorist" under the British, but devotes itself to the elimination of the movements among Palestinians which it (also correctly) describes as terrorist. There is no single all-embracing "terrorism" that can be considered the adversary in what is being called the "war against terrorism". There is no single all-purpose form of "terrorism", as witness the differences between movements so describable which have practised the indiscriminate killing of non-involved persons and those which have specifically avoided it (e.g. ETA and the IRA); between those practising suicide attacks (as in Sri Lanka and some Islamic movements) and others.[8] Consequently the term "terrorism" does not even tell us much about how the way or

---

[8]My source is the unpublished record of a recent comparative colloquium at All Souls' College, Oxford on the subject of "Suicide Attackers".

ways of combating it differ from the major operations of conventional war.

- Second, it confuses the actions of two types of armed forces, One — let us call them "soldiers" — is directed against other armed forces with the object of defeating them. The action of the other — let us call them "police" — has the purpose of maintaining or re-establishing the required degree of law and public order within an existing political entity of public power, typically a state. Victory, which has no necessary moral connotation, is the object of the one, the bringing to justice of offenders against the law, which has a moral connotation, is the object of the other. However, in the situation that has developed in the 20th century, this distinction is easier to draw in theory than in practice, especially when one or both sides do not accept it. Homicide by a soldier in battle is not in itself a breach of the law, unlike homicide in all functioning territorial states. But what if an IRA man regards himself as a belligerent, even though official UK law regards him as a murderer? Were the operations in Northern Ireland a war, as the IRA held, or an attempt to maintain orderly government in one province of the United Kingdom against law-breakers? Since not only a formidable local police-force but considerable national armed forces were mobilized against it for thirty years or so, we may conclude that it was a war, but one systematically maintained in the manner of a police operation, namely in a way that minimized casualties and the disruption of life in the province. It was settled in the end by a negotiated settlement, but one which, typically, has not brought peace so far, but merely a periodically extended absence of fighting. Such are the complexities and confusions of the relations between peace and war at the start of the new century. They are well illustrated by the military and other operations in which the USA and its allies are at present engaged.

5

Let me now consider the problem of armed conflict and its settlement as it faces the world at the start of the 21st century. There is one thing that the two centuries have in common, but there is a major difference between us and the last century, although the contemporary situation has already been developing for some time — roughly since the end of the 1960s.

- What the two centuries have in common is the complete absence of any effective global authority which can control or settle armed disputes.

Globalisation has advanced in almost every respect — economically, technologically, culturally, even linguistically — except one. Politically and militarily, insofar as there are effective authorities on earth, they are still the territorial states. There are officially about 200 of them, but in practice only a handful of them count, among whom the USA is at present overwhelmingly the most powerful. However, no state or empire has ever been large, rich or powerful enough to maintain a hegemony single-handed over the entire political world, let alone complete political and military supremacy over the entire globe. The world is too big, complicated and plural. There is no likelihood that the USA, or any other conceivable single state power, could establish a lasting control over the future politics of the globe, even supposing it wanted to.

- A single super-power cannot compensate for the absence of global authorities, especially in the absence of conventions strong enough to be voluntarily accepted as permanently binding by major states, as, most obviously, in questions of international disarmament and weapons control. Some such authorities exist, notably the United Nations and various technical and financial bodies, such as the IMF, the World Bank and the World Trade Organisation, and some international tribunals. None of them have effective power apart from that granted to them by agreements between states, or given to them by the backing of powerful states, or voluntarily accepted by states. Regrettable as this may be, this is not likely to change in the immediately foreseeable future.
- This is relevant to proposals, now widely canvassed, for the international legal control of various activities generally regarded

as intolerable, notably "war crimes".[9] In the absence of authorities other than states exercising effective power, international institutions risk being either ineffective or lacking universal legitimacy. Even where world courts for these offences are established by general agreement (e.g. the International Criminal Court as by the UN Rome Statute of July 17th 1998), their judgments will not necessarily be accepted as legitimate and binding, so long as powerful states are in a position to refuse submitting to them and do so. Of course a consortium of powerful states may well be strong enough to ensure that some offenders from weaker states are brought before these tribunals, and thus hope to bring some of the cruelties of armed conflict in some areas under control. However, insofar as they do, it is by the traditional exercise of power and influence within an international state system and not as agents of international law.[10] The best that can be hoped for is that in the course of time the accumulation of case-law and jurisprudence on the law of crimes against human rights will gradually create a consensus sufficiently strong to apply to all countries. We are a long way from that point.

6

The major difference is far-reaching. The idea that war takes place essentially in a world divided into territorial areas under the authority of effective governments with a monopoly of the means of public power and coercion, ceased to be realistic in the course of the 20th century. It never really applied to countries at moments of revolution, or to the fragments of disintegrated empires, but until recently most new revolutionary or post-colonial regimes — China between 1911 and 1949 is the main exception — established themselves fairly

---

[9]The best guide to these is Roy Gutman and David Rieff, eds., *Crimes of War: What the public should know* (New York and London, 1999).

[10]This is also the case, by definition, where individual states accept international humanitarian law and unilaterally assert the right to apply it to the citizens of other countries in their national tribunals, as, notably, the Spanish courts, supported by the British House of Lords, did in the case of General Pinochet.

soon within their territories, taking over effective administration over these. They emerged as more or less organized and functioning successor regimes and states.

However, for various reasons in the past 30 years or so the territorial state has lost its traditional monopoly of armed force, much of its former stability and power, and even to an increasing degree, the fundamental sense of legitimacy, or at least of accepted permanence, which allows governments to impose burdens such as taxes and conscription on willing citizens. The material equipment for warfare is now widely available to private bodies, and so are the means for financing non-state warfare. Indeed, in addition to the armed forces of states themselves, we are increasingly faced with warfare conducted by private armed bodies operating for profit, a situation unfamiliar in Europe since the 17th century.[11] The balance between state and non-state organizations has changed.

Armed conflicts within states have become more serious and may continue for decades without serious prospects of victory or settlement: Angola, Sri Lanka, Kashmir, Chechnya, Colombia. In extreme cases, as in parts of Africa, the state may virtually have ceased to exist, or it may, as in Colombia, no longer exercise power over part of its territory. Even in strong and stable states it may be unable to eliminate small unofficial armed groups operating on its territory for periods of decades, like the IRA in Britain and ETA in Spain. The novelty of this situation is indicated by the fact that the most powerful state on the globe, faced with terrorist attack, feels obliged in effect to open formal military operations against a small international non-governmental organisation or network lacking both a territory and a recognizable body of armed forces.

7

How does this affect the balance of war and peace in the coming century? I do not think this is the place to discuss the actual wars

---

[11]Cf. David Shearer, *Private Armies and Military Intervention*, Adelphi Papers 316 (Oxford, 1998).

which are likely to take place in the foreseeable future or their possible outcomes. Nor do traditional inter-state wars raise any problems not present in the 20th century. However both the structure of armed conflict and the methods of settlement have been changed profoundly by the transformation of the world system of sovereign states.

Since the dissolution of the USSR, the "great power system" which governed the international relations of sovereign states for almost two centuries and, with obvious exceptions, exercised some control over conflicts among them, no longer exists. Its disappearance has removed a major brake on the outbreak of inter-state warfare and the armed interventions of states in the affairs of other states, such as that which kept foreign territorial borders largely uncrossed by foreign armed forces during the Cold War. The international system was potentially unstable even then, given the multiplication of small, sometimes tiny, and weak but officially "sovereign" members of the United Nations. The disintegration of the USSR and the European communist regimes plainly increased this instability. Separatist tendencies of varying strength in both new and old, hitherto stable "nation-states" like Britain, Spain, Belgium and Italy risk destabilising it further. At the same time the number of private actors on the world scene of armed conflict has multiplied. Under these circumstances the frequency of cross-border wars and armed interventions since the end of the Cold War is not surprising. Outbreaks of armed conflict in such a situation of instability are to be expected.

8

What mechanisms for controlling and settling such conflict are available? The record is not promising. In the course of the 1990s none of the problems that led to armed conflict in that decade ended with a stable settlement. However, for the time being the instruments for doing so are unusually defective. Even though the community of states has a common interest in finding acceptable solutions to some international problems, economic, humanitarian and politico-military, the survival of institutions, assumptions and rhetoric superseded by the world change since 1989, continued to lock states into the pattern of old suspicions. These may not last too long into the 21st century, but their survival unquestionably exacerbated the post-communist disintegration of South-eastern Europe and made the settlement of the region once occupied by Yugoslavia more difficult.

- The first condition of evolving means of controlling the balance between war and peace will be the liquidation of the assumptions, both ideological and power-political, of the Cold War era. The contest between the USA and the USSR is at an end, but it has left behind the assumption that international relations are a zero-sum game between two global contestants (a "war of civilisations") in which the existence of both is at stake.

- The second necessary change is the recognition that, even though the power relations are today highly skewed in favour of the one surviving super-power, it has failed, and will inevitably fail, to impose a "new world order" (whatever its content) by unilateral force, even supported by what remains of an alliance of supporting states, whose common interests are no longer identical with the USA. The international system will remain multilateral. Its regulation will depend on the ability to agree of several major units, even allowing for the military predominance of one. It is already evident how far international military action of the USA is dependent on the negotiated agreement of other states, without which it could not be effective. It is also evident that the political settlement even of a war in which the superpower is involved will be by negotiation and not by unilateral imposition. The era of wars ending in unconditional surrender will not return in the foreseeable future.

- The third weakness is that of the existing international bodies, notably the United Nations. Although always present, and usually called on, they have no defined or recognized role in the settlement of disputes. Their strategy and operation is constantly at the mercy of shifting power policies. The absence of an international intermediary genuinely considered neutral, and capable of taking action without prior authorisation by the Security Council, has been the most obvious gap in the system of dispute management.

Since the end of the Cold War the management of peace and war has been improvised. At best, as in the Balkans, armed conflicts have been stopped by outside armed intervention and the status quo at the end of hostilities has been maintained by the permanent presence of or threat by the armed forces of third parties. In effect this form of lasting institutionalised foreign intervention has long been applied by individual strong states in what they considered their sphere of influence (as by Syria in Lebanon). As a form of collective action it has been applied only by the USA and its allies (sometimes under UN auspices, sometimes not). This has so far been unsatisfactory for all parties. It commits intervenors to maintain troops indefinitely, and at disproportionate cost, in remote areas in which they have no particular interest and from which they derive no advantage. It makes them dependent on the passivity of the occupied population, which cannot be guaranteed, for, as experience has shown, faced with armed resistance, small forces of armed "peace-keepers" have to be replaced by very much larger military mobilisations. To poor and weak countries it may well be suspect as a new version of the assertion of power by strong rich ones, and a reminder of the institutionalised international inequality of the days of colonies and protectorates, all the more so when much of the local economy becomes parasitic on the needs of the occupying forces. Whether a general model for the future control of armed conflict can emerge from such improvisations, remains unclear.

9

Nevertheless, at bottom the balance of war and peace in the 21st century will not depend on devising more effective mechanisms for negotiation and settlement. It will depend on the avoidance of military conflict between states and on the internal stability of states. With a few exceptions, the potential rivalries and frictions between existing territorial states which led to armed conflict in the past, are less likely to do so today. There are, for instance, comparatively few burning disputes between governments about international borders. On the other hand internal conflicts easily turn to violence, and the main danger of war will lie in the involvement of outside states or military actors in these internal conflicts.

States with wealthy, relatively stable economies and no excessive inequalities in the material condition of their inhabitants are likely to be socially and politically less shaky than poor, highly inegalitarian and economically unstable ones. The dramatic growth of economic and social inequality within as well as between countries is therefore an element undermining peace. However, the avoidance or control of internal armed violence depends, even more immediately, on the powers and effective performance of its tasks, by national governments and their legitimacy in the eyes of the majority of their inhabitants. No government today can any longer take for granted the disarmament of the civilian population and the degree of public order accepted in large parts of Europe. Today, probably no government is in a position completely to eliminate internal armed minorities at all times. Yet the world is increasingly divided into a sector of states capable of administering their territories and citizens effectively, even when faced, as in the United Kingdom, with thirty years of armed action by an internal enemy, and a growing number of territories, bounded with officially recognized international frontiers, but with national governments ranging from the weak and corrupt to the non-existent.

These zones of state disintegration generate the bloodstained combination of internal struggles and international conflicts, as we have seen in Central Africa. There is probably no immediate prospect for lasting improvement in such regions. A further weakening of functioning and effective central governments in the regions in which they still operate, or a further Balkanisation of the world map, would undoubtedly increase the dangers of armed conflict.

10

In conclusion, a tentative forecast: War in the 21st century is not likely to be as murderous as in the 20th. But armed violence, creating disproportionate suffering and loss, will remain omnipresent and endemic, occasionally epidemic in a large part of the globe. The prospect of a century of peace remains as remote as it did a century ago.

Michael W. Doyle[1]

Ideologies and Polities: Liberal Democracy and National Dictatorship in Peace and War

What difference do ideologies make?[2] Must they clash? The "short" 20th century, 1914–1991, in retrospect appears as a period in which liberalism, communism and fascism contested for which would be supreme.[3] Fascism was defeated in a hot war (World War Two) in which liberalism and communism aligned in mutual self-defense. Communism then surrendered after a cold war in which liberalism out-produced its former ally. Were the clashes inevitable? Does the seeming victory of liberalism as the dominant political order of the developed industrial states "end history"? Or does a new rivalry between Islam and Christianity re-play the old patterns?

[1]Edwards S. Sanford, Professor of Politics and International Affairs, Princeton University, currently on a public service leave with the United Nations, serving as Special Adviser to Secretary General Kofi Annan and Assistant Secretary General. This essay reflects the author's views and not necessarily those of the United Nations. It draws on parts of my *Ways of War and Peace* (New York: Norton, 1997). I am grateful for research assistance by Matteo Giglioli and suggestions from the participants and organizers of the Nobel Centennial Seminar, December, 2001.

[2]By "ideology" I mean a system of ideas and ideals forming the basis of an economic or political theory or movement.

[3]For a thoughtful and yet sweeping look at world history in these terms see Philip Bobbit's *The Shield of Achilles* (New York: Knopf, 2002).

These are very large questions. In this essay, I would like to focus on a central contest of the twentieth century, that between liberal democracy and nationalist dictatorship as a single example of clashing ideologies.[4] Does a commitment to freedom or human rights have an effect different from an equally strong commitment to racial or national superiority or glory? Let us begin an answer by noting that ideologies have made large claims.

Promoting freedom produces peace, we have often been told. In a speech before the British parliament in June of 1982, President Reagan proclaimed that governments founded on a respect for individual liberty exercise "restraint" and "peaceful intentions" in their foreign policy. But he then announced a "crusade for freedom" and a "campaign for democratic development".[5] President Bush, similarly, on October 1, 1990, in an address before the United Nations General Assembly, declared: "Calls for democracy and human rights are being reborn everywhere. And these calls are an expression of support for the values enshrined in the Charter. They encourage our hopes for a more stable, more peaceful, more prosperous world".[6] President Clinton continued this tradition, making "Democratic Enlargement" the doctrinal centerpiece of his administration's foreign policy.

In making these claims the presidents and other liberal politicians joined a long list of liberal theorists (and propagandists) and echoed an old argument: the aggressive instincts of authoritarian leaders and totalitarian ruling parties make for war. A modest version of this view led the authors of the US Constitution to entrust Congress, rather than the president, with the power to declare war. A more fiery American revolutionary, Thomas Paine, in 1791 proclaimed: "Monarchical sovereignty, the enemy of mankind, and the source of misery, is

---

[4]In *Ways of War and Peace* (New York: WW Norton, 1997) I explore the other pair — differences between socialism, both Marxist and Communist, and liberalism, pp. 315–380.

[5]President Reagan's speech is printed in *The New York Times*, June 9, 1982.

[6]And perhaps most consequentially, President Bush justified the large cuts in U.S. tactical nuclear forces as a product of the decline in hostility that stemmed from the rise of democratic forces in the former USSR.

abolished; and sovereignty is restored to its natural and original place, the nation.... Were this the case throughout Europe, the cause of war would be taken away".[7]

Liberal states, the argument runs, founded on such individual rights as equality before the law, free speech and other civil liberties, private property, and elected representation are fundamentally against war. When the citizens who bear the burdens of war elect their governments, wars become impossible. Furthermore, citizens appreciate that the benefits of trade can be enjoyed most fully only under conditions of peace. Thus the very existence of liberal states, such as the U.S. Japan and the European allies, makes for peace. Moreover, the growth in the numbers of liberal democracies presages the arrival of world peace, fulfilling the vision of Immanuel Kant's "perpetual peace" among free republics.

A quite different ideology of world politics animates the rhetoric of national fascist dictatorships. Here peoples clash, driven by needs for raw materials, living space and glory. Benito Mussolini announced during Italy's invasion of Ethiopia: "We, certainly, have stated, with the utmost candor, what our objectives are in this colonial undertaking: our security above all and the possibility of expansion for a prolific people which having farmed what was arable in their own unyielding territory will not resign itself to death by starvation".[8] Earlier he made the same point in more general terms: "It is not enough for the established peoples to say: 'let us live calmly', because if we do not know where to send our surplus population, if we do not know where to find the raw materials that will allow us to survive internally, this is a jailer's peace, not a peace of free and truly human men".[9] Adolf Hitler, his fellow national socialist, endorsed the attitudes

---

[7]Thomas Paine, *The Rights of Man*, in *Complete Writings*, Foner, ed., I, p. 342.

[8]Interview with Léo Gerville-Réache, *Le Matin* of Paris, Rome, September 15, 1935, translated in Ronald Cunsolo, *Italian nationalism: from its origins to World War II* (Krieger, Malabar, FL, 1990).

[9]Speech in the Lower House of Parliament (November 15, 1924), in *Mussolini: citazioni — il manuale delle guardie nere*, XX secolo, Rome, 1969, pp. 193–194. All translations that follow from the Italian are by Matteo Giglioli.

and policies Mussolini pursued in similar terms: "Thus the German government in full understanding appreciate the right of the action taken by their Italian friend in Albania, and have therefore welcomed it. Yes, it is not only the right but the duty of Fascism to secure, in the living space undoubtedly allotted to Italy by nature and history, the maintenance of an order on which alone a really flourishing human civilization appears to be based and secured" (Reichstag speech, April 28, 1939).[10]

Mussolini also spelled out in no uncertain terms his rejection of the liberal ideal: "I do not believe in perpetual peace; I think that Kant himself did not believe in it: he chose as the title of his book the wording on a sign over an inn, and the sign represented a graveyard. Understandably, in graveyards you have perpetual peace; but among peoples, in spite of the preaching, in spite of the idealisms, for all their respectability, there are matters of fact, such as race, such as development, such as greatness and decadence of peoples, which lead to conflicts that often are resolved by the force of arms" (in the Lower House of Parliament, February 6, 1923).[11] And, he later added: "Not only do I not believe in perpetual peace, I also find it depressing and in opposition to the fundamental virtues of man, which appear in full light only in bloody struggle" (in the Lower House of Parliament, May 26, 1934).[12]

These are seemingly stark differences: liberty and democracy make for peace; nationalism and dictatorship for war. In this essay, I would like to complicate the picture of a clash of ideologies, explaining when and how liberty or democracy can make for war and nationalism or dictatorship for peace. In this process, I also want to make a case for the importance of ideology in the understanding of world politics, while noting first that ideology does not operate in a historical vacuum. Historians have demonstrated that the impact of ideology exists but that it must be seen in context in the actual

---

[10]Baynes, Norman H. (ed.), *The Speeches of Adolf Hitler (April 1922-August 1939)*, Oxford Univ. Press, London, 1942, 2 vols., p. 1634.

[11]In *Mussolini, op. cit.*, pp. 192-193.

[12]In *Mussolini, op. cit.*, pp. 194-195.

course of world politics.[13] Correspondingly, drawing on classic philosophies of world politics, I would like to illustrate the place of ideologies in constructing theoretical explanations of world politics. Ideologies of freedom and nation count, I will suggest, but only in the context of a more comprehensive political theory. But, in the end, taking into account the intervening complications, I want to defend one generalization, albeit with qualifications and only when democracy and liberalism are joined: together, they can make for an expanding world peace among fellow liberal democracies and this is an outcome well-worth promoting.

Nationalism and Dictatorship and War

The connections leading from nationalism and dictatorship to war are well-established. Benito Mussolini makes the case clearly with his emphasis on the need for national space for a hungry population and his contempt for peacemakers and exultation in "bloody struggle". When such an ideology, or the related views of Adolf Hitler, is combined with a near-monopoly of state power wars are natural outcomes. But to see the connection more clearly, let us disconnect them and see how peace can connect to autocracy or nationalism and then note how the typical nationalist dictatorship is likely to lack what makes some dictatorships and some nationalisms pacific.

Peaceful Dictatorships? First, it is worth noting that empirically, dictatorships have been on average less rather than more likely to be engaged in wars than liberal democracies.[14] (The long history of

---

[13]See for communism and the Cold War, John Gaddis, *We Now Know* (New York: Oxford University Press, 1997); for fascism and Nazism see Aristotle Kallis, *Fascist Ideology: Territory and Expansionism in Italy and Germany, 1922–1945* (London, Routledge, 2000); for liberalism, Tony Smith, *America's Mission* (Princeton University Press, 1994) and empirical debate on the democratic peace in Michael Brown, Sean Lynn-Jones, and Steven Miller, eds., *Debating the Democratic Peace* (MIT Press, 1996).
[14]Melvin Small and David Singer, "The War-proneness of Democratic Regimes", *Jerusalem Jnl of International Relations* (December, 1976), pp. 50–69.

armed intervention or forcible imperial expansion by France, Britain and the United Sates is one reason for this.) Moreover, due to their domestic fragility, dictatorships have good reason to avoid foreign wars because such wars are too likely to either bankrupt regimes that cannot tax efficiently or provoke coups in regimes that lack domestic popular support.[15]

Second, some ("Realist") theorists of world politics have held that dictatorships can be pacific because domestic regimes make little difference. The effects of differing domestic regimes (whether dictators, democracies or anything in between) are overridden by the international system under which all states live. Hobbes thus does not bother to distinguish between "some council or one man" when he discusses the sovereign. Differing domestic regimes do affect the quantity of resources available to the state and the quality of its morale. But the ends that shape policy are determined for Hobbesians by the fundamental quest for power that shapes all politics or the competitive structure of the international system.

At the level of the decisionmaker, Realists therefore argue that peace could be merely the outcome of the diplomacy of a prudent dictator. Indeed, some, including Hobbes, have argued that sovereigns have a natural duty not to act against "the reasons of peace".[16] Individuals established (that is, should establish) a sovereign to escape from the brutalities of the domestic "state of nature", the war of all against all, that follows from competition for scarce goods, scrambles for prestige, and fear of another's attack when there is no sovereign to provide for lawful acquisition or regularized social conduct or personal security. "Dominions were constituted for peace's sake, and peace was sought for safety's sake"; the natural duty of the sovereign is therefore the safety of the people.

Raymond Aron has identified three other types of prudential interstate peace consequent upon the structure of the international

---

[15]Stanislav Andreski, "On the Peaceful Disposition of Military Dictatorships", *Journal of Strategic Studies*, vol. 3, 1980, pp. 3-10.

[16]Thomas Hobbes, *Leviathan* (New York: Penguin, 1980), I. Chap. 13, 62, p. 186.

system: empire, hegemony, and equilibrium.[17] An empire generally succeeds in creating an internal peace. Hegemony can create peace by overawing potential rivals. Peace through equilibrium (the multipolar classical balance of power or the bipolar "cold war") also draws upon prudential sources of peace. An awareness of the likelihood that aggressive attempts at hegemony will generate international opposition should, it is argued, deter these aggressive wars. And distance or weakness can sometimes make states peaceful, simply because they lack the opportunity or capability to engage in war. Much of Latin America, fortunately divided by high mountains and tropical forests, has benefited from an absence of interstate war.[18]

Differing military technologies can also alter the payoffs of security competition: making the costs of non-cooperation high, reducing the costs of being unprepared or surprised, reducing the benefits of surprise attack, or increasing the gains from cooperation. In particular, Robert Jervis has examined insightfully the differing effects of situations in which the offense or the defense has the advantage and in which offensive weapons are or are not distinguishable from defensive weapons. When the offense has the advantage and weapons are indistinguishable, the level of insecurity is high, incentives for preemptive attack correspondingly are strong. When offensive weapons do not have an advantage and offensive weapons are distinguishable the incentives for preemptive attack are low, as are the incentives for arms races. Capable of signaling with clarity a non-aggressive intent and of guaranteeing that other states pose no immediate strategic threat, statesmen should be able to adopt peaceable policies and negotiate disputes.[19]

Prudent dictators clearly can maintain a peace. But the task is difficult and unlikely to be successful over the long run. Prudence can be enhanced by deterrence, transparency, geography, and

---

[17]Raymond Aron, *Peace and War* (New York: Praeger, 1968), pp. 151–154.

[18]Arie Kacowicz, "Explaining Zones of Peace: Democracies as Satisfied Powers", *Journal of Peace Research* 32, 3 (1995), pp. 265–276.

[19]Robert Jervis, "Cooperation Under the Security Dilemma", *World Politics*, 30, 1, 1978, pp. 186–210, 212.

a variety of other factors in complex, strategic standoffs. But these factors vary in hand to predict ways. Military technologies can be changed from defensive to offensive and from distinguishable to indistinguishable and even the "clearest" technical messages appear subject to garbling. The pre-1914 period, which objectively represented a triumph of the distinguishable defense (machine guns, barbed wire, trench warfare) over the offensive, subjectively, as Jervis notes, was a period which appeared to military leaders to place exceptional premiums on the offensive and thus on preemptive war.[20] Bipolar stability discourages polar or superpower wars, not proxy or small power wars. And multipolar balancing of power also encourages warfare to seize, for example, territory for strategic depth against a rival expanding its power from internal growth.

For Hobbes, therefore, safety also enjoins a prudent policy of forewarning (spying) and of forearming oneself to increase security against all other sovereigns who, lacking any assurance that you are not taking these measures, also take them. Safety also requires (morally) taking actions "whatsoever shall seem to conduce to the lessening of the power of foreigners whom they [the sovereign] suspect, whether by slight or force".[21] If preventive wars are prudent, the prudence of rational dictators obviously must allow for frequent wars and preclude a truly stable peace, leaving countries caught in a "state of war" wherein the danger of war for each and every state from each and every state is constant.

Peaceful Nationalism? Perhaps, others have argued, it is nationalism, rather than dictatorship, that makes for war. It is the self-aggrandizement, self-absorption and chauvinism that too often accompany national identification that preclude the rational cooperation that otherwise might occur. But, here too, the argument is mixed. Nationalism can be pacific, when democratic.

---

[20] Jervis examines incentives for cooperation, not the existence or sources of peace.

[21] Hobbes, "De Cive", *The English Words of Thomas Hobbes* (London: J. Bohn, 1841), 2, p. 171.

J. J. Rousseau, the great 18th century philosopher of democratic nationalism, found that the international condition among states was a state of war, but a state of war that could be tamed, at least for a time.[22] In a Rousseauian democracy, each citizen would be asked to pledge all, not to a corrupt monarch or his ministers, but to each other. Sovereignty would be made secure at home; each citizen would also become both equal to all others and free. Inalienable, indivisible, infallible as an expression of the true interests of the people as a whole, and therefore all encompassing, the people assembled would decide laws applying to all on an equal basis, absolutely, and thus constitute the General Will. The General Will would thus be inherently general (meaning national, or coextensive with the polity) and rational — it was the people rightly understanding their long term general interests.[23]

Unlike corrupted monarchies, the Social Contract would pursue no whims or private interests that would lead the state into possibly frequent battles. Wars would only be fought for national purposes that expressed the long term rational interests of the people. Wars thus would only be fought if necessary when the true interests of the people as a whole were at stake.[24]

Peace then becomes possible when the clash of (genuine) national interests is minimized. Corsica is Rousseau's model for such an isolationist peace. It is a small, undeveloped society. The Genoese blockaded the island, devastated the coasts, and slaughtered the native nobility. This tragedy represented a fortunate opportunity for authentic reform. From devastation, a wise Corsican leadership, Rousseau argues, can establish a society and republic of free farmers and small manufacturers, restricting the corrupting effects of trade with the outside world to the barest essentials. Trade under conditions of international anarchy and national egoism is recipe for conflict leading

---

[22]J. J. Rousseau, "Fragment on War", *A Lasting Peace* (London: Constable, 1917), p. 128.

[23]J. J. Rousseau, *Social Contact*, in *The Social Contract and the Discourses* (New York: Dutton, 1950), pp. 28–29.

[24]Rousseau, *Social Contract*, pp. 9–10.

to armed clashes for markets, raw materials and trade routes. But as a new "Sparta", Corsica could cultivate its virtue with its small farms tilled by robust soldiers.[25]

Here, while rural simplicity persists, "Everyone will make a living, and no one will grow rich".[26] Enjoying isolation and guaranteed by the unity a similarity of social circumstances brings, Corsica would present little temptation to and great resistance against any great power seeking a colonial conquest.[27] The Corsicans would gain security in their time, until the increase in population creates a need for extensive manufactures and commerce, and with them an end to virtue, simplicity and the self-dependence that might have for a time made Corsica strong and safe in the surrounding state of war.

In more complicated, interdependent circumstances, Rousseau recommends a step- by-step progressive reform creating as a surrogate for Corsica's island isolation, a non-provocative defense. He refers to the 18th century, contemporary case for Polish independence. By cultivating education, cultural festivals, and a political system rewarding patriotic participation in public life, the Polish nationalists can make Poland indigestible for any foreign conqueror.[28] Combining patriotism with confederalism and a militia army, Rousseau hopes that Poland's enemies will find her slow decision-making and citizen soldiers no offensive threat and her nationalism a deterrent to easy conquest.[29]

The national prudence of the democratic General Will removes wars caused by monarchical and ministerial caprice and isolation contains the conflicts that interdependence induces. Non-provocative defenses assuage conflicts caused by fear of preemptive attack and deter attacks prompted by the likely success of easy conquest.

When states are nationalist dictatorships the threat of war is compounded as the restraints of democratic decision and national

---

[25]Judith Shklar, *Ordinary Vices* (Harvard, 1984), pp. 28-29.

[26]J. J. Rousseau, "Corsica", in *Political Writings*, ed. by Frederick Watkins (Edinburgh, Nelson, 1986), p. 308.

[27]Rousseau, "Corsica", pp. 279-280, 281-283.

[28]Rousseau, "Poland", in Watkins, *Political Writings*, pp. 169-181, 183.

[29]Rousseau, "Poland", pp. 236, 244-254, 268-270.

prudence are both removed. Nonetheless, even rational dictatorships and democratic nations are caught in a "state of war". The perception that some societies — among them the nationalist dictatorships — would have good reasons to want to expand, and that the international system lacks a global sovereign to maintain law and order: all together make rational states fear each other. They feared each other even if they were not inclined to aggress, because they could not be sure that their neighbor was not prepared to aggress on them and so every armament, even defensively motivated, has aggressive potential. The net result is, as Hobbes opined, that "clubs are trumps". Peace is not natural to dictatorships or nationalisms, even rational or democratic ones. It needs to be self-consciously established; the task liberal philosophers set for themselves.

Liberty, Democracy and Peace

Liberal democratic pacifism rests on the view that the aggressive instincts of authoritarian leaders and totalitarian ruling parties make for war. Democratic states, founded on such individual rights as equality before the law, free speech and other civil liberties, private property, and elected representation are fundamentally against war. When the citizens who bear the burdens of war elect their governments, wars become impossible. Furthermore, citizens appreciate that the benefits of trade can be enjoyed only under conditions of peace.

Some liberals, on the other hand, are skeptical of a general liberal democratic peace and of liberalism's responsibility for it. John Locke — the great founder of modern liberal individualism and international law — assumed that liberal states will remain in a near-state of war. It was Immanuel Kant — a liberal republican who calls us to a demanding internationalism — who made the more convincing but much more demanding case for liberal statesmanship. He argued that the liberal peace would be limited to fellow liberals while a dangerous state of war would prevail outside the liberal peace. Some of that danger, moreover, must be attributed to liberal aggressiveness and, one can hope, moderated by liberal statesmanship.

Democratic War? Again, the skeptics warn us that neither democracy nor liberal values are alone sufficient. From Thucydides to Machiavelli, popular government, rather than being a force for peace, was the ideal foundation for imperial power. Democracies free up resources for state power when citizens have a stake in the survival and success of the state. Rather than spending resources in coercing the citizenry, the state can draw upon citizens' resources for what are regarded as public purposes (Thucydides I:17). In addition, democratic institutions provide motives and materiel for imperial expansion. A free society allows an "adventurous spirit" to rule, producing a popular willingness to take risks, to increase production, and to trade far and wide. As Thucydides noted during the Assembly debate that decided to set out to conquer Sicily:

> There was a passion for the enterprise which affected everyone alike. The older men thought they would either conquer the places against which they were sailing or, in any case, with such a large force, could come to no harm; the young had a longing for the sights and experiences of distant places, and were confident that they would return safely; the general masses and the average soldier himself saw the prospect of getting pay for the time being and of adding to the empire so as to secure permanent paid employment in the future. The result of this excessive enthusiasm of the majority was that the few who actually were opposed to the expedition were afraid of being thought unpatriotic if they voted against it, and therefore kept quiet (VI:24).

In other circumstances, more egalitarian, rational national democracies can reduce but not eliminate the state of war, even among each other. That was Rousseau's argument. If popular rule is insufficient to produce peace, are liberal principles sufficient?

Liberal War? Let us examine Locke's international system. Locke's citizens, like Hobbes's, are rational independent individuals. The foreign relations of Locke's states are guided by "national advantage" as judged by the sovereign executive (although Locke's state is based ultimately on consent; while Hobbes's Realism is indifferent to these matters as long as the state is sovereign). There is thus much of

Hobbesian rational unitary egoism in Lockean foreign relations. But we see one crucial difference. Lockean statespersons, like his citizens, are governed by the duties of natural law — life, liberty, and property.

Lockean states then are distinguished, if Locke is correct, by a commitment to legal obligations that can generate mutual trust. In the bargaining literature, trust is crucial for stable agreements, and all rational egoistic bargainers will want to cultivate a reputation for it.[30] But Lockean bargainers, to take a further step, are committed to it by nature (or God).[31]

Lockean states therefore remain at peace with other states unless they have been attacked or find their rights violated. In the first instance, wars are thus created by criminals and criminal states that violates those rights. But the international condition is also fraught with "Inconveniences" that provoke even just, principled states into war.

a. That bias and *ignorance* can cause war among well-meaning liberals, Locke warns us, is the first "Inconvenience" of the state of nature. Even though the laws of nature are clear, we will fail to reflect on their implications or be biased in their consideration in our own case.

b. That *partiality*, passion and revenge can corrupt the adjudication of even clear law, biasing its application in one's own interest, is the second. *Negligence* will make them remiss in the consideration of the others. Both will lack, therefore, adequate *authority* to make adjudication effective.

c. That *weakness* and fear will erode effective execution of the law is the third, Locke concludes. The power to enforce just judgments will thereby be absent and given that absence states will be tempted to act unilaterally and lawlessly.

---

[30] Philip Heymann, "The Problem of Coordination: Bargaining and Rules", *Harvard Law Review* 86, 5 (March 1973) develops these points.

[31] See the seminal essay by John Dunn, "The Concept of Trust in the Politics of John Locke", in Richard Rorty, ed., *Philosophy in History* (Cambridge University Press, 1984).

Put together, these mean that international order will be problematic, achieved only through exceptional statesmanship, not at all the automatic result of liberal principles. Nowhere, therefore, do Lockean states find a state of secure peace or untroubled peace. Avoiding or mitigating the occasions of war is then the Lockean Liberal strategy of peace, corresponding with contemporary conceptions of peace through international organization, legal codification and improved regulation.

Democratic Liberal Internationalism

Kant and the Liberal Internationalists reject the views of Realists and try to fill the gaps in Liberal theory as they illustrate for us the larger potential of the liberal tradition. Immanuel Kant's 1795 essay, "Perpetual Peace", offers a coherent explanation of two important regularities in world politics — the tendencies of liberal states simultaneously to be peace-prone in their relations with each other and unusually war-prone in their relations with nonliberal states.

The first of the effects of liberalism on the foreign relations of liberal states is the establishment of a peace among liberal states.[32]

---

[32]Clarence Streit, *Union Now: A Proposal for a Federal Union of the Leading Democracies* (New York: Harpers, 1938), pp. 88, 90–92) seems to have been the first to point out (in contemporary foreign relations) the empirical tendency of democracies to maintain peace among themselves, and he made this the foundation of his proposal for a (non-Kantian) federal union of the fifteen leading democracies of the 1930's. D. V. Babst, "A Force for Peace", *Industrial Research*, April 1972, pp. 55–58 performed a quantitative study of this phenomenon of "democratic peace". And R. J. Rummel did a similar study of "libertarianism" (in the sense of laissez-faire) focusing on the postwar period in "Libertarianism and International Violence", *Journal of Conflict Resolution* 27 (1983), pp. 27–71. I use liberal in a wider (Kantian) sense in my discussion of this issue in "Kant, Liberal Legacies, and Foreign Affairs, Part 1", *Philosophy and Public Affairs* 12 (1983), pp. 205–235. In that essay, I survey the period from 1790 to the present, and find no war directly between liberal states. But there are partial exceptions to the generalization; for example, Finland, having been attacked by the USSR, was legally at war with the allies in World War Two when the US and the UK allied with the USSR. I discuss hard cases, such as Fashoda, in *Ways of War and Peace*, Chapter 8.

During the nineteenth century, the United States and Great Britain engaged in nearly continual strife — including one war, the War of 1812. But after the Reform Act 1832 defined actual representation as the formal source of the sovereignty of the British parliament, Britain and the United States negotiated their disputes despite, for example, British grievances against the Northern blockade of the South, with which Britain had close economic ties. Despite severe Anglo-French colonial rivalry, liberal France and liberal Britain formed an entente against illiberal Germany before World War One. And in 1914–15, Italy, the liberal member of the Triple Alliance with Germany and Austria, chose not to fulfill its treaty obligations under the Triple Alliance to support its allies. Instead, Italy joined in an alliance with Britain and France that had the result of preventing it from having to fight other liberal states and then declared war on Germany and Austria. And despite generations of Anglo-American tension and Britain's wartime restrictions on American trade with Germany, the United States leaned toward Britain and France from 1914 to 1917, before entering World War One their side. Nowhere was this special peace among liberal states more clearly proclaimed than in President Woodrow Wilson's "War Message" of 2 April 1917: "Our object now, as then, is to vindicate the principles of peace and justice in the life of the world as against selfish and autocratic power and to set up amongst the really free and self-governed people of the world such a concert of purpose and of action as will henceforth ensure the observance of those principles".[33]

Beginning in the eighteenth century and slowly growing since then, a zone of peace, which Kant called the "pacific federation" or "pacific union", began to be established among liberal societies. (The more than forty liberal states currently make up the union. Most are in Europe and North America, but they can be found on every continent.)[34]

---

[33]Woodrow Wilson, *The Messages and Papers of Woodrow Wilson*, ed. Albert Shaw (New York: *The Review of Reviews*, 1924), p. 378.

[34]The expansion of the Liberal Community from the 18th century to the present is summarized in Table 1 below (pp. 20–24).

TABLE 1 *The Liberal Community*

(By date "liberal")[a]

Period		Total Number
18th century	Swiss Cantons[b] French Republic 1790–1795 United States[b] 1776–	3
1800–1850	Swiss Confederation, United States France 1830–1849 Belgium 1830– Great Britain 1832– Netherlands 1848– Piedmont 1848– Denmark 1849–	8
1850–1900	Switzerland, United States, Belgium, Great Britain, Netherlands Piedmont — 1861, Italy 1861– Denmark — 1866 Sweden 1864– Greece 1864– Canada 1867–[c] France 1871– Argentina 1880– Chile 1891–	13
1900–1945	Switzerland, United States, Great Britain, Sweden, Canada Greece — 1911, 1928–1936 Italy — 1922 Belgium — 1940; Netherlands — 1940;	29

TABLE 1 (*Continued*)

(By date "liberal")[a]

Period		Total Number
	Argentina — 1943	
	France — 1940	
	Chile — 1924, 1932	
	Australia 1901	
	Norway 1905-1940	
	New Zealand 1907-	
	Colombia 1910-1949	
	Denmark 1914-1940	
	Poland 1917-1935	
	Latvia 1922-1934	
	Germany 1918-1932	
	Austria 1918-1934	
	Estonia 1919-1934	
	Finland 1919-	
	Uruguay 1919-	
	Costa Rica 1919-	
	Czechoslovakia 1920-1939	
	Ireland 1920-	
	Mexico 1928-	
	Lebanon 1944-	
1945[d]-	Switzerland, the United States,	95
	Great Britain, Sweden	
	Canada, Australia, New Zealand,	
	Finland, Ireland, Mexico	
	Uruguay — 1973; 1985-	
	Chile — 1973; 1990-	
	Lebanon — 1975	
	Costa Rica — 1948, 1953-	
	Iceland 1944-	
	France 1945-	
	Denmark 1945-	
	Norway 1945-	
	Austria 1945-	

TABLE 1 (*Continued*)

(By date "liberal")[a]

Period	Total Number
Brazil 1945-1954, 1955-1964; 1985-	
Belgium 1946-	
Netherlands 1946-	
Italy 1946-	
Philippines 1946-1972; 1987-	
India 1947-1975, 1977-	
Sri Lanka 1948-1961, 1963-1971, 1978-1983, 1988-	
Ecuador 1948-1963, 1979-	
Israel 1949-	
West Germany 1949-	
Greece 1950-1967, 1975-	
Peru 1950-1962, 1963-1968, 1980-	
Turkey 1950-1960, 1966-1971; 1984-1994, 1996-	
Japan 1951-	
Bolivia 1956-1969, 1982-	
Colombia 1958-	
Venezuela 1959-	
Nigeria 1961-1964, 1979-1984	
Jamaica 1962-	
Trinidad and Tobago 1962-	
Senegal 1963-	
Malaysia 1963-	
Botswana 1966-	
Singapore 1965-	
Suriname 1975-1980, 1987-1990, 1991-	
Portugal 1976-	
Spain 1978-	
Dominican Republic 1978-	
Ecuador 1978-	
Peru 1980-1990	
Honduras 1981-	
Papua New Guinea 1982-	
El Salvador 1984-	
Argentina 1983-	

TABLE 1 (*Continued*)

(By date "liberal")[a]

Period	Total Number
Uruguay 1985–	
Guatemala 1985–	
Mauritius 1987–	
South Korea 1988–	
Taiwan 1988–	
Thailand 1988–	
Pakistan 1988–1999	
Panama 1989–	
Paraguay 1989–	
Algeria 1989–1992	
Madagascar 1990–	
Mongolia 1990–	
Namibia 1990–	
Nepal 1990–	
Nicaragua 1990–	
Poland 1990–	
Hungary 1990–	
Czechoslovakia 1990–1993	
Bulgaria 1990–	
Albania 1991–	
Armenia 1991–	
Belarus 1991–1996	
Croatia 1991–	
Estonia 1991–	
Latvia 1991–	
Russia 1991–	
Ukraine 1991–	
Lithuania 1991–	
Slovenia 1991–	
Macedonia 1992–	
Mali 1992–	
Guyana 1992–	
Czech Rep. 1993–	

TABLE 1 (*Continued*)

(By date "liberal")[a]

Period	Total Number
Slovakia 1993–	
Lesotho 1993-	
Guinea-Bissau 1994–	
Malawi 1994–	
Moldova 1994–	
South Africa 1994–	
Ghana 1995–	
Mozambique 1995–	
Georgia 1996–	

[a]I have drawn up this *approximate* list of "Liberal Regimes" (through 2000 including regimes that were liberal democratic as of 1996) according to the four "Kantian" institutions described as essential: market and private property economies; polities that are externally sovereign; citizens who possess juridical rights; and "republican" (whether republican or parliamentary monarchy), representative, government. This latter includes the requirement that the legislative branch have an effective role in public policy and be formally and competitively (either inter- or intra-party) elected. Furthermore, I have taken into account whether male suffrage is wide (that is, 30%) or, as Kant would have had it (*MM*, p. 139), open to "achievement" by inhabitants (for example, to poll-tax payers or householders) of the national or metropolitan territory. (This list of liberal regimes is thus more inclusive than a list of democratic regimes, or polyarchies (Powell, 1982, p. 5). Female suffrage is granted within a generation of its being demanded by an extensive female suffrage movement; and representative government is internally sovereign (for example, including and especially over military and foreign affairs) as well as stable (in existence for at least three years). (Banks and Overstreet, 1983; Foreign and Commonwealth Office, 1980; *The Europa Yearbook*, 1985, 1985; Langer, 1968; U.S. Department of State, 1981; Gastil, 1985; R. Bruce McColm and Freedom House Survey Team, eds., *Freedom in the World 1990-1991* (New York: Freedom House, 1991); and James Finn *et al.*, *Freedom in the World 1994-1995* (New York: Freedom House, 1995).

[b]There are domestic variations within these liberal regimes. For example, Switzerland was liberal only in certain cantons; the United States was liberal only north of the Mason-Dixon line until 1865, when it became liberal throughout. These lists also exclude ancient "republics", since none appear to fit Kant's criteria (Holmes, 1979).

[c]Canada, as a commonwealth within the British empire, did not have formal control of its foreign policy during this period.

[d]Selected list, excludes liberal regimes with populations less than one million. These include all states categorized as "Free" by Freedom House and those "Partly Free" (4 Political and 5 Civil Liberties or more free).

Of course, the outbreak of war, in any given year, between any two given states, is a low probability event. But the occurrence of a war between any two adjacent states, considered over a long period of time, would be more probable. The apparent absence of war between liberal states, whether adjacent or not, for almost two hundred years thus may have significance. More significant perhaps, is that when states are forced to decide on which side of an impending world war they will fight, liberal states wind up all on the same side, despite the complexity of the paths that take them there. And we should recall that medieval and early modern Europe were the warring cockpits of states, wherein France and England and the Low Countries engaged in nearly constant strife. Then in the late 18th century there began to emerge liberal regimes. At first hesitant and confused, and later clear and confident as liberal regimes gained deeper domestic foundations and longer international experience, a pacific union of these liberal states became established. These characteristics do not prove that the peace among liberals is statistically significant, nor that liberalism is the peace's sole valid explanation.[35] But they do suggest that we consider the possibility that liberals have indeed established a separate peace — but only among themselves.

Unfortunately, liberalism seems to carry with it a second effect — what Hume called "imprudent vehemence", or aggression against nonliberals.[36] Peaceful restraint only seems to work in the liberals' relations with other liberals. Liberal states have fought numerous wars

---

[35]Babst (1972) did make a preliminary test of the significance of the distribution of alliance partners in World War One. He found that the possibility that the actual distribution of alliance partners could have occurred by chance was less than 1% (p. 56). This, however, assumes that there was an equal possibility that any two nations could have gone to war with each other; and this is a strong assumption. Nonetheless, given the likelihood of average states getting into wars with each other over the past 200 years, the actual record of no wars among liberal democracies is very unlikely to have been an accident; 2×10^{-21} in Bruce Russett's calculation ("The Democratic Peace — And Yet it Moves", *International Security* 19, 4 (Spring, 1995), pp. 164-175.

[36]David Hume, "Of the Balance of Power" in *Essays: Moral, Political, and Literary* (1741-42) (Oxford University Press, 1963), pp. 346-347. With "imprudent

with nonliberal states. Many of these wars have been defensive, and thus prudent by necessity. Liberal states have been attacked and threatened by nonliberal states that do not exercise any special restraint in their dealings with liberal states. Authoritarian rulers both stimulate and respond to an international political environment in which conflicts of prestige, of interest, and of pure fear of what other states might do, all lead states toward war. War and conquest have thus characterized the careers of many authoritarian rulers and ruling parties — from Louis XIV and Napoleon to Mussolini's fascists, Hitler's Nazis, and Stalin's communists.

But imprudent aggression by the liberal state has also characterized many of these wars. Both liberal France and Britain fought expansionist colonial wars throughout the nineteenth century. The United States fought a similar war with Mexico in 1846-48, waged a war of nearly continuous expansion against the American Indians, and intervened militarily against sovereign states many times before and after World War Two. Liberal states invade weak nonliberals states and display exceptional degrees of distrust in their dealings with powerful nonliberal states.[37]

---

vehemence", Hume referred to the English reluctance to negotiate an early peace with France and the total scale of the effort devoted to persecuting that war, which together were responsible for over half the length of the fighting and an enormous war debt. Hume, of course, was not describing fully liberal republics as defined here; but the characteristics he describes, do seem to reflect some of the liberal republican features of the English eighteenth century constitution (the influence of both popular opinion and a representative [even if severely limited] legislature). He contrasts these effects to the "prudent politics" that should govern the balance of power and to the special but different failings characteristic of "enormous monarchies". The monarchies are apparently worse; they risk total defeat and collapse because they are prone to strategic overextension, bureaucratic, and ministerial decay in court intrigue, and praetorian rebellion (pp. 347-348). In this connection one can compare the fates of Britain with its imprudence to Louis XIV's or Napoleon's France or, for that matter, Hitler's Germany or Mussolini's Italy or Brezhnev's Soviet Union. Over-extension to the extent of destruction is clearly worse, from the strategic point of view, than a bit of imprudence.

[37]For a discussion of the historical effects of liberalism on colonialism, the U.S.-Soviet Cold War, and post World War Two interventions see "Kant, Liberal Legacies, and Foreign Affairs: Part 2", op. cit. and the sources cited there.

Immanuel Kant's theory holds that a stable expectation of peace among states (and war with nonliberals) would be achieved once three conditions are met. We can rephrase the three "definitive articles" of the hypothetical peace treaty he asked states to sign in his "Perpetual Peace" of 1795.

First, Kant argues that the institutions of representative, republican government — including an elected legislative, separation of powers and the rule of law — lead to caution because the government is responsible to its citizens. Representation alone does not guarantee peace, but it should select for popular wars. Kant makes this point in unusually stark words:

> If, as is inevitability the case under this constitution, the consent of the citizens is required to decide whether or not war should be declared, it is very natural that they will have a great hesitation in embarking on so dangerous an enterprise. For this would mean calling down on themselves all the miseries of war, such as doing the fighting themselves, supplying the costs of the war from their own resources, painfully making good the ensuing devastation, and, as the crowning evil, having to take upon themselves a burden of debts which will embitter peace itself and which can never be paid off on account of the constant threat of new wars. But under a constitution where the subject is not a citizen, and which is therefore not republican, it is the simplest thing in the world to go to war. For the head of state is not a fellow citizen, but the owner of the state, and war will not force him to make the slightest sacrifice so far as his banquets, hunts, pleasure palaces and court festivals are concerned. He can thus decide on war, without any significant reason, as a kind of amusement, and unconcernedly leave it to the diplomatic corps (who are always ready for such purposes) to justify the war for the sake of propriety.[38]

Second, he requires a principled respect for nondiscriminatory human rights. This should produce a commitment to respect the rights

---

[38]"Perpetual Peace", p. 100; from Immanuel Kant, *Kant's Political Writings*, in Hans Reiss, ed. and H. B. Nisbet, trans. (Cambridge: Cambridge University Press, 1970).

of fellow liberal republics (because they represent free citizens, who as individuals have rights that deserve our respect) and a suspicion of nonrepublics (because if those governments cannot trust their own citizens, what should lead us to trust them?).[39]

Third, Kant discusses the critical importance of social and economic interdependence. Trade and social interaction generally engender a mix of conflict and cooperation. Liberalism produces special material incentives for cooperation. Among fellow liberals, interdependence should not be subject to security-motivated restrictions and, consequently, tends to be more varied, less dependent on single issues and less subject to single conflicts.

The first principle specifies representative government responsible to the majority; the second and third specify the majority's ends and interests. Together the three generate an expectation of peaceful accommodation among fellow liberals and, unfortunately, suspicious hostility toward nonliberals. Kant thus argues that republican representation, liberal respect, and transnational interdependence are the three necessary and, together, sufficient causes of the two regularities taken together.

Thus no single constitutional, international, or cosmopolitan source is alone sufficient, but together (and only together) they plausibly connect the characteristics of liberal polities and economies with sustained liberal peace. Alliances founded on mutual strategic interest among liberal and nonliberal states have been broken, economic ties between liberal and nonliberal states have proven fragile, but the political bonds of liberal rights and interests have proven a remarkably firm foundation for mutual nonaggression. A separate peace exists among liberal states.

But in their relations with nonliberal states, liberal states have not escaped from the insecurity caused by anarchy in the world political

---

[39]The individual subjects of autocracies, of course, do not lose their rights. It's just that the autocrats cannot claim legitimately to speak for their subjects. Subjects retain basic human rights, such as the rights of noncombatants in war. The terror bombing of civilians — as in the bombings of Dresden, Tokyo, Hiroshima and Nagasaki — constitute, in this view, violations of these rights and of liberal principles and demonstrate weaknesses of liberal models in these cases.

system considered as a whole. Liberal states have not solved the problems of international cooperation and competition. Liberal publics can become absorbed in domestic issues, and international liberal respect does not preclude trade rivalries or guarantee farsighted collective solutions to international security and welfare. Moreover, the very constitutional restraint, international respect for individual rights, and shared commercial interests that establish grounds for peace among liberal states establish grounds for additional conflict (irrespective of actual threats to territorial security) in relations between liberal and nonliberal societies. Kant is no advocate of imperial interventions or ideological crusades. Indeed, he regards both as wrongs that prudent and respectful policies can avoid. But liberal regimes shaped by popular attitudes, representative government, and trade and other transnational ties are susceptible to such policies.

Liberal Ideals, Commercial Interests and Popular Institutions: The Kantian Difference

How is Kant able to explain the peace among liberal states when other democratic and liberal theorists fail? Lockeans acknowledge that purely ideological or normative commitments seem insufficient to account for the peace. Statesmen seem to need some institutional guarantee beyond a normative commitment to international rights in order to regularize a state of peace. Foreign policy responsible to a representative government seems to be what it takes firmly to fix rights-oriented preferences, lock in the solidaristic sentiments of international law, and reduce uncertainty among liberal states (Extensive economic interdependence may also help).

But the interests of free trade alone does not work either. Commercial liberals have argued that democratic states would be inherently peaceful simply and solely because in these states citizens rule the polity and bear the costs of wars. Unlike monarchs, citizens are not able to indulge their aggressive passions and have the consequences suffered by someone else.[40] Since the spoils of war

---

[40]The incompatibility of democracy and war was classically asserted by Paine in *The Rights of Man*. Randall Schweller, "Domestic Structure and Preventive War",

were much less valuable than the profits of industry, Adam Smith saw a strong tendency for manufacturing states to be peaceable. Others, such as Montesquieu, claimed that "commerce is the cure for the most destructive prejudices", and "Peace is the natural effect of trade".[41] Schumpeter argued that laissez-faire capitalism contains an inherent tendency toward rationalism, and that, since war is irrational, liberal capitalisms will be pacifistic. But the historical record of inter-capitalist wars does not support these generalizations. While commercial capitalism can help account for aspects of the liberal peace, a shared ideology of human rights and the institutions of representative government seem to be necessary additional constraints to induce trust among fellow-liberal states.

Democratic popular institutions are also insufficient. Thucydides and Machiavelli saw the rule of the people as the great imperial model of government, but that was because their democracies reflected, or represented, the material interests, fear and glory of either the masses or the political classes. Rousseau's citizens are different and reject imperial expansion. His citizens of the Social Contract are equal, rational and free and constitute through their intensive democratic interaction a General Will. They are not subject to the "particular wills" such as those that dictators and demagogues can exploit to drive citizens into imperial expansion. The exploitation of noncitizens in the empire (the source of so much national revenue for imperial Athens) would be unacceptable in a Rousseauian republic that demanded that all men be free, ruling and being ruled on an equal basis. Rousseauian democracy was thus free, independent, and isolationist, but nonetheless caught in a state of war with its

---

World Politics 44 (January 1992) finds some evidence to support the view that democratic hegemons do not engage in preventive wars. And Carol Ember, Melvin Ember, and Bruce Russett in "Peace Between Participatory Polities", *World Politics* 44 (July 1992) find that pacification is also evident in certain preindustrial tribal societies.

[41] This literature is surveyed and analyzed by Albert Hirschman, "Rival Interpretations of Market Society: Civilizing, Destructive, or Feeble?" *Journal of Economic Literature* 20 (December 1982).

neighbors. How then does the Kantian representative republic establish its partial peace?

Kant's citizens, like Rousseau's, are free, politically equal, and rational. The Kantian state thus is governed publicly according to law, as a republic. Kant's constitutional democracy thus also solves the problem of governing equals. But his citizens are different in two respects. They retain their individuality, whether they are the "rational devils" he says that we egoists often find ourselves to be or the ethical agents (treating other individuals as ends rather than as means) that we can and should become. And they retain their diversity in economic and social circumstance. Given this diversity Kantian republics are experiments in how: "To organize a group of rational beings who demand general laws for their survival, but of whom each inclines toward exempting himself, and to establish their constitution in such a way that, in spite of the fact that their private attitudes are opposed, these private attitudes mutually impede each other in such a manner that their public behavior is the same as if they did not have such evil attitudes".[42]

Like Rousseau's direct democracy, Kant's constitutional democracy exercises democratic caution in the interest of the majority. But unlike Rousseau's General Will, Kant's republics are capable of appreciating the moral equality of all individuals. The Rousseauian citizen cedes all rights to his fellow citizens, retaining only the right to equal consideration. In order to be completely self-determining, Rousseau requires that there be no limit but equality on the sovereignty and authority of the General Will. The resulting communitarianism is intense — every aspect of culture, morality, and social life is subject to the creation and the re-creation of the national citizenry. The tendency to enhance domestic consciousness through external hostility and what Rousseau calls *amour propre* would be correspondingly high. Just as individuality disappears into collective consciousness, so to does an appreciation for the international rights of foreign republics.

---

[42]Kant, "Perpetual Peace". And for a comparative discussion of the political foundations of Kant's ideas, see Judith Shklar, *Ordinary Vices* (Cambridge: Harvard University Press, 1984), p. 453.

These international rights of republics derive from our ability to reconstruct in our imagination the act of representation of foreign individuals, who are our moral equals. Kant appears to think that the General Will, which Rousseau thinks can be realized only within the community, can be intuited by each individual as the Categorical Imperative to treat all human being in accordance with common principles of equal respect. Rousseau's democracy — for the sake of intensifying national identity — limits our identification to fellow citizens.

This imaginative act of Kantian cosmopolitan identification benefits from the institutional process of republican government. Constitutionally divided powers among the executive, legislature, and the judiciary require public deliberation and sometimes compromise and thereby mitigate the effect of particular passions or hasty judgment. Rousseau's direct democracy appears to slight the value of republican deliberation and delay.

Moreover, for the sake of equality and autonomy, Rousseau's democracy precludes the private ties of commerce and social interaction across borders that lead to both domestic diversity and transnational solidarity. These material ties sustain the transnational, or cosmopolitan, identity of individuals with each other that serves as the foundation of international respect, which in turn is the source of the spirit of international law that requires tolerance and peace among fellow constitutional democracies (while exacerbating conflict between constitutional democracies and all other states). Rousseau shares with Kant, democratic rationality. Rousseau, however, excludes both the moral individualism and the social pluralism that provide the foundations for Kant's liberal peace (and make Kantian republics vulnerable to imprudent aggression while protecting overseas interests).

To the extent that these theoretical distinctions tap the actual range of diversity in the development of contemporary democracies, they offer us some useful warnings about the international implications of the current trend toward democratization. While majority rule may be a necessary condition of a state of peace, it is not a sufficient condition. Autarky and nationalism can undermine democratic liberal peace. To establish peace among themselves, democracies must also define individual rights in such a way that the cosmopolitan rights of all mankind are entailed in the moral foundations of the rights of domestic citizens. And they must allow the material ties of transnational society to flourish among themselves.

Liberal regimes must also guard against the danger of being drawn into aggressive wars in pursuit of material advantage or international crusading in the name of liberal principles. Both of these could undermine international order, provoke social collapse, and erode the domestic foundations of liberal regimes. The liberal peace, far from being automatic, will require both moral politics and prudent statesmanship and, given the usual vagaries of human nature and collective decision making, will, as Immanuel Kant noted, be completely achieved only after much "sad experience".

Mahmood Mamdani

Making Sense of Political Violence in Postcolonial Africa

We have just ended a century replete with violence. The 20th century was possibly more violent than any other in recorded history. Just think of world wars and revolutions, and of colonial conquests and anti-colonial resistance, and, indeed, in revolutions and counter-revolutions. Even if the expanse of this violence is staggering, it makes sense to us.

The modern political sensibility sees political violence as necessary to historical progress. Ever since the French Revolution, moderns have come to see violence as the midwife of history. The French Revolution gave us terror and it gave us a citizens' army. The real secret behind Napoleon's spectacular battlefield successes was that his army was not comprised of mercenaries but patriots, those who killed for a cause, who were animated by national sentiment, by what we have come to recognize as a civic religion, nationalism. Reflecting on the French revolution, Hegel thought of man — in the generic sense — as different from animals, in that he was willing to die for a cause higher than life. Hegel should have added: man is also willing to kill for a cause higher than life. This, I think, is truer of modern man and woman, than it is true of humanity in general.

The modern political sensibility is not horrified by all violence. Just put millions in the wrong uniform: citizens and patriots will celebrate their death as the end of enemies. The world wars are proof enough of this. What horrifies modern political sensibility is not violence *per se*, but violence that does not make sense. It is violence that is neither revolutionary nor counter-revolutionary, violence that cannot be illuminated by the story of progress, that appears senseless to us. Not illuminated paradigmatically, non-revolutionary violence appears pointless.

Unable to explain it, we turn our back on history. Two such endeavors are worth noting. The first turns to culture, the second to theology. The cultural turn distinguishes modern from pre-modern culture and then offers premodern culture as an explanation of political violence. If revolutionary or counter-revolutionary violence arises from market-based identities such as class, then non-revolutionary violence is said to be an outcome of cultural difference. On a world scale, it is called a clash of civilizations.[1] Locally, that is, when it does not cross the boundary between the West and the rest, it is called communal conflict as in South Asia, or ethnic conflict as in Africa.

Faced with political violence that arises in a modern context but will not fit the story of progress, theory has tended to take refuge in theology. The violence of the Holocaust is branded as evil that can only be understood outside historical time.[2] Rather than understand the Holocaust as a clue to the debased and grim side of

---

[1]See, for example, Samuel Huntington, *The Clash of Civilizations and the Remaking of World Order* (New York: Simon and Schuster, 1996).

[2]For a discussion of group violence as evil, see, Ervin Staub, *The Roots of Evil: The Origins of Genocide and Other Group Violence* (Cambridge: Cambridge University Press, 1989). On the relationship between evil and historical time, see, Paul Ricouer, *The Symbolism of Evil*; Alain Badiou, *Ethics: An Essay on the Understanding of Evil*; Georges Bataille, *Literature and Evil*; Malcolm Bull, ed., *Apocalypse Theory and the End of the World*; and Alenka Zupancic, *Ethics of the Real*. I am thankful to Robert Meister of the University of Calfornia, Santa Cruz, for suggesting this latter set of readings.

humanity, this kind of thinking turns this horror into a question mark against the very humanity of its perpetrators. There is a huge resistance, moral and political, to thinking through this violence by locating it in a historical context.

Thinking through the Holocaust: The Violence of the Settler

In the corpus of Holocaust-writing, Hannah Arendt stands apart. Rather than talk of the uniqueness of the Holocaust, Arendt insisted on locating the Holocaust in the history of genocide. The history she sketched was that of the settler genocide of the native. It was the history of imperialism, specifically, of twin institutions — racism in South Africa, and bureaucracy in India and Algeria — forged in the course of an earlier European expansion into the non-European world.[3]

> Of the two main political devices of imperialist rule, race was discovered in South Africa, and bureaucracy in Algeria, Egypt and India; the former was originally the barely conscious reaction to tribes of whose humanity European man was ashamed and frightened, whereas the latter was a consequence of that administration by which Europeans had tried to rule foreign peoples whom they felt to be hopelessly their inferiors and at the same time in need of their special protection. Race, in other words, was an escape into an irresponsibility where nothing human could any longer exist, and bureaucracy was the result of a responsibility that no man can bear for his fellow-man and no people for another people.

Not only did genocide have a history but modern genocide was nurtured in the colonies: the "elimination of Hottentot tribes, the wild murdering by Carl Peters in German Southwest Africa, the decimation of the peaceful Congo population — from 20 to 40 million reduced to 8 million people and...worst of all...the

---

[3]Hannah Arendt, *The Origins of Totalitarianism* (New York: Harcourt Brace, 1975), p. 185.

triumphant introduction of such means of pacification into ordinary, respectable foreign policies".[4]

The idea "that imperialism had served civilization by clearing inferior races off the earth" found widespread expression in 19th century European thought, from natural sciences and philosophy to anthropology and politics.[5] When Lord Salisbury, the British Prime Minister, claimed in his famous Albert Hall speech on May 4, 1898 that "one can roughly divide the nations of the world into the living and the dying", Hitler was but 9 years old, and the European air was "soaked in the conviction that imperialism is a biologically necessary process, which, according to the laws of nature, leads to the inevitable destruction of lower races". The paradigmatic example of the destruction of lower races was Tasmania, an island the size of Ireland where European colonists first arrived in 1803, the first massacre of natives occurred in 1804, and the last original inhabitant died in 1869. Similar fates awaited the Maoris of New Zealand, the Native Americans, the Hareros of Southwest Africa, and so on.[6]

By the time the 20th century dawned, it was a European habit to distinguish between civilized wars and colonial wars. Laws of war

---

[4]*ibid.*

[5]Herbert Spencer wrote in *Social Statics* (1850): "The forces which are working out the great scheme of perfect happiness, taking no account of incidental suffering, exterminate such sections of mankind as stand in their way". Charles Lyall pursued this train of thought in *Principles of Geology*: If "the most significant and dimunitive of species…have each slaughtered their thousands, why should not we, the lords of creation, do the same"? His student, Charles Darwin, confirmed in *The Descent of Man* (1871): "At some future period not very distant as measured in centuries, the civilized races of man will almost certainly exterminate and replace throughout the world the savage races". "After Darwin", comments Sven Lindqvist in his survey of European thought on genocide, "it became accepted to shrug your shoulders at genocide. If you were upset, you were just showing your lack of education". See, Sven Lindqvist, *"Exterminate all the Brutes", One Man's Odyssey into the Heart of Darkness and the Origins of European Genocide* (New York: The New Press, 1996), pps. 8, 117, 107.

[6]This paragraph is based on Sven Lindqvist, *"Exterminate all the Brutes"*, pps. 141, 119, 149-151.

applied to wars among the civilized but laws of nature — biological necessity expressed in the extermination of the lower races — applied to colonial wars. In the Second World War, Germany observed the laws of war against Western powers, but not against Russia. As opposed to 3.5% of English and American prisoners of war who died in German captivity, 57% of Soviet prisoners — 3.3 million in all — lost their lives. The gassings of Russians preceded the gassings at Auschwitz: the first mass gassings were of Russian prisoners of war in the southern Ukraine.[7] The first to be gassed in Aushwitz were Russians, beginning with intellectuals and communists. The Nazi plan, writes Sven Lindqvist, was to weed out some ten million Russians with the remainder kept alive as a slave labor force under German occupation. When the mass murder of European Jews began, the great Jewish populations were not in Germany, but in Poland and Russia, forming 10% of the total population and up to 40% of the urban population "in just those areas Hitler was after". The Holocaust was born at the meeting point of two traditions that marked modern Western civilization: "the anti-Semitic tradition and the tradition of genocide of colonized peoples".[8] Here then was the difference in the fate of the Jewish people. They were to be exterminated as a whole. In that, their fate was unique — *but in Europe only*.

This historical fact was not lost on the postwar intellectuals from the colonies. In his *Discours sur le Colonialisme* (1951), Aime Césaire writes that a Hitler slumbers within "the very distinguished, very humanistic and very Christian bourgeois of the 20th century" and yet the European bourgeois cannot forgive Hitler for "the fact that he applied to Europe the colonial practices that had previously been applied only to the Arabs of Algeria, the coolies of India and the Negroes of Africa".[9] "Not so long ago", recalled Fanon

---

[7]Arno J. Mayer, *Why Did the Heavens Not Darken? The Final Solution in History* (New York: Random House, 1988).

[8]Except where indicated, this paragraph is based on Sven Lindqvist, *"Exterminate all the Brutes"*, pps. 158, 160.

[9]Aime Césaire, *Discours sur le Colonialisme* (Paris and Dakar: Présence Africaine, 1995), p. 12.

in *Wretched of the Earth* (1961), "Nazism turned the whole of Europe into a veritable colony".[10]

The first genocide of the 20th century was the German annihilation of the Harero people in southwest Africa.[11] The German geneticist, Eugene Fischer, did his first medical experiments on the "science" of race-mixing in concentration camps for the Harero. His subjects were both Harero and mulatto off-springs of Harero women and German men. Fischer argued that the Harero "mulattos" were physically and mentally inferior to their German parents. Hitler read Fischer's book, *The Principle of Human Heredity and Race Hygiene* (1921), while in prison. The Fuhrer later made Fischer rector of the University of Berlin, where he taught medicine. One of Fischer's prominent students was Joseph Mengele, who would run the gas chambers at Auschwitz. The Holocaust was the imperial chickens coming home to roost.

The link between the genocide of the Harero and the Holocaust was race branding, whereby it is possible not only to set a group apart as an enemy, but also to annihilate it with an easy conscience. To understand the mindset that conceived the Holocaust, one would have to return to political identities crafted by modern imperialism, the settler and the native. Hannah Arendt, and more recently Sven Lindqvist, focused on the agency of the settler, but not on the agency of the native. But it is not just the settler, the native too is a product of the imperial imagination. Framed by a common history, they define

---

[10]Frantz Fanon, *The Wretched of the Earth*, p. 75; for a discussion, see, David Macey, *Frantz Fanon, A Biography* (New York: Picador, 2000), pp. 471, 111.

[11]For details, see Jan-Bart Gewald, *Harero Heroes: A Socio-Political History of the Harero of Namibia, 1890-1923* (Oxford: James Currey, 1999), pp. 141-230; Tilman Dedering, "'A Certain Rigorous Treatment of All Parts of the Nation': The Annihilation of the Harero in German Southwest Africa, 1904", in Mark Levine and Penny Roberts, *The Massacre in History* (New York: Berghahn Books, 1999), pp. 204-222; Regina Jere-Malanda, "The Tribe Germany Wants to Forget", *New African*, London, no. 383, March 2000, pp. 16-21; Horst Dreschler, "Let Us Die Fighting": *The Struggle of the Harero and the Nama against German Imperialism, 1884-1915* (London: Zed Press, 1980).

two sides of a relationship. Unless they are transcended together, they will be reproduced together.

The historians of genocide have sketched half a history for us: that of settler annihilation of the native. To glimpse how this could trigger a counter-tendency, the native annihilating the settler, one has to turn to Frantz Fanon.[12] Hailed as a humanist by most of those who came to pay him homage after death, Fanon has ironically come to be regarded as a prophet of violence following Hannah Arendt's claim that his influence was mainly responsible for growing violence on American campuses in the 1960s.[13] Fanon was recognized as the prophet of decolonization on the publication of his monumental *Wretched of the Earth* (1961); and yet, one needs to recognize that he was also the first critic of decolonization. To understand the central thesis in *Wretched of the Earth* — summed up in a single sentence, "The colonized man liberates himself in and through violence" — one needs to put it in a triple context: that of the history of Algerian colonization, of modernist thought on the historical necessity of violence, and of the post-war movement to decolonization. Put in context, Fanon's thesis was at the same time a description, a claim and a problematization. First, it was a *description* of the violence of the colonial system, of the fact that violence was key to producing and sustaining the relationship between the settler and the native. Second, it was a *claim* that anti-colonial violence is not an irrational manifestation but belongs to the script of modernity and progress, that it is indeed a midwife of history. And third — the more important for this essay — it was a *problematization*, of a derivative violence, of the violence of victims turned killers.

It is in Fanon that one finds the premonition of the native turned perpetrator, of the native who kills not just to extinguish the humanity of the other, but to defend his or her own, and of the moral ambivalence this must provoke in other human beings like

---

[12]Frantz Fanon, *The Wretched of the Earth* (London: Penguin, 1967); also see, David Macey, *Frantz Fanon, A Biography* (New York: Picador, 2000), p. 22.

[13]Hanna Arendt, *On Violence* (New York: Harcourt, Brace and Company, 1970).

us. Although the extermination of colonizers by natives never came to pass, there were enough uprisings that killed many for extermination to hover in the settler imagination as a historical possibility.[14] No one understood the genocidal impulse better than this Martinican-born psychiatrist and Algerian freedom fighter. Native violence, Fanon insisted, was the violence of yesterday's victims, the violence of those who had cast aside their victimhood to become masters of their own lives.

Listen to Fanon: "He of whom they have never stopped saying that the only language he understands is that of force, decides to give utterance by force. ... The argument the native chooses has been furnished by the settler, and by an ironic turning of the tables it is the native who now affirms that the colonialist understands nothing but force". For Fanon, the proof of the native's humanity consisted not in the willingness to kill settlers, but in the willingness to risk his or her own life. "The colonized man", he wrote, "finds his freedom in and through violence".[15] If the outcome was death, natives killing settlers, that was still a derivative outcome. The native who embraces violence to safeguard his and her freedom is the victim-turned-perpetrator.

Legal and Political Identities

If we are to make political violence thinkable, we need to understand the process by which victims and perpetrators become polarized as *group identities*. Who do perpetrators of violence think they are? And who do they think they will eliminate through violence? Even if the identities propelled through violence are drawn from outside the domain of politics — such as race (from biology) or ethnicity or religion (from culture) — we need to de-naturalize these identities

---

[14]For a journalistic account of the spectre of genocide in the White South African imagination, read, Rian Malan, *My Traitor's Heart*.

[15]Frantz Fanon, *The Wretched of the Earth* (London: Penguin, 1967), pp. 33, 66, 68, 73.

by outlining their history and illuminating their links with organized forms of power.

Just as to locate market-based identities such as class in the history of markets to understand them as the outcome of specific historical relations, so we need to turn to the history of state formation to understand the historical nature of political identities. This is particularly so with the modern state which tries to naturalize political identities as anything but political. On the one hand, the modern state enforces particular group identities through its legal project; on the other, it gives depth to these same identities through a history-writing project. It is by giving group identities both a past and a future that the modern state tries to stand up to time.

Settler and native may be drawn from biological discourses on race, but they need to be understood as political identities enforced by a particular form of the state. If they became politically potent, it is because they were legally enforced by a state that made a distinction between those indigenous (natives) and those not (settlers) and turned it into grounds for political, social and civic discrimination. Where indegeneity was stigmatized as proof of lack of civilization and taken as sufficient reason to deny the rights of those conquered, and foreignness valorized as a hallmark of civilization and turned into a guarantee of rights — indeed privileges — for immigrants, there settler and native were racialized as legal and political identities.

Contemporary colonial history of Africa lends itself to a distinction between two distinct modes of rule, each identified with a different form of the colonial state. In the literature on modern colonialism, these two modes are characterized as direct and indirect rule. The transition from direct to indirect rule is one from a modest to an ambitious project. Whereas *direct rule* was preoccupied with shaping elite preferences, *indirect rule* aimed to shape popular preferences. Indirect rule needs to be understood as a response to the crisis of direct rule. Direct rule focused on native elites. It aimed to create native clones of Western modernity through a discourse on civilization and assimilation. Direct rule generated a dual crisis. On the one hand, its civilizational project tended to divide society between an alien minority claiming to be civilized and a native majority stigmatized as backward. On the other hand, the products of this civilizational project — native intellectuals and entrepreneurs — aspired to replace alien rule by self-rule as the basis of a native modernity. The demand for self-rule was the crisis of direct rule.

The colonial response was to subordinate the civilizational project to a law and order project. The big shift was in the legal project: whereas direct rule aimed at introducing rule of law as a single project, indirect rule replaced the project of a single rule of law with a multiple construction of so many sets of "customary" laws. Thus, it bypassed modernizing native elites by championing alternate elites — said to be traditional — who would be as allies in the enterprise to shape mass preferences through a discourse grounded in tradition. But indirect rule did not accept tradition benignly, as a historical given. It treated history as a raw material, putty from which to shape "genuine" tradition. Whereas direct rule was dogmatic and dismissed native tradition as backward and superstitious, indirect rule was analytical. The political project called indirect rule aimed to unpack native tradition, to disentangle its different strands, to separate the authoritarian from the emancipatory, thereby to repack tradition, as authoritarian and ethnic, and to harness it to the colonial project. By repacking native passions and cultures selectively, it aimed to pit these very passions and cultures against one another. I wrote of this in **Citizen and Subject**,[16] an argument I need not elaborate here.

Unlike those who seek to explain political violence by turning to the domain of culture, I intend to argue that even when political identities are drawn from the domain of culture, they need to be understood as distinct from cultural identities. Theoretically, the experience of indirect rule should alert us to the relationship between culture and politics. When the raw material of political identity is drawn from the domain of culture, as in ethnic or religious identity, it is the link between identity and power that allows us to

---

[16]Mahmood Mamdani, *Citizen and Subject: Contemporary Africa and the Legacy of Late Colonialism* (Princeton: Princeton University Press, 1996).

understand how cultural identities are translated into political identities, and thus to distinguish between them. At the same time, to historicize political identity by linking it to political power is to acknowledge that all political identities are historically transitory and all require a form of the state to be reproduced.

Politically, indirect rule was an attempt to stabilize colonial rule by moving away from direct rule that created a volatile context in which the identity of both rulers and ruled was racialized, but the former as a minority and the latter as a majority. Indirect rule did this through a legal project that fractured the singular, racialized and majority identity, *native*, into several, plural, ethnicized, minority identities — called *tribes*.

To understand how political identities may be defined through the force of law, let us take an African example from any indirect rule colony in the first half of the 20th century. Recall that the colonial census classified the population into two broad, overall groups. One group was called *races*, and the other *tribes*. This single distinction illuminates the technology of colonial rule. To elaborate the technology of rule, I would like to make five observations.

First, the census divides the population into two kinds of groups: some are tagged as races and others as tribes. Why? On examination, one can discern a clear pattern: *non-natives* are tagged as *races*, whereas *natives* are said to belong to *tribes*. *Races* — specifically Europeans, Asians, Arabs — were all those the colonial state defined as not indigenous to Africa. *Tribes* — called ethnic groups in the post-colonial period — were all those defined as indigenous in origin.

Second, this distinction had a direct legal significance. All *races* were governed under a single law, civil law. True, civil law was full of discriminations: racial discrimination distinguished between the *master race* (Europeans) from *subject races* (Asians and Arabs). Subject races were excluded from the exercise of certain rights considered the prerogative of only members of the master race. But this discrimination needs to be understood as internal, for the domain of civil law included all races.

The situation was different with tribes and customary law. There was not a single customary law to govern all tribes defined as

one racialized group — natives. Instead, each *tribe* was ruled under
a separate set of laws, called customary laws. It was said that each
tribe was governed by a law that reflected its own tradition. Yet
most would agree that the cultural difference between races — such
as Whites, Asians and Arabs — was greater than that between different
tribes. To begin with, different races spoke different languages,
mutually untelligible. Often, they practiced different religions. They
also came from different parts of the world, each with its own
historical archive. Different tribes, in contrast, spoke languages that
were often mutually intelligible.

My point is simple: even if *races* were as different culturally as
whites, Asians, and Arabs, they were ruled under a single law, imported
European law, called civil law. Even if their languages were similar
and mutually intelligible, *ethnic groups* were governed under separate
laws, called "customary" laws, which were in turn administered by
ethnically distinct native authorities. With *races*, the cultural difference
was not translated into separate legal systems. Instead, it was
contained, even negotiated, within a single legal system, and was
enforced by a single administrative authority. But with *ethnicities*, the
case was the opposite: cultural difference was reinforced, exaggerated,
and built up into different legal systems and, indeed, separate administrative and political authorities. In a nutshell, different races were
meant to have a common future; different ethnicities were not.

My *third* observation: the two legal systems were entirely different
in orientation. We can understand the difference by contrasting
English common law with colonial customary law. English common
law was presumed to change with circumstances. It claimed to
recognize different interests and interpretations. But customary law
in the colonies assumed the opposite. It assumed that law must not
change with changing circumstances. Rather, any change was
considered *prima facia* evidence of corruption. Both the laws and
the enforcing authorities were called "traditional". Indeed, Western
colonial powers were far more concerned to establish the traditional
credentials of their native allies than they were to define the content
of tradition. Their preoccupation was with defining, locating, anointing
the traditional authority. Most importantly, traditional authority in

the colonial era was always defined in the singular. We need to remember that most African colonies had never before had an absolutist state. Instead of a single state authority whose writ was considered law in all social domains, the practice was for different authorities to define separate traditions in different domains of social life. The rule-defining authority thus differed from one social domain to another; besides chiefs, the definers of tradition could include women's groups, age groups, clans, religious groups, and so on.

The big change with the colonial period was that Western colonial powers exalted a single authority, called the chief, as *the* traditional authority. Marked by two characteristics, age and gender, the authority of the chief was inevitably patriarchal. As David Laitin showed in his study of Yorubaland, the practice was to look for those local elites most in danger of being sidelined, local elites that had legitimacy but lacked authority, and then to sanctify their position and enforce their point of view as customary, and reinforce their authority in law, as traditional.[17]

Colonial powers were the first fundamentalists of the modern period. They were the first to advance and put into practice two propositions: one, that every colonized group has an original and pure tradition, whether religious or ethnic; and two, that every colonized group must be made to return to that original condition, and that return must be enforced by law. Put together, these two propositions constitute the basic platform of every religious or ethnic fundamentalism in the postcolonial world.

Fourth, this legal project needs to be understood as part of a political project. The political project was highlighted by the central claim of the indirect rule state, that natives are by nature tribal. Even though this claim was first fully implemented by Britain in those African lands it colonized in late 19th century, in the aftermath of the Berlin Conference, this claim was already made by Sir Henry Maine, Law Member of the Viceroy's Commission in post-1857 India.

---

[17]David Laitin, *Hegemony and Culture: Politics and Religious Change among the Yoruba* (Chicago: Chicago University Press, 1986).

To quote Maine from *Ancient Law*: "I repeat the definition of a primitive society given before. It has for its units, not individuals, but groups of men united by the reality or the fiction of blood-relationship."[18] In time, this very claim, that natives are by nature tribal, would be advanced as reason for why the African colonies have no majority, but only tribal minorities. This claim needs to be understood as political, not because it is not true but because this truth does not reflect an original fact but a fact created politically and enforced legally.

It is not that ethnicity did not exist in African societies prior to colonialism; it did. I want to distinguish between ethnicity as a cultural identity — an identity based on a shared culture — from ethnicity as a political identity. When the political authority and the law it enforces identify subjects ethnically and discriminate between them, then ethnicity turns into a legal and political identity. Ethnicity as a cultural identity is consensual, but when ethnicity becomes a political identity it is *enforced* by the legal and administrative organs of the state. These organs make a distinction between ethnic groups, between those considered indigenous and those not, the former given right of access to rights considered "customary", such as the right to use land, but the latter denied these same rights.

This takes me to my *fifth* observation. When law imposes a cultural difference, the difference becomes reified. Prevented from changing, it becomes frozen. But as the basis of legal discrimination, between those who are said to belong — whether in terms of religion or ethnicity — and those said not to belong, between insiders entitled to customary rights and outsiders deprived of these rights, these culturally symbolic differences become political.

The distinction between cultural and political identities is important for my argument. Cultural identities are as a rule consensual, voluntary, and can be multiple.[19] All post-modernist talk of hybridity

---

[18]Sir Henry Maine, *Ancient Law* (Washington, D.C.: Beard Books, 1861), p. 178.

[19]I write this without any intent to romanticize the domain of consent or to detract from the existence of power relations in the domain of culture.

and multiple identities belongs to the domain of culture. Once enforced by law, however, identities cease to be all of these. A legal identity is not voluntary, nor is it multiple. The law recognizes you as one, and as none other. Once it is enforced legally, cultural identity is drawn into the domain of politics and becomes political. Such an identity cannot be considered a vestige of tradition because of its ancient history, nor can it be dismissed as just an invention of the colonial power because of its legal enforcement. Even if grounded in a genealogy that precedes colonialism, popular identities like religion and ethnicity need to be understood as the very creation of colonial modernity. To distinguish between cultural and legal/political identities is to distinguish between self-identification and state-identification.

Rwanda: A Metaphor for Political Violence

Colonial Rwanda was different in one important respect from the picture I have just described. In colonial Rwanda, the census did not identify any tribes. It only identified races: Hutu as Bantu, and Tutsi as Hamites. The Bantu were presumed to be uncivilized, and the Hamites presumed civilizing agents. We shall see that this difference between Rwanda and other African colonies — that political identities in Rwanda were racialized, but not ethnicized — would turn out to be of great significance. Rwanda is today a metaphor, for political violence, more particularly for senseless violence in politics. I recently wrote a book on Rwanda. Here, I would like to describe the intellectual and political journey that came to be the writing of the book.[20]

Rwanda had a revolution in 1959. On the face of it, the revolution pit Hutu, the indigenous majority, against Tutsi, the immigrant minority. The identity indigenous and immigrant came straight out of colonial history books and colonial law. Within the revolution, there was a debate as to who was the enemy, and thus, who the people. Two

---

[20]Mahmood Mamdani, *When Victims Become Killers: Colonialism, Nativism and Genocide in Rwanda* (Princeton: Princeton University Press, 2001).

tendencies contended for supremacy. Those who lost maintained that
the battle was not of Hutu against Tutsi, but of the majority against
the minority, of the poor against the rich, and of the nation against
the colonizers. This tendency lost not because it lacked support but
because the support it had eroded when the counter-revolution
attempted a restoration of the Tutsi monarchy. With the defeat of the
counter-revolution, the target of revolutionary violence broadened,
from those who had symbolized the local manifestations of power
(such as the chief) to all Tutsi. When the revolutionaries of 1959 talked
of justice, they did not talk of justice for the poor or for Rwandans
but of justice for the Hutu — at the expense of the Tutsi. To ensure
that justice would indeed be done, they insisted that the revolutionary
state continue the colonial practice of issuing cards that identified
every individual as Hutu or Tutsi (or Twa, an insignificant minority).
Henceforth, the Hutu would be the Rwandan nation and the Tutsi
an alien minority.

One can today find two kinds of writings on Rwanda. The first is
preponderant in the academy, the second in the world of journalism.
Academic writing on Rwanda is dominated by authors whose
intellectual perspective was shaped by sympathy with the Rwandan
Revolution of 1959.[21] They saw the Revolution and the political
violence that effected it as progressive, as ushering in a more popular
political and social order. Unable to see the dark underbelly of the
Revolution, and thus to grasp the link between the 1959 Revolution
and the 1994 genocide, this kind of writing portrays the genocide as
exclusively or mainly a state project of a narrow ruling elite. In doing
so, it totally avoids the question of mass participation in the genocide.
In portraying racism and racialized identities as exclusively state-
defined and state-enforced, it fails to explain how these same identities
got socially-embedded and were reproduced socially. In portraying
the genocide as exclusively a *state project*, its singular failing is an
inability to come to terms with the genocide as a *social project*.

---

[21]See, for example, René Lemarchand, *Rwanda and Burundi* (New York: Praeger,
1970); Catharine Newbury, *The Cohesion of Oppression: Clientship and Ethnicity
in Rwanda, 1860-1960* (New York: Columbia University Press, 1989).

But this claim is not easy to make. Massacres in the Rwandan genocide were carried out in the open. Roughly 800,000 Tutsi were killed in a hundred days. The state organized the killings, but the killers were by and large ordinary people. The killing was done mainly by machete-wielding mobs. You were more than likely to be killed by your neighbors or your workmates, or by your teachers or doctors or priests, or even by human rights advocates or your own husband. A few months ago, four civilians stood trial for crimes against humanity in Belgium. Among the four were two nuns and a physicist. How do we explain their participation — and the participation of other sectors in civil society — in the genocide?

In contrast, journalistic writing focuses precisely on this aspect of the genocide.[22] Its peculiar characteristic is to write a pornography of violence. As in pornography, the nakedness is of others, not us. The exposure of the other goes alongside the unstated claim that we are not like them. It is a pornography where senseless violence is a feature of other people's cultures: where they are violent, but we are pacific, and where a focus on their debasedness easily turns into another way of celebrating and confirming our exalted status. In the process, journalistic accounts also tend to reinforce larger claims: that the world is indeed divided into the modern and the pre-modern, whereby moderns *make* culture, but those pre-moderns live by a timeless culture.

If the social science account is overly *instrumentalist*, accenting only the agency of the state and elites, journalists tend to lean heavily on a *premordialist* account that tends to explain contemporary conflicts as replays of timeless antagonisms.[23] If social scientist

---

[22]The most compelling journalistic account is to be found in Philip Gourevitch, *We Wish to Inform You that Tomorrow We Will be Killed with Our Families* (New York: Picador, 1999).

[23]For a cross-over journalistic account that strongly criticizes journalistic voyeurism but gives an unabashed conspiratorial (instrumentalist) explanation, see, Bill Berkeley, *The Graves Are Not Yet Full: Race, Tribe and Power in the Heart of Africa* (New York: Basic Books, 2001).

accounts tend to explain mass participation in the genocide as mass obedience to rulers (for ordinary Rwandans, goes the most widespread explanation, an order is as heavy as a stone), for journalists it explains the agency of masses gripped in ancient passions and antagonisms. In the final analysis, neither the instrumentalist nor the primordial account is able to give a historical explanation of agency in the genocide.

Politically, journalistic writing has given us a simple moral world, where a group of perpetrators face another group of victims, but where neither history nor motivation are thinkable because both stand outside history and context. When journalists did address the genocide as a social project, I thought they failed to understand the forces that shaped the agency of the perpetrator. Instead, they looked for a clear and uncomplicated moral in the story. In a context where victims and perpetrators have traded places, they looked for victims distinguished from perpetrators for all times. Where yesterday's victims are today's perpetrators, where victims have turned perpetrators, this attempt to find an African Holocaust has not worked. Thus I called my book: *When Victims Become Killers*.

How many perpetrators were victims of yesteryears? What happens when yesterday's victims act out of a determination that they must never again be victimized, *never again*? What happens when yesterday's victims act out of a conviction that power is the only guarantee against victimhood, so the only dignified alternative to power is death? What happens when they are convinced that the taking of life is really noble because it signifies the willingness to risk one's own life and is thus, in the final analysis, proof of one's own humanity?

I thought it important to understand the humanity of the perpetrator, as it were, to get under the skin of the perpetrator — not to excuse the perpetrator, and the killing, but to make the act "thinkable", so as to learn something about us as humans. How do we understand the agency of the perpetrator? Framed by which history? Kept alive, reproduced, by which institutions? Who did the Hutu who killed think they were? And whom did they think they were killing in the person of the Tutsi?

The History of Violence between Hutu and Tutsi

The significance of Fanon became clear to me as I tried to understand the history of political violence in Rwanda, specifically, of violence between Hutu and Tutsi. I was struck by one fact: I could not find any significant episode before 1959 where battle lines were drawn sharply between Hutu on one side, and Tutsi on the other. 1959 was the first significant episode where Hutu were pit against Tutsi in a political struggle, so that Hutu and Tutsi became names identifying political adversaries.

I thought this contrasted sharply with earlier political struggles, such as Nyabingi at the outset of the colonial period. Nyabingi was the name of a spiritual cult, also a political movement, in what is today northern Rwanda, the region incorporated into the expanding Kingdom of Rwanda at the beginning of the 20th century. I thought two facts striking about this movement. First, when the Bakiga fought the alliance of German imperial power and the Tutsi aristocracy of the Rwandan kingdom, they did not fight as Hutu against Tutsi. They fought the Tutsi in power, but in alliance with the Tutsi out of power, first under the leadership of a former Tutsi queen, Muhumuza, and then under the leadership of her son, Ndungutse.

Second, these mountain people did not call themselves Hutu, but Bakiga (the people of the mountains). Only when they were defeated, and incorporated into the Rwanda Kingdom, did they cease to be Bakiga, and became Hutu. For Hutu was not the identity of a discrete ethnic group, but the political identity of all those subjugated to the power of the Rwandan state. In Rwanda before colonialism, prosperous Hutu became Tutsi, over generations. True, the numbers involved were too few to be statistically significant. Yet, this was a process of great social and ideological significance. This process of ritual ennoblement, whereby a Hutu shed his Hutuness, even had a name: *Kwihutura*. Its counterpart, whereby an impoverished Tutsi family lost its status, this too over generations, also had a name: *Gucupira*.

Belgian colonialism did not invent Tutsi privilege. There was Tutsi privilege before colonialism. So what was new with Belgian colonialism? Not Tutsi privilege, but the justification for it. For the first time in the history of Rwanda, the terms Hutu and Tutsi came to identify two groups, one branded indigenous, the other exalted as alien. For the first time, Tutsi privilege claimed to be the privilege of an alien group, a group identified as Hamitic, as racially alien. Only with Belgian colonialism did Hutu become indigenous and Tutsi alien, the degradation of the Hutu a native degradation and Tutsi privilege an alien privilege. As Belgian authorities issued identity cards to Hutu and Tutsi, Tutsi became sealed from Hutu. Legally identified as two biologically distinct races, Tutsi as Hamites and Hutu as Bantu, Hutu and Tutsi became distinct and legal identities. The language of race functioned to underline this difference between indigenous and alien.

The point will become clear if we return to the difference between race and ethnicity in 20th century colonial thought. I have pointed out that only natives were classified as tribes in colonial Africa, and as ethnic groups in postcolonial Africa. Non-natives, those not considered African, were tagged as races. Tribes were neighbors, not aliens. In this context, ethnic violence is different from racial violence. Ethnic violence is between neighbors. It is about borders. It is about transgression across borders, about excess. In the conflict between neighbors, what is at issue is not the legitimacy of the presence of others. At issue is an overflow, a transgression. It is only with a race that the very presence of a group can be considered illegitimate, and its claim for power an outright usurpation. This is why when political violence takes the form of a genocide, it is more likely between races, not between ethnic groups.

The racialization of the Tutsi, and of the difference between Hutu and Tutsi, is key to understanding the political violence between Hutu and Tutsi. This was for one reason. It is the language of race that defined insiders and outsiders, distinguishing those indigenous from those aliens. Ultimately, it set apart neighbors from outsiders, and friends from enemies.

Political Identities and the Nationalist Revolution

Colonialism is the genesis of Hutu–Tutsi violence in Rwanda. But colonialism does not explain why this violence continued after the

Revolution. If colonialism is the site of the origin of the Hutu–Tutsi problem as one of racialized political identities, then nationalism reproduced that problem. Here is the dilemma we must confront: Race-branding was not simply a state ideology, it also became a social ideology, reproduced by many of the same Hutu and Tutsi branded as native and alien. That reproduction took place through the nationalist political project that translated the colonial identity of Hutu as the indigenous Bantu race into the post-colonial Rwandan nation, thereby translating the colonial race-branding project into the post-colonial nation-building project. To problematize the nation-building project is simultaneously to critique the revolution of 1959 and the popular agency that it shaped.

The Rwandan Revolution of 1959 was heralded as the "Hutu Revolution". As the revolutionaries built Rwanda into a "Hutu nation", they embarked on a program of justice: justice for Hutu, a reckoning for Tutsi. And in doing so, they confirmed Hutu and Tutsi as political identities: Hutu as native, Tutsi as alien. When does the pursuit of justice turn into revenge? The Revolutionaries turned the world upside down, but they failed to change it. The irony is that instead of transforming the political world created by colonialism, the world of natives and settlers, they confirmed it. Here then is the question for a postcolonial study of nationalism in Rwanda: Why did nationalism fail to transform the colonial political edifice?

Popular agency has been the subject of an ambitious project in history-writing in South Asia, called Subaltern Studies. Taken from Antonio Gramsci, the word subaltern signified popular strata as opposed to those who command. The great historical contribution of Subaltern Studies was to rescue the subaltern from the status of being a victim in world history by illuminating the subaltern as an agent in history, as one capable of changing things. The historical lesson of Rwanda suggests that we accept the limits of this contribution and recognize that subaltern agency too is undergirded by specific institutions. To accept the time-bound nature of subalternity — as did Fanon — is to begin to subvert it. To generate a perspective that can transform existing identities, we need to stand outside the institutions that reproduce our identities so as to understand group identities as institutionally produced and thus of limited historical significance.

Is not every perspective, no matter how popular, locked in the narrow parameters of the relations that generate and sustain it? Untransformed, a subaltern identity is likely to generate no more than an aspiration for trading places, for hegemonic aspirations. This is why a subaltern identity can neither be embraced nor rejected unconditionally. Unless we highlight its historical boundaries and limitations, the subaltern struggle will be locked in a dilemma, a Catch-22. Without a recognition and subversion of limits, without an institutional transformation leading to a transformation of identities, every pursuit of justice will tend to revenge and every reconciliation into an embrace of institutional evil.

Lenin once chided Rosa Luxembourg with being so preoccupied with Polish nationalism that she could not see beyond it and so risked being locked in the world of the rat and the cat. The world of the rat and the cat is the political world of Hutu and Tutsi as produced by colonialism and reproduced by the 1959 Revolution. For the rat, there is no animal bigger in the presence of the cat: neither lion, nor tiger, nor elephant. For the cat, there is none more delicious than the rat. The political world set in motion by the modern state and modern colonialism too generates subaltern identities endlessly, in binary pairs. For every sergeant, there is a subaltern; for every settler, a native. In a world where cats are few and rats are many, one way for cats to stabilize rule is to tag rats by tapping their historicity through a discourse on origins, indigenous and non-indigenous, ethnic and racial. This is why in a world where rats have belled cats, it is entirely possible that rats may still carry on living in the world as defined by cats, fired by the very identities generated by institutions created in the era of cats.

My point is simple and yet fundamental: you can turn the world upside down, but still fail to change it. To change the world, you need to break out of the world view of not just the cat, but also the rat; not only the settler, but also the native. Unless we break out of the world view of the rat, post-colonialism will remain a purgatory punctuated by nonrevolutionary violence. More than any other contemporary event, the genocide in Rwanda poses this dilemma more sharply than ever before.

The Civil War and the Genocide

For a political analysis of the genocide in Rwanda, there are three pivotal moments. The first moment is that of colonization and the racialization of the state apparatus by Belgians in the 1920s. The second moment is that of nationalism and the Revolution of 1959, a turning of tables that entrenched colonial political identities in the name of justice. The third moment is that of the civil war of 1990. The civil war was not borne of a strictly internal process; it was an outcome of a regional development, one that joined the crisis in Rwanda with that in Uganda.

The Tutsi exiles of 1959 found refuge in many countries, including Uganda. Living on the margins of society, many joined the guerrilla struggle against the Obote regime in 1981–85. When the victorious NRA entered Kampala in January 1986, roughly a quarter of the 16,000 guerrillas were Banyarwanda. Banyarwanda had emigrated to Uganda throughout the colonial period. In the Luwero Triangle — the theater of the guerrilla struggle — migrants were nearly half the population. The largest group of migrants was from Rwanda.

Every time NRA guerrillas liberated a village and organized an assembly, they confronted a challenge: Who could participate in an assembly? Who could vote? Who could run for office? The dilemma sprang from the colonial political legacy, which linked rights to ancestry; by defining migrants as not indigenous, it deprived them of political rights. The NRA's answer was to re-define the basis of rights, from ancestry to residence. Simply put, every adult resident of a village was considered as having the right of participation in the village assembly. This new notion of rights was translated into a nationality law after 1986: any one with a 10-year residence in the country had the right to be a citizen. The big change was that the 1959 refugees of the Rwandan Revolution were now considered Ugandans.

This political inheritance was called into question with the NRA's first major political crisis in 1990, triggered by an attempt to honor one of the 10 points in the guerrilla program: the pledge to redistribute absentee land to pastoralist squatters. When it came to distributing the land among a population of mobile pastoralists, there arose the question: Who should get the land? Who was a citizen?

The opposition mobilized around this question, aiming to exclude Banyarwanda as non-citizens. The magnitude of the resulting crisis was signified by an extraordinary session of parliament, lasting three days. At the end of its deliberation, parliament changed the citizenship law from a 10-year residence to a requirement that to be recognized as a citizen you must show an ancestral connection with the land, i.e. show that at least one of your grandparents were born in the territory later demarcated as Uganda. In another month, the RPF crossed the Uganda-Rwanda border. My point is that this was not simply an armed return to Rwanda; it was also an armed expulsion from Uganda.

To understand the explosive impact of the civil war on Rwanda, we need to understand the changing political position of the Tutsi from the First Republic inaugurated by the 1959 Revolution to the Second Republic that began with the 1973 coup that brought Habyarimana to power. We have seen that the First Republic was a culmination of the struggle between two lines in the Revolution. The victorious line, associated with the new President, Kayibanda, defined Hutu and Tutsi as two different *races*, two different *nations*: Tutsi were thus to be treated as aliens in Rwanda, the home of the Hutu nation. In Habyarimana's Second Republic, Tutsi were redefined from a race to an ethnie. From resident aliens in the First Republic, Tutsi became a political minority in the Second Republic. Instead of the distinction between Hutu and Tutsi, the Second Republic highlighted the distinction between Tutsi in Rwanda and Tutsi exiles outside Rwanda: whereas the former were politically elevated as a Rwandan minority that could legitimately expect minority representation in its political institutions, the latter were denationalized as perpetual aliens for whom there was no longer any room in Rwanda. During the Second Republic, the key political division inside Rwanda was not between Hutu and Tutsi, but within the Hutu elite, between those from the North and those from the South.

It is the military organization of the exile Tutsi as the Rwanda Patriotic Army (RPA), and their entry into Rwanda, which triggered the civil war. The civil war, in turn, had multiple political effects. To begin with, it allowed the Habyarimana regime to pose as the defender of the nation against what was said to be an attempt by exiled Tutsi to restore the colonial monarchy — a repeat of 1963 — at a time when the regime was under great pressure from the predominantly Hutu internal opposition to liberalize. Second, it allowed radical Hutu, hitherto marginalized under the Second Republic, to reemerge in the political mainstream. Describing itself as the defenders of "Hutu Power", this tendency organized a variety of media, from radio and television to print media, that claimed the gains of the Revolution were under threat from Tutsi who were indeed a race, not an ethnie, indeed non-Rwandan aliens, not a Rwandan minority.

Third, the more the civil war grew and the RPA gained ground, the more the internal opposition was discredited as a political fifth column tied to the RPA, and its democratic program painted as an anti-national agenda. Fourth, everywhere the RPA gained military control, the local Hutu population either fled or was expelled through administrative pressure. Most observers estimate that, by 1994, as many as 15% of the Rwandan population had been so displaced, some of them for as many as four times. Most now lived in camps in and around Kigali and the southern part of the country. Some of the most enthusiastic participants in the genocide came from the youthful population of these camps. Finally, against the backdrop of the victorious march of the RPA, the plight of the displaced, spread fear among those who were yet to be engulfed by the civil war. The "Hutu Power" media warned them of a fate that the sight of the displaced only confirmed: if the Tutsi returned to power, they would lose both their land and their freedom — in short, everything.

The civil war of 1990–94 hurled Rwanda back into the world of Hutu Power and Tutsi Power. Faced with a possible return of Tutsi power, it provided radical Hutu, a marginal tendency in the

Second Republic, with its first opportunity to return to the political center stage as defenders of the 1959 revolution. Without the civil war, there would have been no genocide.

The Rwandan genocide needs to be located in a context shaped by 3 related moments: the global *imperial* moment defined by Belgian colonialism and its racialization of the state; the *national* moment that was the 1959 Revolution and that reinforced racialized identities in the name of justice; and the *postcolonial* regional moment born of a link between the citizenship crisis in post-Revolutionary Rwanda and its neighbors. True, the crisis of post-colonial citizenship was regional in scope and led to civil wars in not only Rwanda, but also Uganda, and Congo. But only in Rwanda did the civil war unfold in a context that could and did set alight a powder keg born of a distinctive colonial legacy, *race-branding*, that was reproduced as a revolutionary legacy of *race-as-nation*. Though not a necessary but a contingent outcome, it is imperative that we draw lessons from the Rwandan genocide.

Political Power and Political Identity

My argument on the Rwandan genocide linked the violence in the genocide to political identities that drove the violence, and the reproduction of these political identities in turn to a particular form of the state. Instead of taking group identities as a given, I have tried to historicize the process of group formation. By linking political identities to the process of state formation, this makes it possible to distinguish all pre-political — whether cultural, economic, or biological — from political identities. In addition, it allows for an understanding of the dynamics whereby binary political identities, like Hutu and Tutsi, become polarized.

The Rwandan genocide raises three important issues for those who must live in its aftermath, as to those who study it. The *first* concerns the link between political identities and the process of state formation. To understand how Hutu became synonymous with indigenous and Tutsi with alien, I found it necessary to go beyond an analysis of the colonial state to a critique of the nationalist revolution of 1959 which embraced political identities created by colonial power in the name of justice. The *second* issue arises from the combined legacy of colonial rule and nationalist power. It is also the issue that represents the most troublesome legacy of the Rwandan genocide and has bitterly divided those who write on it: Was not the organization of genocidal violence from the summit of political power linked to mass participation on the ground? The evidence shows that this was indeed the case, which is why we need to understand the genocide as both a state project and a social project. The *third* issue highlights the citizenship crisis in the entire region. Just as the civil war that began in 1990 joined the citizenship crisis in Rwanda with that in Uganda, so the entry of Rwandan troops into eastern Congo in 1996 joined the citizenship crisis in Rwanda with that in Congo. If the 1959 Revolution and its aftermath underlined the difference in the colonial experience of Rwanda and its neighbors — that colonial rule in Rwanda created racialized, but not ethnicized, political identities — post-genocidal Rwanda underlines the aspect of similarity in the regional colonial experience. I argued in my book that colonial Rwanda was like a half-way house between direct and indirect rule. Like direct rule, it generated exclusively racialized political identities; at the same time, like indirect rule, it legitimated the despotic power of local chiefs as a carryover of pre-colonial practices rather than a colonial reorganization of the state. The discourse on custom ties citizenship (and rights) to cultural identity and historical origins.

The proliferation of political minorities in the contemporary African context is not a necessary reflection of the cultural map of Africa. Rather, this proliferation is the outcome of a particular form of the state, the indirect rule state, whose genesis lies in the colonial period. The real distinction between race and ethnicity is not that between biology and culture, with race a false biological identity and ethnicity a true and historically created cultural identity. Rather, both race and ethnicity need to be understood as the politicization of identities drawn from other domains: race a political identity of those constructed as not indigenous (settlers) and ethnicity an identity of those constructed as indigenous (natives). Africa's real political challenge, I have argued, is to reform and thus sublate the form of the state that has continued to reproduce race and ethnicity as political identities, alongside a discourse on nativism and "genuine" tradition.

Colonial power not only shaped the agency of popular strata. It was also stamped on the agency of the intellectual. Colonial power was etched not only on the boundaries of the public sphere, it was also imprinted in the table of contents of scholarly works. Just as colonial power set into motion, first the settler and then the native, in the public sphere, so it preoccupied the intellectual imagination with the question of *origins*. How origin was understood depended on the language of power, specifically, on how power framed agency through customary law.

In the African context, customary law framed agency — and "custom" — as ethnic. In another context, such as India, that agency was framed as religious. Is it then mere coincidence that if the postcolonial African preoccupation is with who is a native and who is not, the postcolonial Indian preoccupation has been with who is a convert and who not? Is it any less surprising that if the native imagination in postcolonial Africa tends to absorb the immigrant into a script of invasion, the native imagination in postcolonial India seems to view the agency of the convert as veritable treason, as a transgression so subversive that the convert is seen as forever lacking in an authentic agency?

Why is it that when it comes to postcolonial political vocabulary, Hindu and Muslim in India, or for that matter Sinhala and Tamil in Sri Lanka, like Hutu and Tutsi in Rwanda, sound as political synonyms for native and settler? The challenge, I have argued, is neither to deny separate histories, nor to build on this separation. It is, rather, to distinguish our notion of political community from that of cultural community and, as a consequence, separate the discourse on political rights from that on cultural or historical origins. The point of difference between cultural and political communities is sharpest when we contrast diasporic with immigrant communities. Diasporic communities share a common history, but not necessarily a common future. Immigrant communities, in contrast, are dedicated to build a common future, but may not necessarily share a common past. To distinguish between cultural and political communities is to distinguish between the past — several pasts — and a single future. The single uniting feature of a political community is the commitment to build a common political future under a single political roof. This recognition should be an important step to creating a single political community and citizenship from diverse cultural and historical groups and identities.

Amartya Sen

Global Inequality and Persistent Conflicts[1]

A Cautionary Introduction

In his sagacious essay on "The History of Astronomy", Adam Smith described philosophy as "that science which pretends to lay open the concealed connections that unite the various appearances of nature". The temptation — indeed the determination — to unearth hidden connections between disparate phenomena is the source of much of our understanding of the world in which we live. It informs our interpretation of what we see and shapes the way we think we ought to act and behave. There are few intellectual commitments as productive as the tenacious search for causal connections between diverse phenomena. And yet, as Adam Smith warns, the sense of understanding that is generated from this effort may not invariably be as definitive as we pretend. We have to be cautious.

It is not surprising that possible connection between the two great afflictions that characterize the contemporary world, viz. (1)

[1] I am grateful to Vivienne Taylor, Olav Njølstad and Rosanne Flynn for helpful discussions.

violent and persistent conflicts, and (2) massive economic inequality and poverty, should attract attention. Even though definitive empirical work on the causal linkages between political turmoil and economic deprivations may be relatively rare, the basic presumption that the two phenomena have firm causal links is very common and widespread. Indeed, it is often taken to be a defining characteristic of an enlightened attitude to war and peace to go beyond the immediately political into the "underlying" economic causes of these phenomena, and to look for the roots of discontent and disorder in economic destitution. Sometime this connection is given a very firm shape in the form of what may be called "economic reductionism", whereby social and political strife is explained, ultimately, by its hidden economic roots.

I shall try to argue here that even though the economic factors underlying political violence and social discontent have to be vigorously searched for and investigated, the temptation to opt for economic reductionism can be quite counterproductive. It is important to be clear about this for at least two distinct reasons. First, the economic connections may be quite complex and far from capturable in the simple form in which economic reductionism tends to proceed. Its appealing simplicity may distract attention from important facets of the interrelations — and significant qualifications — that need fuller understanding. For example, the violent history of Afghanistan cannot be unrelated to poverty and indigence that the population have experienced, and yet to reduce the causation of violence there entirely to this singular economic observation would be a great mistake. Much else is clearly involved, and we have to try to understand how the actual processes work, and what part is played by the economic components of the complex structure of interactions that would be involved.

Second, economic reductionism is often taken as a recipe for public policy — presented even as the quintessential argument for going to battle against poverty. This approach, which is often articulated, implicitly down plays the terrible nature of poverty in itself — quite aside from any further harm it might do. Furthermore, the frailty of the presumed relationship can endanger the reasoned basis of policy making aimed at the removal of poverty and inequality.

There has, in fact, been an increasing tendency in recent years to argue in favour of policies of poverty removal on the ground that this is the surest way to prevent political strife and turmoil. To be sure, basing public policy on such an understanding has major attractions. It provides a politically powerful argument for allocating more public resources and efforts on poverty removal because of its presumed political rewards, taking us much beyond the direct economic case for doing this. Given the visibility and public anxiety about wars and disorders, the indirect justification of poverty removal — not for its own sake but for political peace — has become, in recent years, a dominant part of the rhetoric of fighting poverty.

While the temptation to go in that direction is easy to see, the difficulty here lies in the possibility that if wrong, economic reductionism would not only have impaired our understanding of the world, but would also tend to undermine the declared rationale of the public commitment to remove poverty. Indeed, if the justification of poverty removal is based principally on the ground of a causal connection that may, on investigation, turn out to be doubtful, or at least not wholly robust, then the commitment to remove poverty would be dialectically undermined.

This is a particularly serious concern, since poverty and massive inequality are terrible enough in themselves to provide reasons for placing priority on their removal, without any indirect causal presumption. Just as virtue is its own reward, poverty is at least its own penalty. To look for some ulterior reason for fighting poverty through its effects on violence and conflict may make the argument broader with a larger reach, but it can also make the reasoning much more fragile. This is not to deny that poverty and inequality can — and do — have far-reaching connections with conflict and strife, but these connections have to be scrutinized and investigated with an open mind, rather than rapidly invoked to suit a particular argumentation. The temptation to summon economic reductionism prematurely may well be counterproductive for both science and ethics.

Economic Reductionism and Causal Ambiguities

Many countries have experienced — and continue to experience — the simultaneous presence of economic destitution and inequality, on the one hand, and political turbulence and strife, on the other. From Afghanistan and Sudan to Ethiopia and Somalia, there are plenty of examples of the dual adversities faced by people in different parts of the world. Given this observation, it is not at all unnatural to ask whether destitution kills twice — first through economic privation, and second through political carnage. If the quality of mercy is "twice blessed", the quality of destitution may well be "twice cursed".

This possibility is not in doubt. And its underlying logic is not hard to understand either. Penury and deprivation can make people desperate and reckless. It is also not unreasonable to think that people reduced to stark poverty will have reason to fight for tiny rewards, and this could make conflicts and warfare much more likely. The possibility of such linkages must indeed be adequately acknowledged. And yet, I would argue, there are several reasons for caution before jumping into explaining hostility and carnage through poverty and privation.

The first issue concerns empirical evidence. There is, in fact, no dearth of evidence of conflicts and confrontations in economies with a good deal of poverty and much inequality. But, at the same time, there are also other economies with no less poverty or inequality that seem to stay sunk just in economic hardship, without necessarily generating serious political turbulence. Indeed, many famines have occurred without there being much political rebellion or civil strife or inter-group warfare. For example, the famine years in the 1840s in Ireland were among the most peaceful, and there was little attempt by the hungry masses to intervene even as ship after ship sailed down the river Shannon laden with rich food, carrying it to well-fed England from starving Ireland. The Irish do not have a great reputation for pliant docility, and yet that was the major characteristic of the dreadful famine years (with very few exceptions). Looking elsewhere, my own childhood memories in Calcutta include the sight of starving people dying in front of sweet shops with various layers of luscious food displayed behind glass windows, without a single glass being broken, or law and order being disrupted. The Bengalis have been responsible for many violent rebellions against the establishment (a strong uprising against British rule occurred even in 1942, in the year preceding the famine of 1943), but nothing like that happened in the famine year itself. There is more to say on this (on which more presently), but the temptation to invoke economic reductionism needs to be challenged first.

The second issue concerns the need to go beyond empirical observations into causal analysis, and the importance of scrutinising the presumed causal linkages. Surely destitution can give *reason* to defy established rules, but it need not give people the *courage and ability* to do anything very violent. Destitution can be accompanied not only by economic debility, but also by political helplessness. A starving wretch can be too frail and too dejected to fight and battle, and even to protest and holler. It is, thus, not surprising that often enough intense suffering and inequity have been accompanied by peace and quiet.

This issue relates also to the often-observed fact that the agents, and particularly the leaders, of violence, if and when they do occur, often come from not so deprived groups. This has received particular attention in the context of recent burst of global terrorism. It is not only that a leader like Osama bin Laden may be himself a billionaire, but also that many of the prominent leaders come from quite affluent families. However, this does not indicate that the violence that occurs is unrelated to deprivation and destitution, since battles are often fought in the name of the dispossessed, and may not be altogether independent of the existence of severely deprived people. It is rather that in pursuing the connections, there is need for a more sophisticated approach than can be found in the simple mechanics of economic reductionism.

The third issue to consider raises the question of the *direction* of causality in those cases in which the co-existence of economic poverty and violent strife is actually observed. Do these empirical observations provide evidence for the causation of strife (starting from poverty), or for the causation of destitution (connected with strife and disorder)? Indeed, I would argue that there is at least as strong a causal linkage going from war and violence to famines and destitution, than from the latter to the former. I shall discuss some possible connections in the section after next.

Indirect Connections and Complex Processes

Even though economic reductionism is deceptively simple and ultimately self-defeating, there are causal linkages that make poverty and deprivation influence the likelihood of conflict and violence. The chain of linkages are often quite indirect, but no less important for that reason.

Memory of inequity and political disaffection

Even though deprivation or unequal treatment may not generate an immediate revolt, it can remain in the memory of a population and influence the future course of events. While the Irish famines did not generate an immediate uprising, the history of the famines played a major part in the Irish disaffection with English dominance in the century or more following those famines (those "historical memories" are still invoked often enough). The long-run effects of destitution and devastation can linger for a very long time, and can contribute later on to encouraging rebellion and violence.

To a limited extent this happened in India as well. Even when famines typically occurred without substantial violence (taking place often amidst "the peace of the graveyard"), the memory of famines would be frequently recalled later on as proof of inequities of the imperial rule. Causal connections need not be instantaneous for them to be effective, and they can work over decades and even centuries. This is worth bearing in mind in assessing the social and political effects of contemporary poverty and deprivation as well as prevailing perceptions of inequity and injustice.

Recruitment of foot soldiers

While the leaders of terrorist organizations often come from the more prosperous parts of the society, nevertheless poverty can provide rich recruiting grounds for the "foot soldiers" of the terrorist camps. We have to understand better the many dimensions of poverty and inequality, and the far-reaching relevance they have to the process of recruitment, taking explicit account of the different levels of personnel involved in conflicts and terror. The class identity of terrorist leaders may be a deceptive basis for concluding that poverty and destitution do not, in general, help recruitment for violent campaigns.

Public tolerance of terrorism

The tolerance of terrorism by an otherwise peaceful population is another peculiar phenomenon in many parts of the contemporary world, particularly those that feel badly treated, including being left behind by global economic and social progress. People who would find violence entirely unacceptable in personal lives often provide remarkably little opposition — or even condemnation — of political violence when it is perceived to be a part of a fight against injustice. A more equitable sharing of the benefits of globalization can well be an important preventive measure against the emergence of a general climate where terrorism is tolerated — and sometimes even celebrated — by an otherwise gentle population.

Political asymmetry and alienation

More generally, sharp asymmetries in political power in the world can also feed a sense of alienation of the powerless from the idea of a peaceful and collaborative world. Lessening, to the extent possible, massive inequalities of political power may be, in this respect, an important objective for the long-run peace in a world of asymmetries.

Political asymmetry in the current world relates to a considerable extent to the nature of the institutional architecture of the world which emerged in the very special situation of the 1940s, when the United Nations was set up and the Bretton Woods agreement occurred with the establishment of a set of international institutions (like the IMF, the World Bank and others), reflecting a particular reading of global needs and a specific reflection of the-then division of political clout (exemplified by such measures as separating out some "permanent members" of the Security Council from other members of the United Nations, and also by the nature of operational control of the international financial institutions).

The institutional reforms that are needed may include the United Nations, which is the closest we have to a central organization for democratic governance in the world. The UN is playing a bigger — and more constructive — part in global social policies (for example, health care) under the remarkable leadership of Kofi Annan, who is being honoured this week by the award of the Nobel Peace Prize. The reforms that are needed must include expanding the reach of the United Nations and making it financially more secure and viable. However, they may also include demands for a more democratic sharing of the decision-making processes within the United Nations. This can be important not only for reducing the sense of political asymmetry, but also for the direction of practical policy making.

For example, it is hard to curb arms sales in the world, which often plays an escalating role in local and semi-local conflicts, when 81% of those exports emanate from the five permanent members of the Security Council (this figure relates to 1996–2000). This pessimistic reading is not contradicted by actual events occurring in the Security Council, or for that matter, in G-8 gatherings (the G-8 countries together export 87% of the armaments that are traded in the world). In addition to the direct role that is played by the trade in armaments in facilitating violent conflicts, the process of decision-taking, with it clear connection with the financial and other interests of dominant powers, can itself contribute to some far-reaching disquiet and scepticism of leadership of the world order.

Wars, Famines and Destitution

The avoidance of war and violent conflicts, on the one hand, and the removal of deprivation and inequality, on the other, are both important ends, but it is quite plausible that each also serves to a considerable extent as a means to the other. I have so far been concentrating on the effects of asymmetry and inequality on violence and conflict, and I should now look at the other direction of causation. While we must try to avoid political reductionism in explaining poverty in a way that would be similar to economic reductionism in explaining war and violence, nevertheless the political, and in particular military, antecedents of destitution would seem to deserve more serious attention than they tend to get.

For example, it is worth recollecting how famines and severe impoverishment have been very often associated with antecedent military activities and violent encounters. In particular, famines have devastated war-torn countries in sub-Saharan Africa, such as Ethiopia, Somalia, Sudan, Angola, Mozambique, Chad, and many others. The association is not confined to sub-Saharan Africa, and there are terrible examples elsewhere as well, e.g., in Cambodia. Sometimes, famines have also occurred during a war without being directly related to military actions, e.g., the Bengal famine of 1943 which occurred soon after the Japanese army moved into the neighbouring province of Assam and just after Calcutta was lightly bombed.

There is considerable evidence that the preparation for and the execution of wars do often adversely influence the ability of famine-prone countries to escape mass starvation. Some of the connections are easier to see than others. First, the relationship between wars and famines has some simple and easily identifiable aspects. Wars destroy crops; they devastate the economy and ravage the stock of productive capital; they damage transport facilities and disrupt movements of food and other commodities. It is not hard to see that wars can contribute to destitution in a direct and rather gross way. The disruption of health service is also a direct connection, since most people who die from famines perish through illnesses of one kind or another, and the destruction of medical networks can add substantially to famine mortality.[2]

---

[2]On this see my *Poverty and Famines: An Essay on Entitlement and Deprivation* (Oxford: Clarendon Press, 1981), especially Appendix D; and Alex de Waal, *Famines That Kill* (Oxford: Clarendon Press, 1989).

Second, wars and violent conflicts also reduce the economic incentive to make long-run investments. It is not especially smart to set up factories in a would-be battlefield. Nor to invest much to improve the quality of cultivable land. One of the remarkable features of famines in sub-Saharan Africa is their association with stagnation and decline of productive abilities — not just in food production but also in other fields. Indeed, the prospect of industrialization of sub-Saharan Africa has been immensely damaged by military conflicts, and that, along with other problems such as underinvestment in agriculture, injure these economies very deeply. Because of the paucity of investing activities and of capital formation (going well beyond the destruction of the existing capital goods), the devastating effects of wars and war-like situations on productive abilities can be much more extensive and pernicious than is apparent from the statistics of the actual loss of capital and property through war.

A third concern relates to the role of military activities in the accentuation of economic and political divisions. We have to remember that famines are caused by the inability of some sections of the population to command adequate food for survival — not necessarily by the lack of aggregate food supply. The vulnerable groups face starvation as a result of declines in their "entitlements" (i.e., the set of commodity bundles over which a family can establish operative control). Such an entitlement decline can happen in many different ways.[3] Wars and military activities can disrupt the entitlements of vulnerable groups even without destroying crops or disrupting production or transport. With changes of relative prices and opportunities of transaction, the entitlements of different groups can sharply move in different directions. Sometimes the success of one group in commanding food can contribute to the failure of others to get enough for survival.

For example, the Bengal famine of 1943, in which between two and three million people died, was directly fed by the "war boom"

---

[3] On this see my *Poverty and Famines: An Essay on Entitlement and Deprivation* (1981); with Jean Drèze, *Hunger and Public Action* (Oxford: Clarendon Press, 1989).

in Bengal. That province in British India was close to the front line in the war with Japan, and served as a place in which a massive expansion of military as well as war-related civilian expenditures occurred at that time. The increased purchasing power of those favourably affected by the war boom (primarily located in Calcutta and some other urban areas) allowed them to take a considerably bigger share of the available food supply, leaving the rural masses (especially landless labourers) without the ability to compete in the "food battle". This economic divisiveness was made worse by speculative increases in food prices, fed by panic and skilful fomenting of price expectations by professional dealers who benefited much from the war boom.

Fourth, the divisiveness is not only economic, but also political, with extensive economic consequences. To illustrate with the same example, the misery of the rural destitute in the economy of Bengal in 1943 was not moderated by political intervention; in fact just the contrary. It was exacerbated by the Government's decision to favour the urban people, especially those in Calcutta, since this was important for placating them for the success of British war efforts (the rural masses did not count much in this calculation). This led to governmental arrangements to provide subsidized rice for normal residents of Calcutta (through ration shops and "fair price" distribution centres), and those who had been favourably affected by the war boom in earning higher money incomes were *further* helped by the opportunity to buy food at lower prices. Meanwhile, the Devil took the hindmost — the impoverished and debilitated rural workers. The economically divisive consequences of the war were further magnified and strengthened by the political priorities of war.

Fifth, one of the most pernicious effects of wars and war-like situations is a weakening of the opportunity of adversarial politics and social criticism. Authoritarian regimes get a good excuse for further suppressing opposition parties and independent newspapers, and this in turn makes famines and unprevented disasters much more likely. Indeed, studies of famine prevention in different parts of the world have brought out the fact that even in situations of severe decline of total food output and sharp reduction of market-based economic entitlements of particular sections of the population, famines can be altogether prevented by public policies aimed at protecting the vulnerable.[4] This can be done in different ways. One effective means is through public employment for anyone who seeks them (and is ready to do a good day's work), thus providing a good channel of recreating the lost purchasing power of the potential famine victims.

Even though famines are extremely easy to prevent, it is remarkable how often this power is left unused. Those who run the government belong to a different economic class from the famine victims, and the penalties of famine do not typically visit them. However, in a democracy the rulers too have an incentive to stop famines quickly, since elections are hard to win after famines, and since criticisms from the media and censures by opposition parties can hurt the government. When, however, elections do not occur, the media is censured, and the opposition parties are outlawed or suppressed, the government lacks the political incentive to provide protection for famine victims. The invulnerability of rulers is itself strengthened and reinforced by the authoritarianism (including the suppression of opposition parties and the media) that tends to go with war situations.

There are, thus, many different reasons for linking wars and violent conflicts with the occurrence of famines and economic destitution. And what applies in a stark and sharp way to famines has its parallel in the occurrence of less drastic but still very serious impoverishment and privation in less extreme situations.

The Delusion of Civilizational Partitions

We need to look, thus, in both directions in understanding the relationship between economic destitution and political conflict. If economic destitution is "twice cursed", so is political conflict. As

---

[4]On this see Jean Drèze and Amartya Sen. *Hunger and Public Action* (1989).

my final topic in this brief essay, I would like to go beyond this issue of mutuality into the need to recognise that economic and political factors can also sometimes work together in an interactive way. When lines of division on political or social grounds also have economic correlates, they can magnify the forces of divisiveness.

Consider the so-called "clash of civilizations" which has been receiving so much attention lately, especially in the context of the present global confrontations. Many observers, including world leaders such as Prime Minister Blair and President Bush, have argued that the thesis of an inescapable clash is mistaken. This is indeed so, but the inadequacy of the thesis of clashing civilizations begins well before we get to the point of asking whether civilizations must clash. No matter what answer is given to this question, addressing it in this coarse form tends, in itself, to push us into an illusive way of thinking about the people of the world. It is misleading both because the civilizational categories are crude and inconsistent, and also because there are many other ways of seeing ourselves and others (linked to politics, language, literature, class, occupation, and our other affiliations).

The befuddling influence of a singular classification traps those who (like many senior statesmen in Europe and America) dispute the thesis of a clash but respond within its prespecified terms of reference. To talk about "the Islamic world" or "the Western world" (as is increasingly common, in line with Samuel Huntington's categories) is already to reduce people into this one dimension. The same impoverished vision of the world — divided into boxes of civilizations — is shared by those who preach amity among civilizations and those who see them clashing.

There is a serious intellectual dimension in the sense of alienation that breeds global conflicts and hostility. Western writings often take modern civilization as something of an "immaculate Western conception", denying the role of Chinese science and engineering, Indian and Arab mathematics, and other influences from elsewhere that had direct effects on the Renaissance (and later on the European Enlightenment). There is often also a tendency to see such values as tolerance and reasoning as being quintessentially "Western", even though there is much evidence of the championing of these values in all the literate societies in the world (along with detractions, which too are present both in the Western and the non-Western world). Correspondingly, anti-Western fundamentalists are often inclined to view the modern world as being quintessentially Western and hostile to non-Western cultures and traditions. And yet there is a shared history of the world which includes extensive non-Western contributions to what is now seen as "Western science" or "Western mathematics", or for that matter, "Western liberalism".

This historical distortion, based on very selective readings of history (ignoring, for example, the role and impact of African civilizational ancestry, Chinese science and technology, Indian and Arab mathematics, and so on), tends to feed a confrontational approach in global relations. For example, the champions of Arabic or Muslim traditions have just as much reason to take pride in their history of science, mathematics and engineering, their tradition of tolerance and of intellectual "give and take", and their contribution to European renaissance (and through it, to European Enlightenment) as they have to focus on theology or religiosity.[5]

Why is it the case, we have to ask, that a young Arab or Muslim activist tends to feel closely associated with the theological achievements of Islam, but typically not with the contributions of Arab and Muslim mathematicians to world civilization? And why do the defenders of Western values pay so little attention to the global heritage that helped — directly or indirectly — to the progress of civilization across the world? A less slanted reading of global history not only has something to contribute to objectivity, but can also work against unnecessary clashes and divisive confrontations. The

---

[5]There is a slight analogy, which will not be further pursued here, between (1) the practice (in intellectual history) of appropriating, if only implicitly. non-Western innovations within the corpus of the so-called "Western civilization", and (2) the efforts (in business practice) to take out trade patents, in particular Western countries, on well-established traditional medicine (such as "neem") and other artifacts from Asia and Africa.

cause of peace can be helped by a more just acknowledgement of the global roots of contemporary civilization, in addition to a more equitable sharing of economic and social opportunities.

The crudeness of civilizational categories is supplemented by a second problem, to wit, the absurdity of the implicit presumption that this partitioning is uniquely relevant and must drown or swamp other ways of identifying people. That imperious view goes not only against the old-fashioned sentiment that "we human beings are all much the same", but also against the more plausible understanding that we are diversely different. Each of us has many features in our self-conception. Our religion, important as it may be, cannot be an all-engulfing identity. The main hope of harmony in the contemporary world lies not in any imagined uniformity, but in the plurality of our identities, which cut across each other and work against sharp divisions around one uniquely hardened line of impenetrable division.

Even a shared poverty can be a source of solidarity across the borders. The kind of division highlighted by, say, the so-called "anti-globalization" protesters (who, incidentally, run one of the most globalized movements in the world) tries to unite the underdogs of the world economy. Its program goes firmly against religious, national, or "civilizational" lines of division. Indeed, the economic lines of division can be seen to be a factor that works against divisiveness along the so-called "civilizational" lines. In this sense, the anti-globalization protests and the loyalties they try to generate can make a very positive contribution not only in drawing attention to massive inequality and poverty in the world, but also in countering the single-minded concern with religious differences on which the so-called clash of civilizations is parasitic.

The troubling issue to look at, in this context, is the possibility of coupling the so-called civilizational partitioning and economic divisions. The rhetoric of anti-Western and anti-modernist values that the religious fundamentalists present often includes explicit or implicit references to economic exploitation and the fostering of inequality. The Islamic fundamentalist is then seen as pursuing not just an "anti-modern" or "anti-Western" agenda, but also as fighting against injustice visited upon Islamic and other non-Western populations by the Western masters of the global economy. As it happens, at the conceptual level this amounts to a confounding of categories, and even empirically, the economic divisions have, in general, a very different history and character than the religious partitions. But there is enough overlap, along with sufficient ambiguity, between the two classifications to allow the mixing of categories and the use of aggravating rhetoric to bolster religious divisions by the invocation of economic concerns.

This associative misconstruction must be seen as an important challenge to be addressed to make the world less flammable. And it has to be addressed both through economic initiatives and through intellectual resistance. There is a very important need here to facilitate economic opportunities and capabilities for the victims of poverty and gross inequality. This is (as was discussed earlier) important in itself, but additionally in the context of global turmoil and disorder, the economic initiatives can be critically important in preventing the conversion of legitimate complaints against global economic order into explosive "clashes of civilizations". The demands of global economic justice have, in this sense, important political correlates.

Concluding Remarks

To conclude, I have tried to make a number of distinct but interrelated points on the relationship between economic poverty and inequality, on the one hand, and the prevalence of wars and conflicts, on the other. I shall not try to summarize the paper, but highlight a few specific issues.

First, the causal relation between economic destitution and political violence and war can work in both directions, and it is important to investigate and scrutinize critically the distinct routes through which they can interrelate. Indeed, the role of wars and conflicts in generating economic and social destitution may well be manifest and powerful, whereas the contribution of destitution to the generating of wars and conflicts may require more complex investigations.

Second, while the temptation to accept economic reductionism in explaining conflicts and strife is easy to understand, it can sometimes be quite counterproductive. For one thing, the urgency of poverty removal is not parasitic on economic reductionism. Poverty is an evil in itself, and this must be acknowledged, without invoking any further — and ulterior — causal connections. Furthermore, the economic causation may be far more complex than the simple formula of economic reductionism allows. To recognise this does not, of course, require that we deny the relevance of economic factors in political confrontation and warfare. I have tried to identify several different ways in which economic poverty, social inequality and political asymmetry can both influence and be influenced by war and conflicts.

Third, contemporary global confrontations draw substantially on conceptual confounding. The thesis of a "clash of civilizations" is a good example of that. Here the problem arises primarily (1) with the categorization of the world into discrete civilizations, and (2) with treating the civilizational categories as being uniquely more important than other classifications related to other aspects of human identity. Thus, the weakness of the thesis of a clash of civilizations arises well before we get to the question as to whether these civilizations must clash.

Political leaders who dispute the clash of civilizations, but think and act in terms of a unique partitioning of humanity into "the Western world", "the Muslim world", "the Hindu world", and so on, run the risk, against their own intentions, of not only making the world more divisive, but also much more incendiary. They tend also to end up privileging the voice of religious authorities (who then become the *ex officio* spokesmen of the respective "worlds"), while muffling other voices and silencing other concerns. The global fight against economic inequality and poverty can be a casualty of this "civilizational" concentration. On the other hand, to take up that economic fight — even in the noisy and not always well reasoned form of so-called "anti-globalization" movements — can serve as a challenge to the prioritization of religious divisions and intolerance.

In this sense, the global battle against poverty and inequality may have political as well as economic rewards.

Fourth, even though the economic divisions and the religious (or "civilizational") partitions are quite distinct in shape and history, religious fundamentalists often draw on the elements of congruence to add force to their rhetoric. In countering this phenomenon, which is increasingly significant in the contemporary world, conceptual clarity has a critical role.

But there is a need also to rethink global economic policies with note being taken of these connections. It is important in this context to undertake a probing scrutiny of the different economic roles that the major global powers play which impact on the lives of less privileged people across the world. The need, for example, to re-examine and revise patent laws that inhibit affordable use of known drugs against major epidemics (such as AIDS) that better the lives of hundreds of millions of people in Africa and Asia is, of course, strong in itself because of issues of well-being and justice. But additionally these policies have politically incendiary implications which too must also be seized.

Another example to consider is the involvement of the superpowers in the globalized trade in arms. The world leaders who express deep frustration (often with some justice) at the irresponsibility of "anti-globalization" protesters, lead the countries that also make the most money in this terrible trade. During 1996–2000, the G-8 countries sold 87% of the total supply of arms exported in the entire world. The share of the USA alone has just gone up a little to being close to 50% of the total arms sales in the world. And, furthermore, as much as 68% of the American arms exports went to developing countries. The world powers bore an awesome responsibility in the past through their complicity in the subversion of democracy in Africa (and also in Latin America) during the Cold War, and they now have a continuing role in feeding military conflicts today — in Africa and elsewhere — through this dreadful trade.

The idea that those who are anti-Western in the contemporary world are so merely because of the West's value systems and religions or some other cultural feature of the so-called Western civilization overlooks altogether the different ways in which Western countries invade the lives of distant people in every corner of the world. Economic relations can be very important in the way we understand not just the demands of justice in the global economy, but also real inequalities of power and the responsibility — or the lack of it — with which that power is exercised.

The independent importance of distinct concerns does not obviate the need to look at their interrelations and interconnections. The excessive simplicity of economic reductionism, which we must resist, should not be allowed to serve as a barrier to critical scrutiny of the extensive interrelations that shape the world in which we live.

Joseph S. Nye[1]

The Rise and Fall of Great Powers

War is a term that covers many types of violence. Through much of history, war has been the norm rather than the exception in relations among nations. Sixty percent of the years during the last five centuries have seen wars among great powers. Nine of these wars were general or "world wars" involving nearly all the great powers.[2] Although not the most prevalent, such wars are the most devastating. If we divide today's wars into great power, regional power, internal and non-state categories, the first is the least likely, but still the most important in its overall effects on the international system.

As far back as ancient Greece, observers trying to explain the causes of these major world wars have cited the uncertainties associated with shifts in the international distribution of power. As Thucydides explained, the Peloponnesian War appeared to originate in alliance shifts in Epidamnus and Corcyra, but the underlying

---

[1]Joseph S. Nye is dean of the Kennedy School of Government at Harvard University. This paper draws upon his new book, *The Paradox of American Power* (Oxford University Press, 2002).

[2]Jack S. Levy, *War in the Modern Great Power System, 1495–1975* (Lexington: University Press of Kentucky, 1983), p. 97.

cause was the rise in the power of Athens and the fear that created in Sparta. Similarly, World War I is often attributed to the rise in the power of Germany and the fear that created in its neighbors. However, while power transitions provide useful warning about periods of heightened risk, there is no iron law of hegemonic war. If there were, Britain and the United States would have gone to war rather than settled their differences over the Venezuela boundary dispute in 1895.

It is generally agreed that the United States is the leading power at the beginning of the 21st century, but there is less agreement on how long this will last. Some pundits and scholars argue that American pre-eminence is simply the result of the collapse of the Soviet Union and that this "unipolar moment" will be brief.[3] Others argue that America's power is so great that it will last for decades.[4] Whatever the duration, there remains the question of whether a rising challenger — for instance, China or Europe — might lead to a period of great instability.

Scholars who consider themselves "realists" consider it almost a law of nature in international politics that as one nation becomes too strong, others will team up to balance its power. In their eyes, America's current predominance is ephemeral.[5] As evidence, they might cite an Indian journalist who urges a strategic triangle linking Russia, India and China "to provide a counterweight in what now

---

[3]See Charles Krauthammer, "The Unipolar Moment", *Foreign Affairs*, Winter 1990-91, pp. 23-33; Christopher Lane, "The Unipolar Illusion: Why New Great Powers Will Arise", *International Security*, Spring 1993, pp. 5-51; Charles Kupchan, "After Pax Americana: Benign Power, Regional Integration and the Sources of Stable Multipolarity", *International Security*, Fall 1998.

[4]William Wohlforth, "The Stability of a Unipolar World", in Michael Brown *et al.*, *America's Strategic Choices*, rev. ed. (Cambridge, MA: MIT Press, 2000), pp. 305, 309; also from a liberal perspective, G. John Ikenberry, "Institutions, Strategic Restraint, and the Persistence of American Postwar Order", *International Security*, Winter 1998-99, pp. 43-78.

[5]Kenneth Waltz, "Globalization and Governance", *Political Science and Politics*, December 1999, p. 700.

looks like a dangerously unipolar world",[6] or the president of Venezuela telling a conference of oil producers that "the 21st century should be multipolar, and we all ought to push for the development of such a world".[7] *The Economist* argues that "the one-superpower world will not last. Within the next couple of decades a China with up to 1.5 billion people, a strongly growing economy and probably a still authoritarian government will almost certainly be trying to push its interests....Sooner or later some strong and honest man will pull post-Yeltsin Russia together, and another contender for global influence will have reappeared".[8]

Predicting the rise and fall of nations is notoriously difficult. In February 1941, publishing magnate Henry Luce boldly proclaimed the American Century. Yet by the 1980s, many analysts thought Luce's vision had run its course, the victim of such culprits as Vietnam, a slowing economy and imperial overstretch. In 1985, economist Lester Thurow asked why, when Rome had lasted 1000 years as republic and empire, we were slipping after 50.[9] Polls showed that half the American public agreed that the nation was contracting in power and prestige.[10]

The declinists who filled American bestseller lists a decade ago were not the first to go wrong. After Britain lost its American colonies in the 18th century, Horace Walpole lamented Britain's reduction to "a miserable little island" as insignificant as Denmark or Sardinia.[11]

---

[6]Sunanda K. Datta-Ray, "Will Dream Partnership Become Reality?" *The Straits Times* (Singapore), December 25, 1998, p. 46.

[7]Hugo Chavez quoted in Larry Rohter, "A Man with Big Ideas, a Small Country... and Oil", *New York Times*, September 24, 2000, "Week in Review" section, p. 3.

[8]"When the Snarling's Over", *The Economist*, March 13, 1999, p. 17.

[9]Paul Kennedy, *The Rise and Fall of the Great Powers: Economic Change and Military Conflict from 1500–2000* (New York: Random House, 1987); Lester Thurow, *The Zero Sum Solution* (New York: Simon and Schuster, 1985).

[10]Martilla and Kiley, Inc. (Boston, MA), *Americans Talk Security*, no. 6, May 1988 and no. 8, August 1988.

[11]Quoted in Barbara Tuchman, *The March of Folly: From Troy to Vietnam* (New York: Knopf, 1984), p. 221.

His prediction was colored by the then current view of colonial commerce, and failed to foresee the coming industrial revolution that would give Britain a second century with even greater pre-eminence. Similarly, the American declinists failed to understand that a "third industrial revolution" was about to give the United States a second century.[12]

On the other hand, nothing lasts forever in world politics. A century ago, economic globalization was as high by some measures as it is today. World finance rested on a gold standard, immigration was at unparalleled levels, trade was increasing, and Britain had an empire on which the sun never set. As author William Pfaff put it, "responsible political and economic scholars in 1900 would undoubtedly have described the 20th-century prospect as continuing imperial rivalries within a Europe-dominated world, lasting paternalistic tutelage by Europeans of their Asian and African colonies, solid constitutional government in Western Europe, steadily growing prosperity, increasing scientific knowledge turned to human benefit, etc. All would have been wrong".[13] What followed, of course, were two world wars, the great social diseases of totalitarian Fascism and Communism, the end of European empires, and the end of Europe as the arbiter of world power. Economic globalization was reversed and did not again reach its 1914 levels until the 1970s.

Balance or Hegemony?

Many realists extol the virtues of the classic 19th century European balance of power in which constantly shifting coalitions contained the ambitions of any especially aggressive power. They urge the United States to rediscover the virtues of a balance of power at the global level today. Already in the 1970s, Richard Nixon argued that

---

[12]Daniel Bell, *The Coming of Post-Industrial Society: A Venture in Social Forecasting* (New York: Basic Books, 1999 [orig. 1973]), new introduction, passim.
[13]William Pfaff, *Barbarian Sentiments: America in the New Century*, rev. ed. (New York, Hill and Wang, 2000), p. 280.

"the only time in the history of the world that we have had any extended periods of peace is when there has been a balance of power. It is when one nation becomes infinitely more powerful in relation to its potential competitors that the danger of war arises".[14] But whether such multi-polarity would be good or bad for the United States and for the world is debatable. War was the constant companion and crucial instrument of the multi-polar balance of power. Rote adherence to the balance of power and multi-polarity may prove to be a dangerous approach to global governance in a world where war could turn nuclear.

Many regions of the world and periods in history have seen stability when one power has been pre-eminent. Margaret Thatcher warned against drifting toward "an Orwellian future of Oceania, Eurasia, and Eastasia — three mercantilist world empires on increasingly hostile terms... In other words, 2095 might look like 1914 played on a somewhat larger stage".[15] Both the Nixon and Thatcher views are too mechanical because they ignore soft or attractive power. America is an exception, argues Josef Joffe, "because the 'hyperpower' is also the most alluring and seductive society in history. Napoleon had to rely on bayonets to spread France's revolutionary creed. In the American case, Munichers and Muscovites *want* what the avatar of ultra-modernity has to offer".[16]

The term "balance of power" is sometimes used in contradictory ways to express either the existing distribution of power or an equal balance as in a pair of scales. The most interesting use of the term is as a predictor of how countries will behave; that is, will they pursue policies that will prevent any other country from developing a preponderance that could threaten their independence? By the evidence of history, many believe, the current preponderance of the

---

[14]Nixon quoted in James Chace and Nicholas X. Rizopoulos, "Towards a New Concert of Nations: An American Perspective", *World Policy Journal*, Fall 1999, p. 9.
[15]Margaret Thatcher, "Why America Must Remain Number One", *National Review*, July 31, 1995, p. 25.
[16]Josef Joffe, "Envy", *The New Republic*, January 17, 2000, p. 6.

United States will call forth a countervailing coalition that will eventually limit American power. In the words of the realist political scientist Kenneth Waltz, "both friends and foes will react as countries always have to threatened or real predominance of one among them: they will work to right the balance. The present condition of international politics is unnatural".[17]

Such a mechanical prediction misses the mark. For one thing, countries sometimes react to the rise of a single power by "bandwagoning" — that is, joining the seemingly stronger rather than weaker side — much as Mussolini did when he decided, after several years of hesitation, to ally with Hitler. Proximity to and perceptions of threat also affect the way in which countries react.[18] The United States benefits from its geographical separation from Europe and Asia, because it often appears as a less proximate threat than neighboring countries inside those regions. Indeed, in 1945, the United States was by far the strongest nation on earth, and a mechanical application of balancing theory would have predicted an alliance against it. Instead, Europe and Japan allied with the Americans because the Soviet Union, while weaker in overall power, posed a greater military threat because of its geographical proximity, and its lingering revolutionary ambitions. Today, Iraq and Iran both dislike the United States and might be expected to work together to balance American power in the Persian Gulf, but they worry even more about each other.

A good case can be made that inequality of power can be a source of peace and stability. No matter how power is measured, some theorists argue, an equal distribution of power among major states has been relatively rare in history, and efforts to maintain a balance have often led to war. On the other hand, inequality of power has often led to peace and stability because there was little point in

---

[17]Kenneth Waltz, "Globalization and American Power", *The National Interest*, Spring 2000, pp. 55-56.
[18]Stephen Walt, "Alliance Formation and the Balance of Power", *International Security*, Spring 1985, pp. 3-43.

declaring war on a dominant state. The political scientist Robert Gilpin has argued that *"Pax Britannica* and *Pax Americana,* like the *Pax Romana,* ensured an international system of relative peace and security".* And the economist Charles Kindleberger claimed that "for the world economy to be stabilized, there has to be a stabilizer, one stabilizer".[19] Global governance requires a large state to take the lead. But how much and what kind of inequality of power is necessary — or tolerable — and for how long? If the leading country possesses soft power and behaves in a manner that benefits others, effective counter-coalitions may be slow to arise. If, on the other hand, the leading country defines its interests narrowly, and uses its weight arrogantly, it increases the incentives for others to coordinate to escape its hegemony.

Some countries chafe under the weight of American power more than others. "Hegemony" is sometimes used as a term of opprobrium by political leaders in Russia, China, France, and others. The term is used less often, or less negatively, in countries where American soft power is strong. If hegemony means being able to dictate, or at least dominate, the rules and arrangements by which international relations are conducted,[20] then the United States is hardly a hegemon today. It does have a predominant voice and vote in the International Monetary Fund, but cannot alone choose the director. It has not been able to prevail over Europe and Japan in the World Trade Organization. It opposed the International Landmines Treaty, but could not prevent it coming into existence. Saddam Hussein has remained in power for more than a decade despite American efforts to drive him out. The U.S. opposed Russia's war in Chechnya and civil war in Colombia, but to no avail. If hegemony is defined more modestly as a situation where one country has significantly more

---

[19]Robert Gilpin, *War and Change in World Politics* (New York: Cambridge University Press, 1981), pp. 144-145; Charles P. Kindleberger, *The World in Depression, 1929-1939* (Berkeley: University of California Press, 1973), p. 305.

[20]Joshua S. Goldstein, *Long Cycles: Prosperity and War in the Modern Age* (New Haven: Yale University Press, 1988), p. 281.

power resources or capabilities than others,[21] then it simply signifies American preponderance, but not necessarily dominance or control. Even after World War II, when the United States controlled half the world's economic production (because all other countries had been devastated by the war), it was not able to prevail in all of its objectives.[22]

The 20th century bore witness to the rise and fall of several great powers, each with dramatic consequences for world peace and stability. The British Empire collapsed after two world wars, Germany rose to the height of its power at the turn of the century, precipitating the two bloodiest conflicts in modern history, and plunged to its weakest point at the end of World War II. Russia was transformed into a Soviet Empire that, at its apogee, posed a serious challenge to the United States in terms of economic and military power, as well as its cultural and political influence across the globe, but collapsed in 1991. Formerly an agrarian state that

---

[21]See Robert O. Keohane, *After Hegemony: Cooperation and Discord in the World Political Economy* (Princeton: Princeton University Press, 1984), p. 235.

[22]Over the years, a number of scholars have tried to predict the rise and fall of nations by developing a general historical theory of hegemonic transition. Some have tried to generalize from the experience of Portugal, Spain, the Netherlands, France and Britain. Others have focused more closely on Britain's decline in the 20th century as a predictor for the fate for the United States. None of these approaches has been successful. Most of the theories have predicted that America would decline long before now. Vague definitions and arbitrary schematizations alert us to the inadequacies of such grand theories. Most try to squeeze history into procrustean theoretical beds by focusing on particular power resources while ignoring others that are equally important. Hegemony can be used as a descriptive term (though it is sometimes fraught with emotional overtones), but grand hegemonic theories are weak in predicting future events. See Immanuel Wallerstein, *The Politics of the World Economy: The States, the Movements, and the Civilizations: Essays* (New York: Cambridge University Press, 1984), pp. 38, 41; George Modelski, "The Long Cycle of Global Politics and the Nation-State", *Comparative Studies in Society and History*, April 1978; Modelski, *Long Cycles in World Politics* (Seattle: University of Washington Press, 1987). For a detailed discussion, see Nye, *Bound to Lead*, cited, Chapter 2.

played a minimal role on the world stage, the United States became a superpower with global reach. The evolution of power relationships in the 20th century was by no means a smooth series of events.

The world's greatest power in the 19th century, Britain and her empire were already in decline by the beginning of the 1900s. A lengthy list of causes, at the domestic and international levels, have been invoked to explain this decline, though no factor is as important as the enormous strain placed on Britain during World War I. While the Great War demonstrated Britain's impressive military power, particularly its naval and air power, the war did more to hasten the end of British dominance than any other event. Competing with Germany drove up British defense spending and strained the already over-extended British Empire. The final blow was dealt in the Second World War, which devastated the British economy, did major damage to Britain's military resources, and had dramatic political consequences. The impact of the war combined with the rise of anti-colonial nationalism throughout the world ultimately brought an end to the Empire and ended the period of British preponderance.

The turn of the 20th century saw the rapid increase of German power. The speed of Germany's rise was truly impressive. German heavy industry surpassed that of Great Britain in the 1890s, and the growth of German GNP at the beginning of the century was twice that of Britain's. In the 1860s, Britain had 25% of the world's industrial production, but by 1913 that had shrunk to 10% and Germany's share had risen to 15%. Germany transformed its industrial strength into military might, embarking upon a massive naval armaments program. The response in Europe to Germany's rising power contributed to the increasing rigidity of the alliance system and directly contributed to the outbreak of World War I. Germany came out of the war tremendously weakened. It lost 7 million citizens and 25,000 square miles of territory, its army was drastically reduced, and the Treaty of Versailles ordered Germany to pay $33 billion in reparations for the damage caused during the war. Germany was severely crippled by the Great War, but was not destroyed, and 20 years later, Europe was engulfed in the most catastrophic war in history. The Second World War finally ended the

German challenge and ushered in an era dominated by the increasing power of two states of enormous scale — the United States and the Soviet Union.

Because of their continental scale and disproportionate military power, the two largest victors of World War II became known as superpowers. The subsequent growth of their nuclear arsenals reinforced this bipolar distribution of power. For four decades, the American alliances with Europe and Japan were designed to contain the expansion of Soviet power and the nuclear balance produced prudence. Nonetheless, proxy wars were fought in peripheral areas like Vietnam and Afghanistan. The centrally planned economy of the Soviet Union, however, was unable to adapt to the changes in technology often referred to as the "Third Industrial Revolution". Soviet economic productivity began to lag behind that of the United States. Its military expenditure increased to over a quarter of its GNP, while America's declined from 10 percent at the height of the Cold War to three and a half percent at its end. The Soviet Union succumbed to "imperial overstretch" but the United States did not. When the USSR finally collapsed in 1991, it left an unbalanced U.S. power and a world that many called unipolar or hegemonic.

"Pax Britannica" in the 19th century is often cited as an example of successful hegemony, even though Britain ranked behind the United States and Russia in GNP. Britain was never as superior in productivity to the rest of the world as the United States has been since 1945, but Britain also had a degree of soft power. Victorian culture was influential around the globe, and Britain gained in reputation when it defined its interests in ways that benefited other nations (for example, opening its markets to imports or defending freedom of the seas). America lacks a global territorial empire like Britain's, but instead possesses a large continental scale home economy and has greater soft power. These differences between Britain and America suggest a greater staying power for American predominance. Political scientist William Wohlforth argues that the United States is so far ahead that potential rivals find it dangerous to invite America's focused enmity, and allied states can feel confident that they can continue to rely on American protection.[23] Thus the usual balancing forces are weakened. Whether other countries will unite to balance American power will depend on how the United States behaves as well as the power resources of potential challengers.

China

Many view China, the world's most populous country, as the leading challenger and possible source of war.[24] As an Australian analyst argues, "Almost every commentator has for some years regarded China as the likeliest of the usual suspects for future 'peer competitor' status".[25] Polls show half the American public thinks China will pose the biggest challenge to U.S. world power status in the next 100 years (compared with eight percent for Japan, and six percent for Russia and Europe).[26] Some observers compare the rise of authoritarian China to that of the Kaiser's Germany in the period preceding World War I. Sinologist Arthur Waldron, for example, argues that "sooner or later, if present trends continue, war is probable in Asia…China today is actively seeking to scare the United States away from East Asia rather as Germany sought to frighten Britain before World War I". Similarly, the columnist Robert Kagan claims "the Chinese leadership views the world in much the same way Kaiser Wilhelm II did a century ago. …Chinese leaders chafe at the constraints on them and worry that they must change the rules of the international system before the international system changes them".[27] Chinese leaders have often complained about U.S. "gunboat diplomacy", and invited Russia, France and others to join it in resisting

---

[23]Wohlforth, cited.

[24]Michael E. Brown, Owen R. Coté Jr., Sean M. Lynn-Jones, Steven E. Miller, *The Rise of China* (Cambridge, MA: MIT Press, 2000).

[25]Coral Bell, "TK", *The National Interest*, Fall 1999, p. 56.

[26]"American Opinion", *Wall Street Journal*, September 16, 1999, p. A9.

[27]Arthur Waldron, "How Not to Deal with China", *Commentary*, March 1997; Robert Kagan, "What China Knows That We Don't", *The Weekly Standard*, January 20, 1997.

U.S. "hegemonism".[28] Moreover, "in government pronouncements, stories in the state-run press, books and interviews, the United States is now routinely portrayed as Enemy No. 1".[29] As two sober analysts put it, "it is hardly inevitable that China will be a threat to American interests, but the United States is much more likely to go to war with China than it is with any other major power".[30]

We should be skeptical, however, about drawing conclusions solely from current rhetoric, and flawed historical analogies. In both China and the U.S., perceptions of the other country are heavily colored by domestic political struggles, and there are people in both countries who want to see the other as an enemy. As for history, it is important to remember that by 1900, Germany had surpassed Britain in industrial power, and the Kaiser was pursuing an adventurous, globally oriented foreign policy that was bound to bring about a clash with other great powers. In contrast, China lags far behind the United States economically, and has focused its policies primarily on East Asia and on its own economic development, and its official communist ideology holds little appeal. Nonetheless, the rise of China recalls Thucydides' warning that belief in the inevitability of conflict can become one of its main causes.[31] Each side, believing it will end up at war with the other, makes reasonable military preparations which then are read by the other side as confirmation of its worst fears.

In fact, the "rise of China" is a misnomer. "Re-emergence" would be more accurate, since by size and history the Middle Kingdom has long been a major power in East Asia. Technically and economically, China was the world's leader (though without global reach) from 500 to 1500. Only in the last half millennium was it

---

[28]"China Lashes Out at U.S. 'Gunboat Diplomacy'", *Financial Times* (London), September 4, 1999, p. 4.

[29]John Pomfret, "U.S. Now a 'Threat' in China's Eyes", *Washington Post*, November 15, 2000, p. 1.

[30]Richard K. Betts and Thomas J. Christensen, "China: Getting the Questions Right", *The National Interest*, Winter 2000–01, p. 17.

[31]Thucydides, *History of the Peloponnesian War*, p. 62.

overtaken by Europe and America. The Asian Development Bank has calculated that in 1820, at the beginning of the industrial age, Asia made up an estimated three-fifths of world product. By 1940, this fell to one-fifth, even though the region was home to three-fifths of world population. Rapid economic growth has brought that back to two-fifths today, and the Bank speculates that Asia could return to its historical levels by 2025.[32] Asia, of course, includes Japan, India, Korea and others, but China will eventually play the largest role. Its high annual growth rates of 8 to 9 percent led to a remarkable tripling of its GNP in the last two decades of the 20th century. This pragmatic economic performance enhanced China's soft power in the region.

Nonetheless, China has a long way to go, and faces many obstacles to its development. At the beginning of the 21st century, the American economy was about twice the size of China's. If the American economy grows at a 2 percent rate and China at 6 percent, the two economies would be equal in size sometime around 2020. Even so, the two economies would be equivalent in size, but not equal in composition. China would still have a vast underdeveloped countryside — indeed, assuming 6 percent Chinese growth and only 2 percent American growth, China would not equal the United States in per capita income until somewhere between 2056 and 2095 (depending on the measures of comparison).[33] In terms of political power, per capita income provides a more accurate measure of

---

[32]Asian Development Bank, *Emerging Asia* (Manila, 1997), p. 11.

[33]Figures were calculated using data from *CIA World Fact Book 2000* (http://www.cia.gov/cia/publications/factbook/) — purchasing power parities — and the World Bank (http://www.worldbank.org/data/wdi2001/pdfs/tab1_1.pdf) — official exchange rates. Measured by purchasing power parities which correct for the costs of goods in different currencies. Equality in size would not occur until 2056 if measured by official exchange rates. If the US grows at 3 percent per year, the convergence would occur between 2022 and 2075 (depending on the measure). My thanks to Kennedy School graduate students Ebrahim Afsah and Francisco Blanch for lending their computational skills.

the sophistication of an economy. The Asian Development Bank projects Chinese per capita income will reach 38 percent of the United States by 2025, about the same level relative to the U.S. that South Korea reached in 1990.[34] That is impressive growth, but a long way from equality. And since the United States is unlikely to be standing still during that period, China is a long way from posing the kind of challenge to American preponderance that the Kaiser's Germany posed when it passed Britain at the beginning of the last century.

Moreover, linear projections of economic growth trends can be misleading. Countries tend to pick the low hanging fruit as they benefit from imported technologies in the early stages of economic take-off, and growth rates generally slow as economies reach higher levels of development. In addition, the Chinese economy faces serious obstacles of transition from inefficient state-owned enterprises, a shaky financial system, and inadequate infrastructure. Growing inequality, massive internal migration, an inadequate social safety net, corruption and inadequate institutions could foster political instability. Coping with greatly increasing flows of information at a time when restrictions can hinder economic growth presents a sharp dilemma for Chinese leaders. As the Harvard economist Dwight Perkins points out, "much of the early success of market reforms…resulted from the basic simplicity of the task". The process of creating a rule of law and adequate institutions in the economic area will be "measured in decades, not years or months".[35] Indeed, some observers fear instability caused by a collapsing rather than a rising China.[36] A China that cannot control population growth, flows of migration, environmental effects on the global climate, and internal conflict poses another set of problems.

---

[34]Ibid.

[35]Dwight Perkins, "Institutional Challenges for the Economic Transition in Asia", paper presented at Australian National University, September 2000, p. 48.

[36]See Merle Goldman, Raja Menon, Richard Ellings, "Letters from Readers" *Commentary*, February 2001, pp. 13, 19.

As long as China's economy does grow, it is likely that its military power will increase, thus making China appear more dangerous to its neighbors, and complicating America's commitments in the region. A RAND study projects that by 2015, China's military expenditure will be more than six times higher than Japan's and its accumulated military capital stock would be some five times that of Japan (measured at purchasing power parity).[37] The Gulf War of 1991, the tensions over Taiwan in 1995-96, and the Kosovo campaign of 1999 showed Chinese leaders how far China lagged behind in modern military capabilities, and as a result they nearly doubled military expenditures over the course of the 1990s. Nonetheless, China's total military budget actually declined from two and a half to two percent of GDP in the last decades of the 20th century, and the weakness of its political system makes it inefficient at converting economic resources into military capacity.[38] Some observers think that by 2005 China might achieve a military capability similar to that of a European country in the early 1980s. Others, citing imported technology from Russia, are more concerned.[39] In any event, growing Chinese military capacity would mean that any American military role in the region will require more resources.

Whatever the accuracy of such assessments of China's military growth, the key question for our purposes is comparative assessment, and that depends on what the United States (and other countries) will be doing over the next decades. The key to military power in the information age depends on the ability to collect, process, disseminate and integrate complex systems of space-based surveillance, high speed computers, and 'smart' weapons. China (and others)

---

[37] Charles Wolf, Jr., Anil Bamezai, K.C. Yeh, Benjamin Zycher, *Asian Economic Trends and Their Security Implications* (Santa Monica, RAND, 2000), pp. 19-22.

[38] David M. Lampton and Gregory C. May, *A Big Power Agenda for East Asia: America, China and Japan* (Washington, The Nixon Center, 2000), p. 13. These calculations use constant dollars at market exchange rates and are higher than official Chinese figures.

[39] David Shambaugh, "Containment or Engagement in China? Calculating Beijing's Responses", *International Security*, Fall 1996, p. 21.

will develop some of these capabilities, but according to the
Australian analyst Paul Dibb, the revolution in military affairs (RMA)
"will continue to favor heavily American military predominance.
It is not likely that China will, in any meaningful way, close the
RMA gap with the U.S".[40]

The fact that China is not likely to become a peer competitor to
the United States on a global basis, does not mean that it could not
challenge the United States in East Asia, or that war over Taiwan is
not possible. Weaker countries sometimes attack when they feel
backed into a corner, such as Japan did at Pearl Harbor or China did
when it entered the Korean War in 1950. "Under certain conditions
Beijing will likely be fully undeterable. If, for example, Taiwan were to
declare independence, it is hard to imagine that China would forgo
the use of force against Taiwan, regardless of the perceived economic
or military costs, the likely duration or intensity of American intervention, or the balance of forces in the region".[41] But it would be unlikely
to win such a war, and prudent policy on both sides can make such
an outcome unlikely. There is no need for the United States and
China to go to war in this century, and it is important for analysts
on both sides to keep pointing this out to leaders and publics.

Europe

The closest thing to an equal that the United States faces at the
beginning of the 21st century is the European Union. Although
the American economy is four times larger than that of Germany —
the largest European country — the economy of the European Union
is roughly equal to that of the U.S., and its population is considerably
larger, as is its share of world exports. These proportions will
increase if, as planned, the European Union gradually expands to

---

[40]Paul Dibb, "The Revolution in Military Affairs and Asian Security", paper presented
at the IISS 35th Annual Conference in Singapore, p. 29.

[41]Thomas J. Christensen, "Posing Problems without Catching Up: China's Rise and
Challenges for U.S. Security Policy", *International Security*, Spring 2001, p. 36.

include the states of Central Europe over the next decades. Europe spends about two-thirds of what the United States does on defense, has more men under arms, and includes two countries that possess nuclear arsenals. In terms of soft power, European cultures have long had a wide appeal in the rest of the world, and the sense of a Europe uniting around Brussels has had a strong attraction to Eastern Europe as well as Turkey. Governments and peoples there have begun to shape their policies to fit in with Brussels. Europeans have been important pioneers and played central roles in international institutions. As Samuel Huntington argued a decade ago, a cohesive Europe "would have the population resources, economic strength, technology, and actual and potential military strength to be the preeminent power of the 21st century".[42] And some today see America and Europe on the road to political conflict. A 1995 article in the *National Review* provides a good example of this, arguing that "a political bloc is emerging in the form of the European Union that likes to see itself as a challenge to America".[43]

The key question in assessing the challenge presented by the EU is whether it will develop enough political and social-cultural cohesion to act as one on a wide range of international issues, or whether it will remain a limited grouping of countries with strongly different nationalisms and foreign policies. The uniting of Europe has been a slow but steady process for half a century, and the pressures of globalization have added to the incentives to strengthen European regional institutions.

Already, the European Union has effectively constrained American power. On questions of trade and influence within the World Trade Organization, Europe is the equal of the United States. European countries successfully defied American trade sanctions against Cuba and Iran. The creation of the European Monetary Union and the

---

[42]Samuel P. Huntington, "The U.S. — Decline or Renewal?" *Foreign Affairs*, Winter 1988–89, p. 93.

[43]David Pryce-Jones, "Bananas Are the Beginning: The Looming War between America and Europe", *National Review*, April 5, 1999.

launching of the Euro at the beginning of 1999 were greeted by a number of observers as a major challenge to the United States and to the role of the dollar as the dominant reserve currency.[44] While such views overly discounted the unique depth and breadth of American capital markets which make countries willing to hold dollars, the European role in monetary affairs and the International Monetary Fund is nearly equal to that of the U.S. The size and attraction of the European market has meant that American firms seeking to merge have had to seek approval from the European Commission as well as the U.S. Justice Department — as GE found out to its consternation when the EU rejected its proposed takeover of Honeywell in 2001. And in the Internet age, American policy makers are concerned to make sure American practices do not contravene European regulations on privacy of information. "Whether you like it or not, the EU is setting the standards for privacy protection for the rest of the world".[45]

At the same time, Europe faces significant limits on its degree of unity. National identities remain stronger than a common European identity, despite fifty years of integration, and national interests, while subdued in comparison to the past, still matter.[46] Integration was driven for years by the engine of Franco-German cooperation. As Germany grew with reunification, developed a more "normal" foreign policy, and insisted on more weight in votes on European issues, French attitudes towards EU institutions became more cautious. As French Prime Minister Lionel Jospin put it, "I want Europe, but I remain attached to my nation. Making Europe without unmaking France, or any other European nation, that is my political choice".[47]

---

[44]Martin Feldstein, "EMU and International Conflict", *Foreign Affairs*, November–December 1997.

[45]Cherise M. Valles, "Setting the Course on Data Privacy", *International Herald Tribune*, May 28, 2001, p. 13.

[46]Pippa Norris, "Global Governance and Cosmopolitan Citizens", in Nye and Donahue, eds., cited, p. 157.

[47]John Vinocur, "Jospin Envisions and Alternative EU", *International Herald Tribune*, May 29, 2001, p. 1.

Moreover, the continuing enlargement of the European Union to include Central Europeans means that European institutions are likely to remain *sui generis*, but tending to the confederal rather than the federal end of the spectrum. The prospects for a strong federal Europe may have disappeared when the original six countries agreed upon expansion that included Britain and parts of Scandinavia. On the question of whether the EU is becoming a state, political scientist Andrew Moravscik summarizes succinctly: "most informed observers prefer to speak of a 'postmodern polity' in which the EU rules alongside, rather than in place of, national governments".[48]

The other key question for whether the EU becomes a global challenger to the United States rests on the nature of the linkages across the Atlantic.[49] Some foresee a progressive erosion of ties. Harvard's Stephen Walt cites three serious reasons: the lack of a common threat reduces cohesion in the alliance; the United States now trades one and a half times as much with Asia as with Europe; and there are growing cultural differences among elites on both sides of the Atlantic as generations change.[50]

On the other hand, reports of trans-Atlantic differences are often over-stated. Direct investment in both directions is higher than with Asia and helps knit the economies together. Nearly a third of trade occurs *within* transnational corporations. Moreover, while trade inevitably produces some degree of friction in the domestic politics of democracies, it is a game from which both sides can profit if there is a will to cooperate, and U.S.-European trade is more balanced than U.S. trade with Asia.

At the cultural level, Americans and Europeans have sniped at and admired each other for more than two centuries. For all the

---

[48]Andrew Moravscik, "Despotism in Brussels?" *Foreign Affairs*, May–June 2001, p. 121.

[49]Joseph S. Nye, "The US and Europe: Continental Drift?" *International Affairs*, January 2000, pp. 51–59.

[50]Stephen M. Walt, "The Ties That Fray", *The National Interest*, Winter 1998–99, pp. 3–11.

complaints about McDonald's, no one forces the French (and other Europeans) to eat there, though millions do each year. In some ways, the inevitable frictions show a closeness rather than a distance. As Karsten Voigt, a senior German politician put it, "The distinction between foreign and domestic policy has blurred as our societies have interwoven. That is why emotional issues like genetically altered food or the way we treat the children of international divorces rise to the surface. In a way foreign policy was easier when it dealt with interests rather than emotions and morals".[51] Yet it is also true that American consumers can benefit from European efforts to raise standards in anti-trust actions or internet privacy. And in a larger sense, Americans and Europeans share the values of democracy and human rights more thoroughly with each other than with any other region of the world. As Ambassador Robert Blackwill has written, at the deepest level, neither the US nor Europe threatens the vital or important interests of the other side.[52]

The Distribution of Power in the Global Information Age

The United States had already become the world's largest economy by the end of the 19th century. America's economic domination reached its peak (at between a third and a half of world product) soon after 1945.[53] For the next 25 years, the American share declined to its long-term average as others recovered and developed.[54] Before World War I and again before World War II, the United States

---

[51]Roger Cohen, "Tiffs over Bananas and Child Custody", *New York Times*, May 28, 2000, 'News of the Week' section, p. 1.

[52]Robert D. Blackwill, *The Future of Transatlantic Relations* (NY, Council on Foreign Relations, 1999).

[53]See Nye, *Bound to Lead: The Changing Nature of American Power* (New York: Basic Books, 1990), Chapter 1.

[54]Herbert Block, *The Planetary Product in 1980: A Creative Pause?* (Washington, D.C.: U.S. Dept. of State, Bureau of Public Affairs, 1981), p. 18; Simon Kuznets, *Economic Growth and Structure* (New York: W.W. Norton, 1965); Council on Competitiveness, *Competitiveness Index* (Washington, D.C., 1988), Appendix II.

accounted for about a quarter of world product, and it remains roughly equal to that level today. The American share of the GDP of the seven largest economies that hold annual economic summits was 48.7% in 1970, 46.8% in 1980, and 45.2% at the end of the century. "What has appeared to keep the US safely at the top of the league has been its traditional strengths — a huge single market fostering competition, a stable currency and a sound financial system — allied to rapid technological progress in its information technology sector".[55]

Can this degree of economic dominance continue? Probably not. As globalization stimulates economic growth in poor countries that are able to take advantage of new technology and world markets, their share of world product should increase much as did that of East Asian countries over the past few decades. If the US and other wealthy countries grow at about two and a half per cent per year but the fifteen largest underdeveloped countries grow between four and five and a half per cent per year "over half of world gross output 30 years hence will be in countries that are poor today whereas 1990s rich ones, the current members of the OECD, will see their share fall from 70% of the world total to about 45%. The United States share falls from about 23% to 15%".[56] The U.S. would still have the largest economy, but its lead would be more modest than today. Of course such linear projections can be foiled by political change and historical surprises, and growth in developing countries may not be this fast. Nonetheless, it would be surprising if the U.S. share did *not* shrink over the course of the century. Nonetheless, as a Canadian political scientist concludes, "unless the United States suffers a major catastrophe (and one, moreover, that does not also affect other major powers), there is only one way that the relative balance of power capabilities between the United States and the

---

[55]Richard Adams, "U.S. the Dominant Economic Model", *Financial Times Annual Survey: Markets 2000*, January 11, 2000, p. 24.

[56]Harry Rowen, "The Prospects Before Us: A World Rich, Democratic, and (Perhaps) Peaceful", unpublished manuscript, June 1993, p. 29.

other major powers extant at the turn of the millennium will change: very slowly, and over many decades".[57] Such catastrophes would have to be multiple and many times larger than the events of September 2001 to have such effects.

Even in the likely event that the United States remains the largest country well into the century, there are other changes occurring in the distribution of power, particularly the rise in the importance of non-state actors. After the collapse of the Soviet Union, some have described the resulting world as unipolar; some as multi-polar. Both are right and both wrong, because each refers to a different dimension of power that can no longer be assumed to be homogenized by military dominance. Unipolarity is misleading because it exaggerates the degree to which the United States is able to get the results it wants in some dimensions of world politics, but multipolarity is misleading because it implies several roughly equal counties.

Instead, power today is distributed among countries in a pattern that resembles a complex three-dimensional chess game.[58] On the top chessboard, military power is largely unipolar. As we have seen, the U.S. is the only country with both intercontinental nuclear weapons and large state-of-the-art air, naval, and ground forces capable of global deployment. But on the middle chessboard, economic power is multi-polar, with the U.S., Europe and Japan representing two-thirds of world product, and with China's dramatic growth likely to make it a major player early in the century. As we have seen, on this economic board, the United States is not a hegemon, and often must bargain as an equal with Europe. This has led some observers such as Samuel Huntington to call it a hybrid uni-multipolar world.[59] But the situation

---

[57]Kim Nossal, "Lonely Superpower or Unapologetic Hyperpower? Analyzing American Power in the Post-Cold War Era", paper for the South African Political Studies Association, July 1999, p. 12.

[58]My friend Stanley Hoffmann first introduced me to the metaphor of multiple (though not three-dimensional) chessboards. See his *Primacy or World Order* (New York, McGraw-Hill, 1978), p. 119.

[59]Samuel P. Huntington, "The U.S. — Decline or Renewal?", cited.

is even more complicated and difficult for the traditional terminology of the balance of power among states to capture. The bottom chessboard is the realm of transnational relations that cross borders outside of government control. This realm includes actors as diverse as bankers electronically transferring sums larger than most national budgets at one extreme, and terrorists transferring weapons or disrupting Internet operations at the other. On this bottom board, power is widely dispersed, and it makes no sense to speak of unipolarity, multipolarity or hegemony.

Because of its leading edge in the information revolution, and its past investment in traditional power resources, the United States will likely remain the world's single most powerful country well into this new century. While potential coalitions to check American power could be created, it is unlikely that they would become firm alliances unless the United States handles its hard power in an overbearing unilateral manner that undermines its soft power. As Joseph Joffe has written, "unlike centuries past, when war was the great arbiter, today the most interesting types of power do not come out of the barrel of a gun.... Today there is a much bigger payoff in 'getting others to want what you want', and that has to do with cultural attraction and ideology and agenda setting and holding out big prizes for cooperation, like the vastness and sophistication of the American market. On that gaming table, China, Russia and Japan, even the West Europeans, cannot match the pile of chips held by the United States".[60] The United States could squander this soft power by heavy-handed unilateralism. As Richard Haas, the Director of Policy Planning in the Bush Administration State Department has warned, any attempt to dominate, "would lack domestic support and stimulate international resistance, which in turn would make the costs of hegemony all the greater and its benefits all the smaller".[61]

---

[60]Josef Joffe, "America the Inescapable", *New York Times* [Sunday] *Magazine*, June 8, 1997, p. 38.

[61]Quoted in R.W. Apple Jr., "As the American Century Extends Its Run", *New York Times*, January 1, 2000, p. 3.

But the prospect that the rise of new state challengers will threaten a declining United States and plunge the world into the uncertainty and danger of hegemonic transition and war seems unlikely.

At the same time, this more complex distribution of power and the rise of non-state actors in the 21st century mean that there are more and more things outside the control of even the most powerful state. Although the United States does well on the traditional measures of power, there is increasingly more going on in the world that those measures fail to capture. Under the influence of the information revolution and globalization, world politics is changing in a way that means not even the strongest state can achieve all its international goals acting alone. September 11, 2001 dramatized a change that was already occurring in world politics. The U.S. lacks both the international and domestic prerequisites to resolve conflicts that are internal to other societies, and to monitor and control transnational transactions that threaten Americans at home. There is no alternative to mobilizing international coalitions and building institutions to address shared threats and challenges. The national interest will have to include global interests and the production of global public goods. As a British observer has written, "the paradox of American power at the end of this millennium is that it is too great to be challenged by any other state, yet not great enough to solve problems such as global terrorism and nuclear proliferation. America needs the help and respect of other nations".[62]

---

[62]Sebastian Mallaby, "A Mockery in the Eyes of the World", *Washington Post*, January 31, 1999, p. B5.

Mary Kaldor

Beyond Militarism, Arms Races
and Arms Control

Introduction

Since the end of the Cold War, a profound restructuring of armed
forces has taken place. During the Cold War period, armed forces
tended to resemble each other all over the world. They were
disciplined, hierarchical, and technology intensive. There were, of
course, guerrilla and/or terrorist groups but they were considered
marginal and their demand for weapons was small in relation to the
overall demand for weapons.

The Cold War could be described as the final stage of what
has come to be known as modernity, or to use Anthony Giddens'
terminology, the final stages of the first phase of modernity.[1] By
modernity, I mean that period of human development that began
somewhere between the 15th and the 18th centuries, characterised
by the development of science and technology, the nation state,
modern industry, and, I would argue, Clausewitzean or modern war.
By modern war, I mean war between states, fought by armed forces,

---

[1]Giddens A., *The Consequences of Modernity*, Polity Press, 1990; *Global Civil Society
2001* (Oxford: Oxford University Press, 1990).

for state interest; the type of war that was theorised so brilliantly by Clausewitz. The development of modern war cannot be disentangled from the development of modern states. It was in war that European states, which were to provide the model for other states, established their monopoly of organised violence within the territorial confines of the state; they eliminated competitors, centralised administration, increased taxation and forms of borrowing, and, above all, created an idea of the state as the organisation responsible for protection of borders against other states and for upholding a rule of law within the state. The sharp distinctions between the military and civilians, public and private, internal and external, are a product of these developments. As Charles Tilly put it in a famous phrase: "States made war and war made the state".[2]

After 1945, the whole world was parcelled up into individual states, each with their own currency and their own armed forces. Each state was a member of a bloc (West, East and non-aligned) and within each bloc, there were transfers of weapons and other types of military assistance according to a very similar model of warfare. The idea of war and of preparations for war was bound up with the ways in which states established their political legitimacy.

Since the end of the Cold War, military spending by governments has fallen substantially. But what we have witnessed is less a contraction of military forces than a restructuring and increased diversity of types of military forces. There is a parallel with the pre-modern period, which was also characterised by a diversity of military forces — feudal levies, citizens militias, mercenaries, pirates, for example — and by a corresponding variety of types of warfare.

Two inter-linked developments have been critical, in my view, in bringing about these changes. One is the sheer destructiveness of modern warfare. As all types of weapons have become more lethal and/or more accurate, decisive military victory has become

---

[2]Tilly C., *Coercion, Capital and European States AD 990-1992* (Oxford: Backwells, 1992).

more and more difficult. The scale of destruction in World War II (some 50 million dead) is almost unbearable to contemplate. The Cold War could be understood as a way of evading or psychologically suppressing the implications of that destructiveness. Through the system of deterrence, the idea of modern war was kept alive in the imagination and helped to sustain the legitimacy and discipline of modern states. The military planners and scenario builders imagined wars, even more destructive than World War II, and developed competitive new technologies that, in theory, would be used in such wars. There were, of course, real wars and some 5 million people have died in wars in every decade since 1945 but, among the dominant powers, these were regarded as "not-war" or marginal to the main contingency — a global inter-state clash. With the end of the Cold War, we have to come to terms with the impossibility of wars of the modern type.

The second development is the process known as globalisation. By globalisation, I mean increasing interconnectedness, the shrinking of distance and time, as a result of the combination of Information and Communications Technology (ICT) and air travel. A central issue for theorists of globalisation has to do with the implications for the modern state.[3] Some argue that the state has become an anachronism and that we are moving towards a single world community. Some take the opposite view, that globalisation is an invention of the state and can easily be reversed. Yet others insist that globalisation does not mean the end of the state but rather its transformation. I share the last position but I would argue that there is no single method of transformation. States are changing in a variety of ways and, moreover, these changes, I shall argue, are bound up with changes in the types of armed forces and the forms of warfare.

The terms "militarism", "arms races" and "arms control" are expressions drawn from the Cold War era and before. Militarism refers to excessive levels of military spending by the state and excessive influence of armed forces over civilian life. "Arms races"

---

[3]See Held, David *et al.*, *Global Transformations* (Cambridge: Polity Press, 1999).

refer to the competition between similar types of military forces. "Arms control" refers to the process of treaty making between states based on the assumption that stability can best be preserved through a "balance of power (or terror)" between states.

In this essay, I shall start by describing militarism, arms races and arms control in the period before 1989, and I shall then distinguish between the different types of armed forces that are emerging in the post-Cold War world, only some of which can be characterised in terms of militarism and arms races, and discuss how they are loosely associated with different modes of state transformation and different forms of warfare. I have identified four different types of armed forces. They could be described as Weberian idealtypes. They are probably not comprehensive and no single example fits a particular type exactly. There is also a lot of overlap. The point is to provide a schematic account of what is happening in the field of warfare so as to be able to offer some new ways of thinking about the possibilities for controlling or limiting the means of warfare and why we need a new terminology beyond militarism, arms races and arms control. I shall suggest that the emphasis that has been increasingly accorded to international law, particularly humanitarian law, offers a possible way forward.

Militarism, Arms Races and Arms Control in the Period Before the End of the Cold War

The striking feature of 20th century militarism is the application of science and technology to warfare and the industrialisation of the armed forces. A key invention of the 20th century was the weapons system — hardware, which combined a weapons platform, like a ship, a tank or an aircraft; a weapon, such as a gun or a missile or a bomb; and means of communication and targeting. The weapons system came to dominate the organisation of armed forces, in much the same way as the machine came to dominate the organisation of modern industry. Thus competition between armed forces took the form of competitive improvements to successive generations of weapons systems.[4] This is why arms races have been so important in the 20th century.

In war, the effectiveness of improved systems was proved or disproved on the battlefield and the struggle for supremacy provided an important stimulus to science and technology. In peacetime, the competition for improved weapons system took the form of arms races, which provided an outlet for new developments in science and technology within the subjective parameters of the military planners. There have been two major arms races in the 20th century — the first before the First World War, and the second after the Second World War. One ended in war and the other in peace. Are there lessons to be learned from these two cases?

The origins of 20th century militarism can be traced to the last decades of the 19th century when private industry began to obtain military contracts. The entry of companies like Vickers and Armstrong in Britain or Krupp in Germany into the arms business marked the beginning of a military industrial complex. The arms race that preceded World War I largely took the form of naval competition — bigger and better battleships culminating in the Dreadnought monstrosities, which began to be built in 1906. This arms race can be explained in two ways. First of all, the battleships were a symbol of growing militarism and nationalism, which developed in the 19th century in response to both domestic and international tensions as a consequence of the huge changes brought about by industrialisation and inter-imperial rivalry. For Britain, in particular, they were visible affirmations of British naval power. Although the late 19th century battleships incorporated immense technological advance, as wood giving way to iron and steel, sail to steam, and as ships and guns got bigger, in form and function, they were still recognisable as the capital ship of Nelson' day, epitomising Britain's victory at Trafalgar. "On them as we conceived" wrote Churchill "floated the majesty, dominion, and power of the British Empire".[5]

---

[4]See Mary Kaldor, "The Weapons Succession Process", *World Politics*, July 1986.
[5]Quoted in Philip Noel-Baker, *The Private Manufacture of Arms* (London: Victor Gollancz, 1936), pp. 411–412.

Other countries, especially Germany, chose to acquire battleships as a way of competing with Britain. At the turn of a century, some South American countries were spending a quarter of their national income on battleships; such was their international political prestige.

The second factor that explains the naval arms race is competition among the arms companies. The first private contracts were issued in the 1880s when Britain was facing its first serious depression. As steel and engineering companies began to face competition from Germany and America, they sought Admiralty contracts using the argument that their capacity represented a reserve that might be needed in wartime. As they became more dependent on military contracts so they competed to offer improvements, such as greater firepower, better protection or more speed, in order to convince the government to issue new contracts, aided by periodic public outcries about German naval construction.

"The modern warship" wrote Engels "is not only a product but at the same time a specimen of modern large-scale industry, a floating factory — producing mainly, to be sure, a lavish waste of money…in this competitive struggle between armour-plating and guns, the warship is being developed to a pitch of perfection which is making it both outrageously costly and unusable in war".[6]

The outbreak of the First World War has to be primarily explained in terms of growing militarism and nationalism.[7] The arms race was significant indirectly, it can be argued, as a symbol of militarism, as a cause of paranoia as vested interests exploited public scares, and in the way that it diverted domestic resources from more productive uses thus contributing to social tension. In the event, Engels was right and warships were of little use in World War I. The armourers had to restructure in order to mass-produce machine guns and other small

---

[6]"The Force Theory", in *Anti-Duhring* (first published in 1894), (London: Lawrence and Wishart, 1975), pp. 207–208.

[7]See Fritz Fischer, *Germany's Aims in the First World War*, Chatto and Windus, 1967; Mazower, Mark, *Dark Continent: Europe's Twentieth Century*, Berghan Books, 1997.

arms whose significance the government had failed to anticipate.[8] The First World War was the first truly industrial war although industrial innovations had already been introduced in the American civil war and in the Franco-Prussian war. Millions of young men were killed in the stalemate produced by the use of lethal industrial inventions within the framework of 18th century ideas about warfare. It was only towards the end of the war that the invention of the tank and the military aircraft broke through the lines of vulnerable young men.

The second major arms race was after World War II — the arms race between the United States and the Soviet Union. It is often argued that the arms race and the so-called nuclear balance kept the peace in Europe. I have another explanation. The origins of World War II, it can be argued, lie in the failure to resolve the tensions that led to World War I. In World War II, it can be argued, both the United States and the Soviet Union hit upon solutions. For the United States, the war enabled America to break the constraints of world trade and development imposed by the colonial powers and to increase demand through public spending and through lendlease so as to utilise the massive surplus capacity generated by increased productivity. For the Soviet Union, the war provided a form of discipline both political and economic, which was lacking in a bureaucratically regulated system; war provided a kind of test of efficiency akin to market relations. The Cold War provided a way of sustaining those solutions, while avoiding the destructiveness of actual war. This is why I call the Cold War the "Imaginary War". Through the arms race, through military exercises and scenarios, through espionage and warlike rhetoric, we lived as though we were still at war.[9] This explanation was anticipated by George Orwell in *1984*:

---

[8]See John Ellis, *The Social History of the Machine Gun* (New York: Pantheon Books, 1973). Machine guns had been widely used in the colonies to devastating effects. In the Battle of Omdurman in Sudan in 1898, 11,000 dervishes were killed as against twenty British and twenty Europeans. Somehow, it was thought that these weapons would not be used against Europeans.

[9]See Mary Kaldor, *The Imaginary War* (Oxford: Basil Blackwell, 1990).

"War, it will be seen, is now a purely internal affair. In the past,
the ruling groups of all countries of all countries, although they
might limit their common interest and limit the destructiveness of
war, did fight against one another, and the victor always plundered
the vanquished. In our own day, they are not fighting against one
another at all. The war is waged by each ruling group against
its own subjects, and the object of war is not to make or prevent
conquests of territory but to keep the structure of society intact.
The very word 'war' therefore has become misleading. It would
probably be accurate to say that by becoming continuous war
has ceased to exist.... The effect would be much the same if the
three super-states, instead of fighting one another, should agree
to live in perpetual peace, each inviolate within its own
boundaries.... A peace that was truly permanent would be the
same as permanent war. This — although the vast majority of
Party members understand it only in a shallower sense — is the
inner meaning of the Party slogan: *War is Peace*"[10]

Military spending during the Cold War period was higher in
absolute terms than in any previous peacetime period — much
higher than before the First World War. In particular, a key component
of military spending was spending on research and development,
which accounted for over half the overall science budgets in both
the United States and the Soviet Union. As in the case of the
Anglo-German naval arms race, two factors were particularly
important:

- First of all, the missiles, aircraft and tanks that were developed
  were symbols of the victory in 1945. If we study the evolution of
  weapons and strategy in both countries, it is easier to understand
  in terms of a competition against a phantom German army, which
  had continued to develop in a linear fashion, than in terms of
  competition with each other. Take, for example, the development
  of missiles. For the Americans, these were seen as pilotless aircraft

---

[10]Orwell, George 1983, *1984*, Penguin Books, London (first published in 1948),
p. 173.

and as a continuation of the strategic bombing mission of World War II. Organisationally, they were part of Strategic Air Command and the emphasis was on long-range missiles. The Russians never had a strategic bombing mission and used aircraft tactically in support of ground operations; Stalin described aircraft as the "handmaiden of artillery". Hence when missiles were developed, they were housed in the artillery school and the emphasis was on medium and short-range missiles. Of course, all this can partly be explained in terms of the predilection of generals to fight the last war and to be conservative organisationally. But this predilection also expresses a way of reminding others about the achievements of the last war as a way of sustaining political dominance.

• Secondly, the arms race is to be explained by pressure from the laboratories and defence companies responsible for development and production of the new weapons systems — what was coined by President Eisenhower in his farewell speech, the military-industrial complex. Like British steel and engineering companies in the 1880s, American aircraft companies in the late 1940s argued that contracts needed to be issued to sustain the capacity for producing military aircraft and, indeed, new orders were made even before the formation of NATO and the outbreak of the Korean war. Subsequently, competition among defence companies led to efforts to produce improved accuracy, firepower, speed, and protection, as well as ever more complex and elaborate systems.[11] Competitive pressure to innovate was less in the Soviet Union because companies were not threatened with bankruptcy; there was more emphasis on quantity than quality — to keep production going — and innovation was more conservative or evolutionary than in the West.

As was the case in the pre-1914 arms race, this process was not confined to the main protagonists. 20th century militarism and

---

[11]See Mary Kaldor, *The Baroque Arsenal* (London: Andre Deutsch, 1982).

successive generations of weapons systems were spread throughout the world through alliances, military assistance, arms exports and so on. Minor arms races were reproduced between India and Pakistan, for example, or between Israel and the Arab states.

Pressures to halt of restrain the arms race already began in the 1950s with the emergence of an anti-nuclear movement, starting in Japan, after a Japanese fishing boat, the Lucky Dragon, had been caught up in a nuclear test. It is difficult to believe that the military planners understood the implications of nuclear weapons since tens of thousands were acquired during the 1950s. The movement did, I believe, strongly influence public consciousness about nuclear weapons, and, after the Cuban missile crisis, the idea of "arms control" was borne. This was the idea of managing the most dangerous aspects of the arms race. It was not disarmament, it did not involve a reversal of the arms race; rather it was another way of sustaining the imaginary part of the Cold War. The idea was to keep the Cold War going while lessening its most dangerous consequences. The Vietnam War further dented the idea of imaginary war and produced strong domestic opposition in the United States. Arms control was taken a stage further together with its political counterpart détente — relaxation in the conflict.

But détente and arms control were profoundly contradictory. It was difficult to sustain the idea of conflict and to justify new generations of weapons systems when political leaders were engaged in negotiations and co-operation. Moreover, the beginnings of globalisation made it harder to sustain the closed societies of the East. In the late 1970s, military-industrial pressure mounted within both blocs for a new Cold War. But unlike the first Cold War, the proposals, in the West, for a new generation of nuclear weapons produced polarisation not cohesion and led to a new peace movement. And in the East, the war in Afghanistan and the crackdown in Poland led to the stirrings, albeit repressed, that were to burst forth in 1989.

It is sometimes argued that the West won the Cold War because the arms race bankrupted the Soviet Union. I believe the opposite. I think the Cold War helped to sustain the Soviet system long after it ceased to function effectively. The Cold War allowed the Soviet Union to maintain a permanent war economy; without the arms race, the system would have collapsed or would have been forced to change much earlier. What ended the Cold War were the revolutions in Eastern Europe. But the Western peace movement also played a part, in supporting Eastern activists and providing the arguments that Gorbachev was able to use in winding down the arms race in the late 1980s. Pressure from the peace movement meant, I would argue, that, even without the 1989 revolutions, the West would have had to reduce its arsenals of nuclear weapons. Above all, the notion that war of a traditional kind between typical twentieth century industrial armed forces, can no longer be fought, results from the debate generated by peace movements.

In the aftermath of the end of the Cold War, the new types of armed forces that seem to be emerging can be understood as either ways of getting around the impossibility of twentieth century type warfare or else, in the case of the US or the neo-modern states, of trying to resuscitate twentieth century warfare in new ways. Legacies from the Cold War still exist in both the United States and Russia and are shaping their new roles in the so-called war against terror. I shall describe these new types of armed forces in turn.

Netforce: Informal or Privatised armed forces

A typical new phenomenon is armed networks of non-state and state actors. They include: para-military groups organised around a charismatic leader, warlords who control particular areas, terrorist cells, fanatic volunteers like the Mujahadeen, organised criminal groups, units of regular forces or other security services, as well as mercenaries and private military companies.

The form of warfare that is waged by these networks is what I call "new war"[12] New wars, which take place in the Balkans, Africa,

---

[12]Kaldor, M., *New and Old Wars: Organised Violence in a Global Era* (Cambridge: Polity Press, 1999).

Central Asia and other places, are sometimes called internal or civil wars to distinguish them from intra-state or Clausewitzean war. I think this terminology is inappropriate for a number of reasons. First, the networks cross borders. One of the typical features of the "new wars" is the key role played by Diaspora groups either far away (Sudanese or Palestinian workers in the Gulf states, former Yugoslav workers in Western Europe, immigrant groups in the new "melting pot" nations like North America or Oceania) or in neighbouring states (Serbs in Croatia and Bosnia, Tutsis in Burundi or the DRC). Secondly, the wars involve an array of global actors — foreign mercenaries and volunteers, Diaspora supporters, neighbouring states, not to mention the humanitarian actors such as aid agencies, NGOs or reporters.

And thirdly, and most importantly, the "new wars" tend to be concentrated in areas where the modern state is unravelling and where the distinctions between internal and external, public and private, no longer have the same meaning. Such areas are characterised by what are called frail or failing states, quasi or shadow states. These are states, formally recognised by the outside world, with some of the trappings of statehood — an incomplete administrative apparatus, a flag, sometimes a currency — but where those trappings do not express control over territory and where access to the state apparatus is about private gain not public policy. In particular these are states where the monopoly of legitimate organised violence is eroding.

In many of the areas where new wars take place, it is possible to observe a process that is almost the reverse of the process through which modern states were constructed. Taxes fall because of declining investment and production, increased corruption and clientilism, or declining legitimacy. The declining tax revenue leads to growing dependence both on external sources and on private sources, through, for example, rent seeking or criminal activities. Reductions in public expenditure as a result of the shrinking fiscal base as well as pressures from external donors for macro-economic stabilisation and liberalisation (which also may reduce export revenues) further erode legitimacy. A growing informal economy associated with increased inequalities, unemployment and rural-urban migration, combined with the loss of legitimacy, weakens the rule of law and may lead to the re-emergence of privatised forms of violence: organised crime and the substitution of "protection" for taxation; vigilantes; private security guards protecting economic facilities, especially international companies; or para-military groups associated with particular political factions. In particular, reductions in security expenditure, often encouraged by external donors for the best of motives, may lead to break away groups of redundant soldiers and policemen seeking alternative employment.

Of course, the networks that engage in new wars are not all to be found in these failing states. They include nodes in advanced industrial countries and, in the inner cities of the West, it is possible to observe gang warfare that has many of the characteristics of "new wars". Nevertheless, this type of state provides a fertile environment for this type of network.

There are three main characteristics of the "new wars". First of all, I use the term "war" to emphasis the political character of the new wars, even though they could also be described as organised crime (illegal or private violence) or as massive violations of human rights (violence against civilians). Because networks are loose horizontal coalitions, unlike vertical disciplined armies of the past, a shared narrative, often based on a common identity, ethnic or religious, is an important organising mechanism. In the case of the netforce, the networks engaged in the new wars, what holds them together is a generally an extreme political ideology based on the exclusive claim to state power on the basis of identity — ethnic chauvinism or religious communalism. I stress access to state power because these ideologies are not about substantive grievances, such as language rights or religious rights, although these may be indirectly important; rather they are about control of power and resources for an exclusively defined group of people.

I take the view that these ideologies are politically constituted. Even though they are based on pre-existing cleavages of tribe, nation and religion, and even though they may make use of memories and experiences of past injustices, they are constructed or accentuated for the purpose of political mobilisation.

Modern communications are important for the new networks both as a way of organising the network and as a form of mobilisation. Constructions of the past are developed and disseminated through radio, videos and television. Thus hate radio was of key importance in Rwanda. In Serbia, television was effectively used to remind people of the injustices of the past — the defeat of the Serbs by the Turks in 1389 and the fascist Croat treatment of Serbs during World War II. In the Middle East, videocassettes of Bin Laden's speeches circulate widely. The effect of television and radio in speeding up mobilisation especially in the countryside or among newly arrived urban migrants, who do not have the reading habit, should not be underestimated. There is an important contrast here with 19th century "imagined communities" which were propagated through the print media and involved the intellectual classes. The more populist electronic media are designed to appeal primarily to the least educated members of the public. In general, it is states that control the radio and television. But non-state groups can make use of other forms of media; Diaspora broadcasts through satellite television, which were important in Kosovo; the circulation of videos; or local radio in areas under political control.

A second characteristic of the "new wars" is that war itself is a form of political mobilisation. In what I have called wars between states, the aim of war was, to quote Clausewitz, "to compel an opponent to fulfil our will". In general this was achieved through the military capture of territory and victory in battle. People were mobilised to participate in the war effort — to join the army or to produce weapons and uniforms. In the new wars, mobilising people is the aim of the war effort; the point of the violence is not so much directed against the enemy; rather the aim is to expand the networks of extremism. Generally the aim is to control territory through political means and military means are use to kill, expel or silence those who might challenge control. This is why the warring parties use techniques of terror, ethnic cleansing or genocide as deliberate war strategies. In the new wars, battles are rare and violence is directed against civilians. Violations of humanitarian and human rights law are not a side effect of war but the central methodology of new wars. Over 90% of the casualties in the new wars are civilian and the number of refugees and displaced persons per conflict has risen steadily.

The strategy is to gain political power through sowing fear and hatred, to create a climate of terror, to eliminate moderate voices and to defeat tolerance. The political ideologies of exclusive nationalism or religious communalism are generated through violence. It is generally assumed that extreme ideologies, based on exclusive identities — Serb nationalism, for example, or fundamentalist Islam — are the cause of war. Rather, the spread and strengthening of these ideologies are the consequence of war. "The war had to be so bloody", Bosnians will tell you, "because we did not hate each other; we had to be taught to hate each other".

A third characteristic of the new wars is the type of economy they generate. Because these networks flourish in states where systems of taxation have collapsed and where little new wealth is being created, and where the wars destroy physical infrastructure, cut off trade and create a climate of insecurity that prohibits investment, they have to seek alternative, exploitative forms of financing. They raise money through loot and plunder, through illegal trading in drugs, illegal immigrants, cigarettes and alcohol, through "taxing" humanitarian assistance, through support from sympathetic states and through remittances from members of the networks. All of these types of economic activity are predatory and depend on an atmosphere of insecurity. Indeed, the new wars can be described as a central source of the globalised informal economy — the transnational criminal and semi-legal economy that represents the underside of globalisation.

The logical conclusion that can be drawn from these three characteristics is that the new wars are very difficult to contain and very difficult to end. They spread through refugees and displaced persons, through criminal networks, and through the extremist viruses they nurture. We can observe growing clusters of warfare in Africa, the Middle East, Central Asia or the Caucasus. The wars represent a defeat for democratic politics, and each bout of warfare strengthens those with a vested political and economic interest in continued violence. There are no clear victories or defeats because the warring parties are sustained both politically and economically by continuing violence. The wars speed up the process of state unravelling; they destroy what remains of productive activities, they undermine legitimacy, and they foster criminality. The areas where conflicts have lasted longest have generated cultures of violence, as in the jihad culture taught in religious schools in Pakistan and Afghanistan or among the Tamils of Sri Lanka, where young children are taught to be martyrs and where killing is understood as an offering to God. In the instructions found in the car of the hijackers in Boston's Logan Airport, it is written: "If God grants any one of you a slaughter, you should perform it as an offering on behalf of your father and mother, for they are owed by you. If you slaughter, you should plunder those you slaughter, for that is a sanctioned custom of the Prophet's".

It should be noted that there are other private or informal forces that do not correspond to this analysis. For example, in many of the new wars, villages or municipalities establish citizens' militias to defend local people — this was the case in among some groups in Rwanda and also in Tuzla and Zenica during the Bosnian war. There are also more traditional guerrilla groups, whose strategy is to gain political control through winning hearts and minds rather than through sowing fear and hatred; hence they attack agents of the state and not civilians, at least in theory. Finally, there are numerous private security companies, often established to protect multinational companies in difficult places, and mercenaries, who fight for money; tactics and forms of warfare, in these cases, depend largely on the paymasters.

The New American Militarism

It could be argued that if September 11 had not happened, the American military-industrial complex might have had to invent it. Indeed, what happened on September 11 could have come out of what seemed to be the wild fantasies of "asymmetric threats" that were developed by American strategic analysts as they sought a new military role for the United States after the end of the Cold War. A reporter for the London Observer claimed to have found in one of the headquarters for terrorist training in Afghanistan, a photocopy of the "terrorist cookbook" which circulates among the American fundamentalist right.

World military spending declined by one third in the decade after 1989. America military spending also declined but by less than the global average and began to rise again after 1998. As of the year 2000, American military spending in real terms is equivalent to its spending in 1980, just before the Reagan military build-up. More importantly, what took place during the 1990s was a radical shift in the structure of US military expenditure. Spending on military research and development declined less than overall military spending and has increased faster since 1998. As of 2000, US military R&D spending is 47% higher in real terms than in 1980.[13] Instead of ushering in a period of downsizing, disarmament and conversion (although some of that did take place at local levels in the US), the end of the Cold War led to a feverish technological effort to apply information technology to military purposes, known as the Revolution in Military Affairs (RMA).

Indeed, it can be argued that the cuts of the early 1990s are equivalent to the reductions that can be expected in the normal procurement cycle. The high points in the procurement cycle were in the early 1950s, late 1960s and early 1970s, and the early 1980s. During the downturns, military R&D is always sustained, designing and developing the systems to be procured in the next upturn. As new systems reach the more expensive development and procurement phases, this has always coincided with renewed preoccupations with threats of various kinds. The North Korean invasion of South Korea in 1950, for example, occurred at a moment when pressure to increase military spending was mounting as a result of over-capacity in the arms industry, especially the aircraft industry, and of fears about the return of mass unemployment after the end of the post-war consumer boom. NSC 68, the famous report, which

---

[13]See SIPRI, Stockholm International Peace Research Institute, *SIPRI Yearbook 2001: Armaments, Disarmament and International Security* (Oxford: Oxford University Press, 2001).

recommended an increase in military spending to meet the Soviet threat, was published just before the Korean invasion. A parallel can be drawn with the current situation since the systems developed under the rubric of the RMA are reaching the development and production phase and there is over-capacity in the aerospace industry.

During the 1990's, great efforts were expended in "imagining" new "worst-case scenarios" and new post-Soviet threats. With the collapse of the Soviet military-industrial complex, strategic planners have come up with all sorts of inventive new ways of attacking America, through spreading viruses, poisoning water systems, causing the collapse of the banking system, disrupting air traffic control or power transmission. Of particular importance has been the idea of state-sponsored terrorism and the notion of "rogue states" who sponsor terrorism and acquire long range missiles as well as WMD (Weapons of Mass Destruction). These new threats emanating from a collapsing Russia or from Islamic fundamentalism are known as "asymmetric" threats as weaker states or groups develop WMD or other horrific techniques to attack US vulnerabilities to compensate for conventional inferiority. Hence what happened on September 11, and the subsequent anthrax scare, seems like a confirmation of these anticipations of horror.

RMA consists of the interaction between various systems for information collection, analysis and transmission and weapons systems — the so-called "system of systems". It has spawned a suitably Sci fi jargon — "battlespace" to replace "battlefield" connoting the three dimensional character of contemporary battle; "dominant battlespace knowledge"; "precision violence"; "near-perfect mission assignment"; C^4I/BM (command, control, communications, computers, intelligence, and battle management); "co-operative engagement capability" (Navy); "digitalized ground forces" (Army); and (one of my favourites) "just-in-time warfare" (referring to reduced logistical requirements).[14]

---

[14]See Freedman, L., "The Revolution in Strategic Affairs" *Adelphi Paper 318*, (London: International Institute of Strategic Affairs, 1998).

The cruise missile, the target of peace movement campaigns in the 1980s, can be described as the "paradigmatic" weapon of RMA. It is a "system that can be delivered by a variety of platforms (i.e. all three services can use it) and strike in a precise manner and with low collateral damage" (Freedman, 1998: 70). It was the cruise missile that was used in the summer of 1998 against terrorist camps in Afghanistan and an alleged chemical weapons factory in Sudan after the bombings of the US embassies in Kenya and Uganda.

Enthusiasts for RMA suggest the introduction of information technology is akin to the introduction of the stirrup or gunpowder in its implications for warfare. Unlike these earlier innovations, however, RMA takes place within the traditional force structures inherited from the past. Earlier innovations were only adopted when force structures changed in such a way as to be capable of assimilating the new technologies. Thus the introduction of the stirrup depended on the evolution of feudal relations and the emergence of knights, while gunpowder was only applied to warfare after capitalist development made possible the use of mercenaries.

The origins of the RMA can be traced to the 1970s when the effect of growing accuracy and lethality of munitions was observed in the wars in Vietnam and the Middle East. The so-called military reformers suggested that this implied an historic shift to the defence. The offensive manoeuvres characteristic of World War II and planned in Europe for World War III were no longer possible since tanks and aircraft were almost as vulnerable as troops had been in World War I. In particular, it was argued that this historic shift lessened the need for nuclear weapons to compensate for Soviet conventional superiority since this could be nullified by improvements in conventional defence. The opponents of this view argued that the offence was even more important in the context of information technology because it made possible unmanned guided offensive weapons and because of the importance of area destruction munitions, which could destroy widely scattered defensive forces. It was the latter view that prevailed, perhaps because it left force structures undisturbed and sustained defence companies, retaining an emphasis on offensive manoeuvres and delivery platforms in a more or less linear extension from the strategic bombing missions of World War II.

The consequence was what became known as "emerging technologies" in the 1980s. These were long-range strike weapons using conventional munitions that were nearly as lethal as nuclear weapons. Terms such as "deep strike", "airland battle", and the "maritime strategy" became the buzzwords of the 1980s. The idea was that the West would meet any Soviet attack by striking deep into Soviet territory. When Iraq invaded Kuwait in 1990 and the Pentagon was asked to present the military options, they were able to roll out a plan that had been prepared in the event of a southward Soviet thrust.

The Gulf war provided a model for what can be described as casualty-free war — that is to say the use of high technology either directly to attack an enemy or to support a proxy, say the KLA in Kosovo or the Northern Alliance in Afghanistan. The idea now is that this high-tech warfare can be used against "rogue states" sponsoring terrorists. The same techniques were used against Iraq in December 1998, in Yugoslavia in 1999 and now in Afghanistan. They satisfy a confluence of interests. They fulfil the needs of the scientists, engineers and companies that provide an infrastructure for the American military effort. They allow for a continuation of the imaginary war of the Cold War period from the point of view of Americans. They do not involve American casualties, and they can be watched on television and demonstrate the determination and power of the United States government — the "spectacles" as Der Derian has put it, that "serve to deny imperial decline".[15] It is this imaginary character from an American perspective that explains Jean Baudrillard's famous remark that the Gulf War did not happen.

The programme for national missile defence has to be understood in the same vein. Even if the system cannot work, it provides

---

[15]See Der Derian, J. and Shapiro, M. (Eds), *International/Intertextual Relations: Postmodern Readings of World Politics* (Lexington, MA: Lexington Books, 1989).

imaginary protection for the United States, allowing the United States to engage in casualty-free war without fear of retaliation. This notion is evident from the way in which Donald Rumsfeld, the US defence secretary, talks about how NMD will enhance deterrence through a combination of defensive and offensive measures. The weakness of deterrence was always the problem of credibility; a problem that lead to more and more useable nuclear weapons. With casualty-free war, the credibility of US action is more convincing; after all, it is said, that the attack on the World Trade Towers was equivalent to the use of a sub-strategic nuclear weapon. NMD, at least psychologically, extends the possibilities for casualty-free war.

However, from the point of view of the victims, these wars are very real and not so different from new wars. However precise the strikes, it is impossible to avoid "mistakes" or "collateral damage". It does not make civilian casualties any more palatable to be told they were not intended. Moreover, the destruction of physical infrastructure and the support for one side in the conflict, as in the case of proxies, results in many more indirect casualties. In the case of the Gulf War, direct Iraqi casualties can probably be numbered in the tens of thousands but the destruction of physical infrastructure and the ensuing wars with the Kurds and the Shiites caused hundreds and thousands of further casualties and seem to have entrenched the vicious and dangerous rule of Saddam Hussein. In the current war in Afghanistan, there have probably been thousands of casualties, both civilian and military as well as thousands of people fleeing their homes and a humanitarian disaster because aid agencies have not been able to enter the country. The help provided to the hated Northern Alliance reduces the prospects of a broad- based Afghan government that might begin a process of stabilisation. Far from extending support for democratic values, casualty-free war shows that American lives are privileged over the lives of others and contributes to a perception of the United States as a global bully.

Terms like imperialism are, however, misleading. The United States is best characterised not as an imperial power but as the "last nation state". It is the only state, in this globalised world, that still has the capacity to act unilaterally. Its behaviour is determined less by imperial considerations than by concerns about its own domestic public opinion. Casualty-free war is also in a sense a form of political mobilisation. It is about satisfying various domestic constituencies, not about influencing the rest of the world, even though such actions have a profound impact on the rest of the world.

Neo-Modern Militarism

Neo-modern militarism refers to the evolution of classical military forces in large transition states. These are states that are undergoing a transition from a centralised economy to a more internationally open market-oriented system and, yet, which are large enough to retain a sizeable state sector. Typical examples are Russia, India and China. They are not large enough to challenge the US and they are constrained by many of the imperatives of globalisation, subject to many of the pressures that are experienced by frail or failing states. They tend to adopt extreme ideologies that resemble the ideologies of the "new wars" — Russian or Hindu chauvinism, for example. And there are often direct links to and even co-operation with the shadier networks, especially in Russia. Israel should probably also be included in this category, although its capacity to retain a sizeable military sector is due less to its size than to its dependence on the United States.

These states have retained their military forces, including nuclear weapons. In the case of India, there has been a significant increase in military spending throughout the 1990s and it could be argued that term "arms race" could be applied to India and Pakistan, especially after the 1998 nuclear tests. Pakistan, however, could be said to be closer to the networks of the new wars with its links to militants in Kashmir and Afghanistan; in other words somewhere between netforce and neo-modern militarism. In the case of Russia, there was a dramatic contraction of military spending after the break-up of the Soviet Union and a deep crisis in the military-industrial complex. But pressure to increase military spending has increased and the demands of the war in Chechnya is leading to a reassessment of the relative importance of conventional versus nuclear weapons. The proposed cuts in nuclear weapons discussed between Putin and Bush will release funds for conventional improvements. China is also engaged in military expansion especially since 1998, when the military were prohibited from engaging in commercial activities. Given the reductions in Russian nuclear capabilities and the new generation of Chinese systems, China will come to look more like a competitor to Russia, especially in the nuclear field.

The type of warfare that is associated with neo-modern militarism is either limited inter-state warfare or counter-insurgency. These states envisage wars on the classic Clausewitzean model. They engage in counter-insurgency in order to defeat extremist networks as in Chechnya or Kashmir. Or they prepare for the defence of borders against other states, as in the case of the Kargil war between India and Pakistan in 1998. Unlike the United States, these states are prepared to risk casualties and, in the case of the Chechen war, Russian casualties have been extremely high. The typical tactics used against the networks are shelling from tanks, helicopters or artillery, as well as population displacement to "clean" areas of extremists or "terrorists". The impact on civilians is thus very similar to the impact of the "new wars". Yet precisely because of the growing destructiveness of all types of weapons, military victory against an armed opponent is very difficult. Grozny has virtually been reduced to rubble. Yet still resistance persists.

The networks have understood that they cannot take territory militarily, only through political means, and the point of the violence is to contribute to those political means. The states engaged in neo-modern militarism are still under the illusion that they can win militarily. The consequence is either self-imposed limits, as in the case of inter-state war, or exacerbation of "new wars" as in the case of Kashmir, Chechnya or Palestine, where counter-insurgency merely contributes to the political polarising process of fear and hate. In other words, the utility of modern military force, the ability to "compel an opponent to fulfil our will" is open to question nowadays.

Protectionforce: Peace-Keeping/Peace-Enforcement

An important trend in the last decade has been the increase in peacekeeping operations. At the start of the decade, there were only 8 United Nations peacekeeping operations; they involved some 10,000 troops. As of the end of 2000, there were 15 United Nations operations involving some 38,000 military troops.[16] In addition, a number of regional organisations were engaged in peace-keeping: NATO in Bosnia, Kosovo and Macedonia; the Commonwealth of Independent States (CIS), mainly Russia, in Tajikistan, Transdinestr, Abkhazia, and South Ossetia; the Economic Community of West African States (ECOWAS) in Sierra Leone, Liberia and Guinea.

Peacekeeping has not only increased in scale; there have been important changes in the tasks peacekeepers are asked to perform and in the way we think about peacekeeping. During the Cold war period, peacekeeping was based on the assumption that wars were of the Clausewitzean type. The job of peacekeepers was to separate the warring parties and to monitor cease-fires on the basis of agreements. Peacekeeping was sharply distinguished from peace enforcement, which was equated with war fighting, i.e. intervening in a war on one side, authorised under Chapter VIII of the UN Charter.

In terms of organisation, peacekeeping has more in common with the networks than with classic military forces. Peacekeeping forces are generally loose transnational coalitions. Although they usually have a clearly defined multinational command system, peacekeepers are also subject to national commands, which erodes the vertical character of the command system. Because they are often far away from the decision-makers and because of the nature of their tasks, individual initiative is often more important than unquestioning obedience. Moreover, peacekeepers have to work together with a range of other agencies, international organisations like UNHCR or UNDP and also NGOs involved in humanitarian assistance or conflict

---

[16]See Anheier, H., Glasius, M. and Kaldor, M. (Eds)., *Global Civil Society 2001* (Oxford: University Press, 2001).

resolution. A shared narrative based on humanitarian principles is critical in holding the networks together.

The new tasks for peace-keepers include the protection of safe havens, where civilians can find refuge, the protection of convoys delivering humanitarian assistance, disarmament and demobilisation, providing a secure environment for elections or for the return of refugees and displaced persons, or capturing war criminals. These tasks reflect the changes in the nature of the warfare. New terms like "second-generation peace-keeping", "wider peace-keeping" or "robust" peacekeeping have been used to describe these new roles. Peacekeepers nowadays operate in the context of continuing wars or insecure post-conflict situations, and they are more likely to risk casualties than were traditional peacekeepers.

A number of recent reports have emphasised that the new role of peacekeeping is, first and foremost, the protection of civilians since they are the main targets of the new wars.[17] The new peacekeeping is indeed somewhere between traditional peacekeeping (separating sides) and peace enforcement (taking sides). I have argued that outright military victory is very very difficult nowadays, at least if we are unwilling to contemplate mass destruction. The job of the new protectionforce is not to defeat an enemy but to protect civilians and stabilise war situations so that non-extremist tolerant politics has space to develop. The task is thus more like policing than warfighting although it involves the use of military forces. Techniques like safe havens or humanitarian corridors are ways of protecting civilians and also increasing the international presence on the ground so as to influence political outcomes.

In practice, peacekeeping has not lived up to this description. Partly this is due to lack of resources. Not nearly enough has been invested in peacekeeping and in providing appropriate training and

---

[17]See, for example, Brahimi, *Report of the Panel on United Nations Peace Operations* (UN Doc.A/55/305-S/2000/809, 21 August) New York, United Nations, 2000; International Commission on Intervention and State Sovereignty, *The Responsibility to Protect* Stylus publishers, 2002.

equipment. More importantly, international lives are still privileged over the lives of the civilians they are supposed to protect. OSCE monitors left Kosovo hurriedly when the bombing of Yugoslavia began, leaving behind a terrified population who had believed rightly or wrongly that the orange vans of the OSCE monitors were some protection; the local OSCE staff left behind were all killed. Likewise, Dutch peacekeepers handed over the 8000 men and boys of Srebrenica to Serb forces in July 1995 and they were all massacred. In Rwanda, UN forces were withdrawn just as the genocide of 800,000 Tutsis began, despite the impassioned plea of the Canadian UN Commander, General Dallaire, to establish safe havens. There are, of course, also moments of heroism, like the Ukranian peacekeepers in Zepa or the British in Goradze, or the UN staff in East Timor who refused to evacuate their headquarters unless the people who had sought refuge there were also saved. But, as yet, these moments are insufficient to be seen to justify the commitment in resources and will that would be necessary for a serious and sustained use of peacekeeping.

Peace-keeping/peace enforcement is associated with states that could be described as post-modern or globalising.[18] These are states that have come to terms with the erosion of their autonomy (their ability to retain control over what happens in their territory), in the context of growing interconnectedness. They have thus adopted a deliberate strategy of multilateralism, of trying to influence the formation of global rules and participating actively in the enforcement of those rules. The British Prime Minister Tony Blair attempted to articulate this position in his speech on the "Doctrine of the International Community" during the Kosovo war. "We are all internationalists now whether we like it or not" he told an audience in Chicago. "We cannot refuse to participate in global markets if we want to prosper. We cannot ignore new political ideas in other

---

[18]Clark, Ian, *Globalisation and International Relations Theory* (Oxford: Oxford University Press, 1999) Cooper, Robert; *The Postmodern State and the World Order* (London: Demos/Foreign Policy Centre, 2000) 2nd edition.

countries if we want to innovate. We cannot turn our backs on conflicts and the violation of human rights in other countries if we still want to be secure".[19]

The states that fit this category include most European states, Canada, South Africa, Japan, as well as a number of others. Of course, most states, including the United States and Russia, engage in this type of peace operation. But it is not viewed as the main contingency for which they prepare. The new globalising states are reorienting their military doctrines along these lines. The wars in the Balkans have had a profound impact in Europe, where concern about Balkan stability and experience in the region is shaping military thinking.

Controlling War?

During the Cold War period, the main concern was how to prevent a war of global annihilation. Arms control was seen as one of the most important methods of prevention; it was a way of stabilising the perception of a balance of power. A true balance of power is a war that no side can win. Because armed forces were roughly similar during the Cold War period, it was possible to estimate a surrogate balance of power based on quantitative estimates of military forces, which could be codified in arms control treaties. This surrogate balance of power was seen as a way of preventing perceptions of imbalance, which might have tempted one or other side to start a war. In practice, of course, numbers are irrelevant since any nuclear war is likely to lead to global annihilation but the exercise of measuring a balance of power shored up the notion of an imaginary war that could not be won.

The danger of a war of global annihilation has, thankfully, receded since the end of the Cold War. What we are now witnessing, however, is a series of real wars that cannot be won. There are no surrogate balances, except perhaps between the neo-modern military forces.

---

[19]Blair, T., *Doctrine of the International Community,* April 23, 19991, http://www.primeminister.gov.uk

The US no longer has what is known in the jargon as a "peer competitor" and other types of armed forces are too varied to be compared. What I have tried to argue is that the first three types of armed forces (the networks, the new American military forces, and the neo-modern military forces) all engage in real wars with very similar consequences — indiscriminate suffering for civilians (even though the Americans claim that their greater precision and discriminateness minimises such suffering). Nowadays, therefore, the emphasis of those who are concerned about such suffering has to be directly with the ways to control war. Limitations on weapons may be part of that wider goal but have to be viewed from a different perspective than in the Cold War period.

Perhaps the most hopeful approach to the contemporary problem of controlling war, nowadays, is not through arms control but through the extension and application of international humanitarian law (the "laws of war") and human rights law. During the 1990s, much greater importance was accorded to humanitarian norms — the notion that the international community has a duty to prevent genocide, violations of humanitarian law (war crimes) and massive violations of human rights (crimes against humanity). The idea of overriding state sovereignty in the case of humanitarian crises became much more widely accepted. The establishment of the Yugoslav and Rwanda Tribunals paved the way for the establishment of an International Criminal Court. The Pinochet and Ariel Sharon cases removed the principle of sovereign immunity.

Humanitarian law is not, of course, new. Its origins lie in the codification of "laws of war", especially under the auspices of the International Red Cross, in the late nineteenth century. The aim was to limit what we now call "collateral damage" or the side effects of war, above all, to prevent the indiscriminate suffering of civilians, and to ensure humane treatment for the wounded and for prisoners of war. These laws codified rules in Europe, which dated back to the Middle Ages and underlay a notion of "civilised" warfare, which was important in order to define the role of the soldier as the legitimate agent of the state, as a hero not a criminal. (Of course, these rules were not applied outside Europe against "barbarians" or the "rude nations").

Humanitarian law was greatly extended after World War II. The Nuremberg and Tokyo trials marked the first enforcement of war crimes and, indeed, crimes against humanity. The Genocide Convention of 1948 as well as further extension of the Geneva Conventions, and, the newly developing human rights law, all represented further strengthening of humanitarian law, albeit marginalised by the dominant Cold War confrontation.

What has changed in the last decades is the change in the nature of warfare, even though some aspects were presaged in the holocaust and the bombing of civilians in the Second World War. As argued above, violations of humanitarian law and human rights law are no longer "side effects" of war, they represent the core of the new warfare. Therefore taking seriously humanitarian law is one way of controlling the new warfare.

This is the context in which the limitation of armaments should also be understood. Recent efforts to limit or eliminate categories of weapons, like the Land Mines Convention or the protocol to the Biological Weapons Convention, or the efforts to control small arms are not based on the assumption of a balance between states. Rather they are the outcome of pressure by global civil society to uphold humanitarian norms and prevent indiscriminate harm to civilians. The 1996 International Court of Justice decision about nuclear weapons, as well as several recent cases in Scotland, is based on the same line of thinking.

Taken seriously, a humanitarian approach would outlaw netforce and would restructure legitimate, i.e. state, military forces from classic war fighting tasks to a new and extended form of protectionforce. It would outlaw WMD as well as weapons like land mines that cause indiscriminate harm. Peace keeping and peace enforcement could be reconceptualised as humanitarian law enforcement, with appropriate equipment.

Such an approach would be consistent with the transformation of states along the lines of the post-modern or globalising states. It would imply a strengthening of global rules and greater participation in the enforcement of rules. All three of the other types of warfare I have described are based on particularist assumptions about the need to protect particular communities, networks or states, and to privilege their lives over others. There is no reason why growing interconnectedness should be combined with particularism and fragmentation; indeed that is the characteristic of the contemporary world. But it is no longer possible to insulate particular communities or states; even the United States is now vulnerable to transnational networks. If we are to find ways to cope with the uneven impact of globalisation and to deal with the criminal and violent underside of globalisation, then the main task is to construct some form of legitimate set of global rules. This is not the same as a global state; rather it is about establishing a set of global regimes underpinned by states, international institutions and global civil society. The humanitarian regime would be at the heart of such a set of rules because of the legitimacy that derives from the assumption of human equality.

How would this approach have changed the reaction to the events of September 11? What happened on September 11 was a crime against humanity. It was interpreted, however, in the US as an attack on the US and a parallel has been repeatedly drawn with Pearl Harbour. Bush talks about a "war on terrorism" and has said that "you are either with us or with the terrorists". The approach of casualty-free war has been adopted, using high tech strikes and a proxy, the Northern Alliance, to destroy the state sponsoring terrorism, the Taliban, and to destroy the Al-Qaeda network. (At the time of writing, some US Special Forces and Marines have been deployed on the ground). We do not know how many people have died as a result of the strikes or have fled their homes but it undoubtedly numbers in hundreds if not thousands. The chances of stabilising Afghanistan exist but are reduced by the dominant role played by the Northern Alliance. Most importantly, perhaps, the approach contributes to a political polarisation between the West and the rest, both because of the privileging of American lives and the language in which the war is conducted. While the Taliban has been overthrown, there is unlikely to be any clear military victory. As I have argued, the political narrative, in this case of jihad against America, is central to the functioning of the network. Casualty-free war confirms the political narrative and sets up exactly the kind of war envisaged by the Al-Qaeda network.

A humanitarian approach would have defined September 11 as a crime against humanity. It would have sought United Nations authorisation for any action and it would have adopted tactics aimed at increasing trust and confidence on the ground, for example through the establishment of safe havens in the North as well humanitarian corridors. It would have established an International Court to try terrorists. It would have adopted some of the means already adopted to put pressure on terrorist networks through squeezing financial assets, for example, as well as efforts to catch the criminals. Such an approach would have to eschew double standards. Catching Mladic and Karadic, the perpetrators of the Srebrenica massacre is just as important as catching Bin Laden. Human rights violations in Palestine and Chechnya are no less serious than in Kosovo or Afghanistan.

A humanitarian approach, of course, has to be part of a wider political approach. In wars, in which no military victory is possible, political approaches are key. An alternative political narrative, based on the idea of global justice, is the only way to minimise the exclusive political appeal of the networks. What this involves is, no doubt, being discussed in other sessions of this symposium.

I am aware that all this sounds impossibly utopian. Unfortunately, the humanitarian approach may be seen in retrospect as a brief expression of the interregnum between the end of the Cold War and September 11, 2001. We are, I fear, on the brink of a global new war, something like the wars in the Balkans or the Israel-Palestine war, on a global scale with no outsiders to constrain its course. Sooner or later, the impossibility of winning such a war must become evident and that is why we need to keep the humanitarian approach alive. Even if it cannot solve these conflicts, it can offer some hope to those caught in the middle.

Louise Fawcett

Rivalry over Territory and Resources and the Balance of Peace and War: The 20th Century[1]

Introduction

To generations of historians it seemed unsurprising and uncontroversial to state a clear linkage between the outbreak of war and the struggle for territory and resources. For end-of-the-century social scientists this linkage may need qualification.

During past centuries empires, states and peoples have struggled to acquire and defend territory and resources for reasons of power, prestige, security, or ideology. These struggles, conflicting as they did with the interests and aspirations of other empires, states and peoples, often led to war: not perpetual war — periods of war were followed by periods of peace — but wars were seen as a normative feature of international relations. Further, the 'right of conquest': the proposition that a state emerging victorious in war was entitled to claim jurisdiction over captured territory was uncontested.[2]

---

[1]I am particularly grateful to Martin Ceadel, Eduardo Posada, Adam Roberts and Ngaire Woods for their helpful comments and suggestions on an earlier version of this paper.
[2]See Sharon Korman, *The Right of Conquest* (Oxford: Clarendon Press, 1996), p. 1.

This notion of war as part of the natural order of things, a reflection of states' appetites and interests, and with it the acceptance of territorial gain, had come into question long before the 20th century,[3] but such liberal thinking yielded to the reality of two world wars: wars of territory and resources par excellence. In the interwar period too, the sort of imperial expansion so characteristic of the 19th century continued, albeit in a somewhat tempered form. The Cold War that followed World War II was, for all its coldness, as much about territory and resources as it was about ideology, particularly for the USSR. And the conflicts that accompanied decolonization also demonstrated the continued salience of territorial and resource issues in a new post-colonial order (for both super-powers and the former colonies themselves).

The legacies of some such conflicts remain, notably in the Middle East, but also in Africa and South Asia, and have seen little let up in the post-Cold War order, as the Palestine-Israel, Central African or India-Pakistan cases demonstrate. To them must now be added the new wave of post-imperial crises resulting from the break up of the USSR and Yugoslavia. Here we find territorial and to some extent resource issues tangled with those of ethnicity, religion and nationalism. The Gulf War, in contrast, was nothing if not a manifestation of Saddam Hussein's desire to expand Iraq to incorporate the Kuwaiti oil reserves. And the West's decision to intervene was in turn influenced by the region's significance in resource terms. More generally, in ways that are perhaps less immediately obvious, struggles over resources and territory are played out at the sub-state level — within nations — by local groups and ethnic communities on the one hand, and at the supra-state or global level by international institutions on the other.

On this reading little of substance has changed. The 20th century looks much like those that preceded it in terms of state motivation,

---

[3]See for example, Martin Ceadel, *Origins of War Prevention: The British Peace Movement and International Relations 1730–1854* (Oxford: Clarendon Press, 1996).

the balance of peace and war and even the causes of war. The players may to some extent have changed, but the game is still the same.

We know, of course, that things are not that simple. First, it can be argued that rivalry over territory and resources is not the only, or indeed in itself a sufficient explanation of war, and this applies not only to the 20th century.[4] Second, changes have taken place in the course of the 20th century that would lead some scholars to challenge the dominant notion that the major determinant of the balance of peace and war is territorial and resource rivalry.[5] In short, both the balance of peace and war, and the relationship between territorial rivalry and war appear to have changed in fundamental ways, or at least for certain states.

Strong, stable and (now) democratic states, in a clear shift from 19th century European practice, will eschew territorial expansion and/or direct control of other states' resources.[6] They refrain from fighting as a means of solving disputes, except in self defence or other circumstances defined by the United Nations. The right of conquest is denied. For such states, war is unnecessary: the road to power and prestige no longer requires the direct acquisition of the territory and resources of others. It is also undesirable: war, unless it is 'virtual' is both too costly and dangerous and often politically unacceptable as a way of proceeding.[7]

Other states, often weak, unstable and non-democratic, continue to regard war an acceptable extension of policy, desire the territory and resources of others and see the latter as vital in the quest for status and security. The balance of war and peace has then changed,

---

[4]See for example, John Vasquez, *The War Puzzle* (Cambridge: Cambridge University Press, 1993).

[5]For example, Richard Rosecrance, *Rise of the Virtual State* (New York: Basic Books, 1999).

[6]There are exceptions: India's seizure of Goa in 1961 which was justified (by India) in terms of the latter's status as colony; a justification which failed (though for somewhat different reasons) to uphold Argentina's claim to the Falkland Islands in 1982.

[7]Michael Ignatieff, *Virtual War: Kosovo and Beyond* (London: Vintage, 2001).

not so much in terms of numbers of wars: a recent study found that
the number of significant conflicts remain at 30–40 per annum,[8]
but in terms of the types of states and actors that engage in wars
with each other, and the types of wars that are fought.[9]

In this paper I examine the nature of this evolving relationship.
To this end I first review the major conflicts of the 20th century to
demonstrate the shifting balance of war and peace and the relative
salience of territory and resource issues as determinants of conflict.
I then look at some of the problems and challenges associated with
this approach, as well as some alternative readings of events, in
particular how changes at the domestic and international level have
affected the policies and practices of states. Lastly, I attempt a balance
sheet from the perspective of the turn of the century, and assess
the lessons for the future.

I argue that if the nature and purpose of war has changed for
some states, conflict and competition over territory and resources
continue to dominate the balance of war and peace. They remain
central to our understanding of wars between and within states:
very few conflicts have *no* territorial or resource component. And
while this component may be harder to distinguish for the still quite
small band of developed, satisfied states whose ambitions no longer
include direct territorial gain, it remains present in their dependence
on the territory and resources of others, and in their ability to
influence global agendas to serve their security needs. For a much
bigger band of underdeveloped, and dissatisfied states, territory and
resources remain highly salient, and both a direct and indirect cause
of war: direct, where states and non-state groups compete both for
territory and political control, or where existing states seek to expand

---

[8]See Michael Clarke, 'War in the New International Order', *International Affairs*,
(Summer, 2001), p. 663. For an alternative survey of war type and frequency see
Ted Robert Gurr, 'Containing Internal War in the Twenty-First Century', in Fen Osler
Hampson and David M. Malone, *From Reaction to Conflict Prevention. Opportunities
for the UN System* (London: Lynne Reinner, 2002), pp. 41–42.
[9]This point is powerfully made by Kalevi Holsti, in *The State, War and the State of
War* (Cambridge: Cambridge University Press, 1996).

for reasons of security and prestige; indirect, where weak states feel insecure and dis-empowered by the existing balance of power in global institutions which is seen to privilege the strong and marginalise the weak. In this way, the whole process of globalization may have contributed to a new form of territorial and resource rivalry. Overall it is unlikely that the incidence of wars will decrease, or the salience of territorial and resources issues will decline, unless and until more states share the political and economic conditions which enable them to decouple such issues from their basic security dilemma as states. This will mean a far greater degree of domestic stability and meaningful participation in regional and global institutions than has existed hitherto.

Wars in the 20th Century: An Overview

The territorial advances of the major European powers in the 19th century — whether in the form of overseas expansion, or state building and unification (in the cases of Germany and Italy) were, in themselves, a major source of war. They also laid the bases for patterns of future conflict well into the 20th century. Imperialism helped create the image of a 'premier league' of European powers, which rising states like Germany felt they must struggle to join or remain forever a second rank power. The parallel process of Europeanization, which involved both rule-setting by Europe and denial of sovereignty to non-European peoples, sowed the seeds of a series of colonial and post-colonial conflicts whose consequences affected the balance of war and peace throughout the 20th century. Emulation of European practices of influence and control, by states like Japan and China, had similar consequences.[10]

The unstable decade or so before the First World War witnessed intense territorial ambition and rivalry. The Russo-Japanese War 1904–05 was in large part the result of clashing interests in the Far

---

[10]In this section, I am influenced by the excellent study by Jeremy Black, *Why Wars Happen* (London: Reaktion Books, 1998) especially Chapter 4, pp. 150–71.

East. Designs on territory lay also behind crises in North Africa and
the Far East where, in E.H. Carr's words, 'there was a hasty scramble
by the European powers to secure the few eligible sites which were
still vacant'.[11] Territorial challenges were implicit in the nationalist
uprisings within the still existing Habsburg and Ottoman empires,
pulling in friends and foes alike; they were explicit in France's wish
for the return of Alsace Lorraine. Such designs were not, in
themselves, the only cause of war as we shall see, but must be seen
as a major underlying factor in slide towards war in 1914.

If territorial rivalries — both in the colonies and the Balkans —
had played a major role in the onset of the First World War, they
remained a source of conflict and competition in the interwar period,
despite the efforts of US President Woodrow Wilson and others to
supply the foundations of new international order. This order, of
which the League of Nations was intended as the central construct,
was sorely challenged by a host of competing claims between minor
and major states (including Turkey, Hungary and Poland) almost before
the ink on the Versailles treaties had dried. The ambitions of Germany
— which had lost territory to Denmark, Belgium, France, and Poland
— as well as Italy and Japan, were scarcely disguised. Post-
revolutionary Russia also emerges as a major revisionist power, despite
the early repudiation of all imperialist war aims. Britain and France
were not immune, staking out new claims for influence and territorial
control in Africa, and what became known as the Middle East, via
the mandate system. To that system incorporating as it did the notion
of a Jewish homeland into a new state framework including Iraq,
Jordan, Syria and Palestine, can be attributed the sources of some of
the most persistent and violent conflicts of the 20th century.

In the interwar period, these conflicts (as in other parts of the
imperial system) were limited struggles between colonized and
colonizers for greater independence. These were the beginnings of
a 'revolt against Western dominance': a struggle for liberation,
sovereignty, equality, and justice, aimed to wrest first territory and

---

[11]EH Carr, *The Twenty Years' Crisis 1919-1939* (London: Macmillan, 1981), p. 61.

then resources away from external control.[12] This struggle, with few exceptions, was not completed until well after the Second World War; for some states it remains incomplete even today.

It was not colonial rivalry that provided the impetus for the new cycle of war that commenced in the 1930s, at least not directly. If the Japanese seizure of Manchuria in 1931 carried many of the hallmarks of imperial expansion and the Italian invasion of Ethiopia (1935-36) was distinguished as the 'last of the European wars of colonial annexation',[13] these conflicts did not of themselves provoke a general war. General war must be attributed first to the actions of Hitler's Germany, with its plans for expansion and domination of territory and peoples, second to Japan's restless quest for resource control in the name of 'co-prosperity' which extended its reach to South East Asia, and third to the determination of the Allied powers to curtail such aspirations.

For the Axis powers, comprehensive defeat in the Second World War, and the changed domestic and international environment which ensued, squashed permanently territorial and resource ambitions. For the colonial powers also, long years of imperial expansion came to an end. But if territorial aggrandisement ceased to be a great power game, rivalries over territory and resources continued, conditioning the new balance of peace and war. The two new, and not unrelated contexts for these rivalries were the Cold War and decolonization.

In the Cold War the rhetoric of two contrasting ideologies merely disguised a new version of an old form of indirect territorial control: the sphere of influence. The Soviet position was prefigured by Stalin's wartime observation: 'whoever occupies a territory also imposes on it his own social system. Everyone imposes his own system as far as his army has power to do so. It cannot be otherwise.'[14] Rivalries over the definition and extension of the two superpowers' respective

---

[12]Hedley Bull, 'The Revolt against the West', in Hedley Bull and Adam Watson, *The Expansion of International Society* (Oxford: Clarendon Press, 1984), pp. 217-228.
[13]Black, *Why Wars Happen*, p. 188.
[14]Milovan Djilas, *Conversations with Stalin* (London: Penguin Books, 1962), p. 90.

spheres became acute at certain high points of the Cold War, though
not all led to outright conflict: Berlin and Korea were two early
examples; Cuba and Afghanistan were others. Within its own sphere
the USSR was forced to intervene twice, in Hungary and
Czechoslovakia, to reassert its model of political control. The uprising
in Hungary, in particular, was seen as a direct threat to the integrity
of the Soviet sphere.

For its part, the decolonization process which gathered
momentum in the 1950s and 60s, was in the first instance more
about the newly independent states gaining control of their own
territory and resources. And this process, in itself, engendered rivalries
between both former colonies and colonizers, as in Algeria, Angola,
or Malaya, but also between rival factions within the colonies
themselves, as was the case in Burma, Congo or Vietnam. But
decolonization quickly fed into and became subsumed by the
dynamics of the Cold War, where rivalry for influence and control
over the newly independent states soon became vital to the bloc
building process. In this regard, one cannot but note the paradoxical
transformation of superpower anti-imperialism into a form of
superpower neo-imperialism in which rivalry over territory and
resources once more enjoyed pride of place.

Few wars took place entirely outside the Cold War framework.
An important exception was the Falklands War: a colonial hangover
in which a threat to British sovereignty and territorial integrity was
dealt with in the style of the 19th century British statesman,
Palmerston: by the sending of gunboats. Another was the Iran-Iraq
war 1980–87, originating over the long-disputed Shatt al-Arab
waterway, and displaying all the characteristics of a classical territory
and resources war. The early Arab-Israel conflicts, whose origins and
development were only tangentially linked to the Cold War, resulted
in the successful, if still contested, transfer of territory to Israel (the
Golan Heights and East Jerusalem).

My summary of the 20th century would be incomplete without
a brief look at the post-Cold War order, for this was not a 'short

century' as far as war was concerned.[15] But if its last decade or so was characterised by continuing conflict, it also saw new shifts in the relationship between territory and resource rivalry and the balance of peace and war. The end of the bipolar order necessarily meant the end of bloc building and maintenance, and the struggles over territory that this entailed. But there was also relative stability in the Cold War structure, as noted by many theorists, based on some fixed assumptions of international order.[16] When this was broken, a new instability ensued. In particular it was the ending, on the Soviet side, of the more coercive forms of control exercised to keep satellite states in line, that has given way to new rivalries and tensions. Yet again, one form of territorial rivalry has replaced another where different factions or groups battle for political control and space in states once within the Soviet sphere. To some extent the post-Cold War period mirrors earlier end of empire struggles, before and after the First and Second World Wars where reallocation of territory and political power took place, often amid violence and conflict.

Where superpower rivalry for control of Eastern Europe or Third World states may be a thing of the past, both Russia and the USA retain a watchful eye on conflicts deemed still to be within their respective spheres, ready to intervene if need dictates. Hence, Russia looks to states of the former Union, the United States to Latin America. These regions remain off limits to external actors and agencies without the consent of the power in question. In this regard the USA is, of course, more favourably placed to dictate outcomes. Its sphere, unlike that of the former USSR, with its looser and more consensual character, not only survived the Cold War, but extended its reach. Where the Warsaw Pact folded, NATO has shown capacity to reinvent itself, taking on new roles of mediation and conflict

---

[15]See Eric Hobsbawm, *Age of Extremes. The Short 20th Century 1914-1991* (London: Abacus, 1994).

[16]John Mearsheimer, 'Back to the Future', Instability in Europe after the Cold War', *International Security* 15 (Summer, 1990), pp. 5-56.

resolution. Clearly these roles do not, in themselves, incorporate any overt territorial agenda, but when NATO, or for that matter any state or international institution intervenes, for whatever reason, in the affairs of another state or states, there are necessarily motives and outcomes more complex than merely peacemaking or the delivery of humanitarian assistance. Put simply: today's wars, like yesterday's wars, both for those who fight and those who intervene, have profound territorial and resource implications. And this applies to all conflicts, not only in the former Soviet or Yugoslav spheres, but also in many developing countries where post-colonial tensions and struggles over nation and state building continue, unrestrained by the effects of superpower overlay;[17] it also applies to the inter-state wars or interventions that have taken place involving Western powers. Given the resilience of the norms of territorial integrity and sovereignty (discussed in the last section) it could hardly be otherwise.

The wars of the contemporary era, 'new' wars or wars of the 'third type', as Mary Kaldor and Kalevi Holsti respectively call them,[18] may be different from some of the other types of war described here. Seen from a longer perspective, however, they are less new than one might suppose, and their territorial and resource component is hardly in doubt for their being intrastate. Often, the strategic aim of such conflicts is to secure territory through political control. Indeed ethnic conflicts, writes Chaim Kaufmann, 'are primarily military struggles in which victory depends on physical control of the disputed territory'.[19] These are wars emanating from within new and weak states: state-nation wars, wars from below or peoples wars, struggles over identity, community and political control: Bosnia-

---

[17]Barry Buzan, *Peoples States and Fear* (London: Harvester Wheatsheaf, 1991), p. 208.

[18]Mary Kaldor, *New and Old Wars* (Cambridge, Polity Press, 1999); K. J. Holsti, *The State, War and the State of War* (Cambridge: Cambridge University Press, 1996).

[19]Chaim Kaufmann, 'Possible and Impossible Solutions to Ethnic Civil Wars', *International Security*, 20: 4, (Spring, 1996), p. 140; Mary Kaldor (ed.), *Global Insecurity* (London: Pinter, 2000), p. 6.

Herzegovina is a classic example. Such wars have the capacity to spread both regionally and internationally, refusing to remain within their 'internal limits',[20] so in this sense at least territorial rivalry continues to condition the overall balance of war and peace. Outside Europe, Colombia offers a model of a different kind of 'new' war, where a weak central government has struggled to retain political and even territorial control against a backdrop of competing demands from different rebel groups, inevitably with severe regional and increasingly international repercussions.

If such intrastate wars prevail, and define the current topology of war, interstate wars over territory and resources remain a threat. In contemplating new types of war we cannot so readily dismiss the old type, as both the Iran-Iraq and Gulf Wars demonstrated. Both of these incorporated territorial and resource claims which have lost none of their salience. Even the most recent conflict in Afghanistan throws serious doubt on the obsolescence of wars of old type. At the onset of the crisis it was widely reported that this war was quite different from past wars: as Gerard Barker wrote in the *Financial Times*: 'there are no territorial acquisitions to be reversed, no enemy troops to be targeted, no surrender terms'.[21] But is this statement really true and illustrative of the new war puzzle? Within days and weeks an enemy state *had* been defined, enemy troops targeted; quite soon it became possible to imagine the kind of surrender terms that would be offered at the appropriate time. The United States sought no territorial revision of Afghanistan as such, but successfully demanded a change of regime from the Taliban to one more friendly to Western interests, so that Afghan territory will not again be use as a base of attack against the USA. (A similar position could well be adopted to unseat the present Iraqi regime). Furthermore, if the attack on the United States was carried out by a non-state actor, it still flagrantly violated US territory and sovereignty,

---

[20]See I. William Zartman, 'Putting Humpty-Dumpty Together Again', in David A. Lake and Donald Rothchild (eds.), *The International Spread of Ethnic Conflict* (Princeton: Princeton University Press, 1998), p. 330.

[21]*Financial Times*, 20 September 2001.

and as such could be seen as an act of war entitling the United States to take self defence measures — measures endorsed by the United Nations. And in some ways, the attack on the United States did reflect, albeit it in some rather tortuous fashion, the resistance of parts of the world to the kind of territorial and resource control implied by US hegemony: its dominance of markets, of institutions, of security and even ideas.

The targets and actors in the war game may have shifted, but many of the familiar features of war are here, even a fear of nuclear weapons use. It was said of the Gulf crisis (because of the obvious violation of Kuwaiti sovereignty, the broad based support for the US coalition, including non-use of the veto by Security Council members) that this was a unique sort of war or the 'last of the old wars',[22] representing the concatenation of a particular set of circumstances unlikely to recur. The continuing Afghan crisis, and increasingly likely risk of future crises of similar genre, throw this assumption into doubt.

This view was endorsed by statements made by the former Australian foreign minister, Gareth Evans, at an Asia-Pacific security conference in Singapore in late February 2002: 'Until very recently, war between states seemed a much less real threat than internal conflict. Interstate conflict had become rare and seemed likely to remain so. The ideology that saw virtue and nobility in war had all but disappeared in advanced countries. Globalization was making national borders ever less important. And the united international response to Iraq's invasion of Kuwait gave further pause to those thinking that territorial aggression might be cost-effective'. But recent events, Evans continued, had changed this view. In particular he referred to 'a different phenomenon... now capturing most attention — war between states being waged for self-defence purposes, as permitted under Article 51 of the UN Charter in response to armed attack'.[23]

---

[22]Ignatieff, *Virtual War*, p. 5.

[23]Gareth Evans, 'Iraq and the UN Security Council', *International Herald Tribune*, 28 February 2002.

In short, interstate wars look set to continue. Consider also the long-standing regional rivalries, that still condition interstate relations in the Middle East, Africa and parts of Asia. At the end of the 20th century, the war between Ethiopia and Eritrea was one of the few conflicts between two countries fighting over territory;[24] to this we now can add the recent flare-ups in the India-Pakistan and Israel-Palestine conflicts. The China-Taiwan relationship is another that could spill over into a regional, even a general war, given the possibility of US involvement. Territory is central to all such disputes.

More generally, in a growing and a globalizing world, the struggle for territory and finite resources will continue to cause tensions if not wars. In this regard we cannot ignore the steady growth in world population (predicted at 8.9 billion in 2050) and related resource implications. Already, intense competition for resources like water, fish and oil have conditioned conflict in the West Bank, the China Sea or the Persian Gulf, to note just a few examples. Where territorial waters and boundaries are contested (Peru v Ecuador), or where the discovery of new resources provoke disputes over ownership (Romania v Ukraine), the risk of conflict is real and unlikely to diminish.[25] The threat to international order, or put differently, the continuing struggle over territory and resources, comes not only from wars of the third kind, but from the veritable cocktail of threats comprising new and old war types. With the possible exception of the World Wars of the 20th century, it surely cannot be asserted that the world is free from any type of war.

Beyond Territorial War?

All this pessimistic reflection will cause liberals to sigh. I have deliberately and perhaps provocatively spent the first half of the essay looking at the evolving relationship between rivalry over territory and resources and war. I have argued that if this relationship

---

[24]Dennis C. Jett, *Why Peacekeeping Fails* (London:Palgrave, 1999), xiii.
[25]Jeremy Black, *War* (London: Continuum, 2001), pp. 21-22, 49-50.

has changed, both normatively, and in terms of types of rivalries and range of actors, it has also endured. I have taken liberties with the notion of territory, including not just classic territorial wars, but all wars that have, in John Vasquez's words a dimension of 'territoriality'.[26] This broader definition includes 'ethno-territorial wars', blurring the distinction between conflicts over territory and resources, and over populations, to incorporate wars of self-determination and secessionism like Chechenya versus Russia; South Ossetia and Abkhazia versus Georgia; or Slovenia, Croatia, and Bosnia versus Serbia-Montenegro. In this way I have hoped to give purchase to the tenacity of territorial issues in determining the balance of peace and war.

It is not the intention of this paper, however, merely to reinforce what has been the dominant paradigm in International Relations: the so-called realist school, which holds that international relations are still best characterised by a struggle for power in which territorial conquest remains a principal objective to advance state interests.[27] With this in mind, I would now like to use the remainder of this paper to contemplate alternative views. I turn first to those arguments and approaches that point to a more complex array of factors explaining states' decisions to go to war, and second to the school of thought that suggests that territorial and resource rivalries have become less salient as a cause of war, or indeed that war itself has become less salient as an normative feature of International Relations.

The notion that we should consider war as the result of a more complex set of processes and decisions than an animal or hunter-like response to acquisition and defence of territory and resources, or the inevitable behaviour of states in international anarchy, has long held currency among leading scholars on the causes of war. Writing on the complex causes of war, John Vasquez distinguishes between underlying and proximate causes. Territory is a fundamental

---

[26]Vasquez, *War Puzzle*, p. 129.
[27]Robert Gilpin, *War and Change in World Politics* (Cambridge: Cambridge University Press, 1981), pp. 7, 23.

underlying cause of war, but we need to examine the global institutional context to determine whether or not states will fight.[28] It is the dovetailing of desire and need, circumstance and opportunity, that leads states to war. States that feel insecure for instance, may embrace war as a means of acquiring territory to defend their borders: historically German, Soviet and Israeli expansion may be seen in this way. States may act precipitately, even foolishly, but they also weigh up the costs and benefits of war, they seek to strike at the right moment, when early advantage is assured, or when appropriate domestic and international conditions are met. A belief in easy conquest is one reason why states will adopt expansionist or aggressive policies.[29] When such a belief is unfounded, fortunes turn quickly against the aggressor as the Argentine generals found in the Falklands, or Saddam Hussein in Kuwait. The point here is that states calculate the risks of war: they are not warlike just for the sake of it, and here one might draw a contrast with the plundering hordes of Genghis Khan.

This calculation of risk and gain, and with it the notion that war is not inevitable, but susceptible to management, opens up endless prospects for prevention or limitation, both of states' war aims and of their bellicosity. As interesting as a study of the wars that have happened is a study of wars that have not happened. Many states *have* eschewed war as a means of resolving territorial or other rivalries. This type of thinking already goes some way to modifying our understanding of the conditions in which states will go to war. It does not shift us very far from understanding that territory and resources remain primary variables, nor that states remain the main actors, nor that states have a built in tendency to war. But it is not difficult to see how a new group of theorists have moved on from such evidence to construct some quite different theories about war. Such theories are pegged to the post-Cold War order, but with their

---

[28]Vasquez, *War Puzzle*, pp. 7-8.

[29]Stephen Van Evera, *The Causes of War* (Ithaca and London: Cornell University Press, 1999), pp. 5-6.

origins in previous orders. They focus on the absence of territorial ambition, even aggressive intent, as well as normative and institutional constraints, and with these the non-use of force, except in certain prescribed conditions, by a growing number of states. This is interesting and worth exploring, for if we can determine the conditions under which states eschew war, can we not then promote an international order in which war and force are outlawed as legitimate policy tools, one in which territorial and resource rivalries are things of the past? If states have become less warlike, the salience of territorial rivalry as a source of war has necessarily decreased.

The pacific tendency of some states, or of some state types, has long been noted. A model was set by Immanuel Kant's prediction of a peaceful order based around an international federation of true republican states. Liberals like Norman Angell, writing just before the First World War, thought that economic interdependence had rendered territorial control obsolete and war irrational.[30] He was wrong in implying that great power war would therefore not happen, but right in the sense that along with the spread of liberal ideas and free trade, economic interdependence contributed to a radical rethinking about peace and war. Thorstein Veblen, renowned American economist and social critic, distinguished in 1917 between what he called the 'predatory dynastic state' and the 'live and let live' democratic state. States of the latter category, it is true, were still prone to colonial expansion as the interwar experience would show, but also represented the emergence of a new state type whose propensity to go to war would be circumscribed and whose predatory ambitions had been 'tamed'. War then is not an underlying trait of human nature, but a habit which can be lost just as it is acquired: for Veblen a lasting peace would await the development and spread of a non-predatory way of life, 'the social construction of conditions conducive to peace'.[31]

---

[30]Norman Angell, *The Great Illusion* (London: William Heinmann, 1912).

[31]Thorstein Veblen, *The Nature of Peace* (London: Transaction, 1998), introduction to the *Transaction Edition*, pp. vii-xxix.

Among a core group of states the construction of such conditions proceeded apace, and was reflected in an emerging security and normative architecture in which the right to conquest and war was progressively curtailed: in the League of Nations, the Kellogg Briand Pact, the United Nations.[32] If the experience of two World Wars had, it seemed, inoculated states against war; the development of nuclear weapons supplied the booster dose. Why contemplate war in the face of such vistas of destruction and death? Despite the Cold War's angry, even predatory side, the parallel growth of international law and institutions bore witness to the propensity of states to curb and contain aggressive behaviour. And finally, the kind of economic interdependence that Angell had identified, really did make nonsense of the idea of classical territorial war, certainly in Western Europe, but to some extent elsewhere. It became possible to identify peaceful communities, or zones of peace whose members were increasingly defined by state type: from the republican order prescribed by Kant and others, through the live and let live democracies that Veblen had identified, to the constitutionally secure liberal states where, in Michael Doyle's words, 'the political bond of liberal rights and interests have proven a remarkably firm foundation for mutual non-aggression'.[33]

In states where such a foundation exists, territorial and resource rivalry is resolved not by conflict, but by other means, and the right to conquest is denied. The uses and methods of war are highly circumscribed, and warfare is more humane.[34] The corollary, of course, is that outside the zone of peace such rivalries continue. But the democratic peace idea has had many followers, multiplied, unsurprisingly by the possibilities and prospects for both peace and

---

[32]On the legal side of these developments see Korman, *Right of Conquest*, Chapter 7, pp. 179–248.

[33]Michael Doyle, 'Kant, Liberal Legacies and Foreign Affairs', *Philosophy and Public Affairs*, 12/3 (1983), p. 220.

[34]On this changing aspect of war, see Christopher Coker, *Humane Warfare*, (London: Routledge, 2001).

democracy were opened up by the end of the Cold War. New states have signed up for the peace zone, but membership conditions are notoriously hard to fulfil, with democratization, a more accurate condition for many states, providing often as many motives for war as for peace.[35] Still, core members can feel increasingly secure within the union and institutions that their shared values and interests have helped to create.

The very existence of such a union is motive enough to reconsider the doctrines of Clausewitz and the hitherto robust relationship between territorial rivalry and war. Other recent strands of liberal thinking, however, introduce new elements into this equation. Proponents of globalization find that the territorial state has decreased in salience, and with the territorial state, territorial rivalries. 'Deterritorialization', a clumsy, but fashionable term, captures the notion of the seamless and shrinking world in which territorial location, distance, and borders no longer have a determining influence.[36] Clearly, our world is far from globalized, but behind the globalizing idea lies the understanding that traditional interstate rivalry is old fashioned, even eccentric and will have a diminishing role in the international politics of the twenty first century.

Others argue in not dissimilar vein, that if globalization is a contested reality, the power of states has become separated from territorial control, and now resides in economic, cultural and other forms of 'soft' power. Territory no longer confers advantage and occupation is costly and unnecessary.[37] In this way developed states, argues Richard Rosecrance, are 'putting aside military and territorial ambitions as they struggle not for political dominance, but for a

---

[35]Edward D. Mansfield and Jack Snyder, 'Democratization and the Danger of War', *International Security* 20 (1995), pp. 5-38.

[36]Jan Aart Scholte, 'Global Civil Society', in Ngaire Woods (ed.), *The Political Economy of Globalization* (London: Macmillan, 2000), p. 179.

[37]Fred Halliday, *The World at 2000* (London: Palgrave, 2001), p. 6; Leonard Johnson, 'The Decline of International War', in A. Walter Dorn, (ed.) *New Order for a New Millennium* (London, 1999), pp. 65-66.

greater share of world output'.[38] States will remain territorial entities, but the obsession with land will decline with focus on state capacity rather than size. In this context military power matters, but its nature and utility has changed because the threats to states' security, and the nature and role of the state, have also changed.

All of this around the millennium literature points to fundamental changes in the relationship between war, territory and resources: democratic states will not fight, and the 'language of national interest' is disappearing from the 'discourse of war'; war is too costly financially and emotionally, and armies are 'withering away'; borders do not matter, markets do, and state power is independent of territory.[39] Should we then revise our assumptions, particularly in the light of some solid empirical evidence which suggests that 'territorial aggrandizement is no longer the dominant motif for interstate politics'?[40]

Powerful states adhere to the territorial sovereignty norm and ensure others do also. This makes redistribution difficult if not impossible. As Mark Zacher notes, there has not been a case of *successful* territorial aggrandisement since 1976,[41] though this has not prevented efforts to change the status quo. Indeed the norm must be imposed by force. So territorial rivalry may cause two kinds of wars: wars by states motivated by traditional considerations of territorial gain, and wars of intervention designed to stop them. In this sense a narrowing of the definition of territory and resources may be unhelpful. In any time period some rivalries wax and others wane. If strong states, for all the reasons outlined above, at present eschew territorial gain, their place has been taken by a bevy of new states and other actors which still covet territory and the fruits of

---

[38]Richard Rosecrance, *The Rise of the Virtual State* (New York: Basic Books, 1999), p. 3.

[39]John Keegan, *War and Our World* (London: Pimlico, 1998), pp. 34, 58; Coker, *Humane Warfare*, p. 148.

[40]Mark W. Zacher, 'The Territorial Integrity Norm: International Boundaries and the Use of Force', *International Organization* 55/2 (2001) p. 234.

[41]*Ibid*, p. 244.

war. (The fact that war is not solely a state activity does not of itself necessarily change the balance of peace and war.) Indeed a major problem in approaching this question is one of perspective. From the standpoint of the strong, secure democratic states one answer suggests itself; from the standpoint of the weak and insecure states, which still constitute the majority, another. We know that poor states with fragile cultures are insecure, often suffer from internal conflicts, and engage in war. And given the propensity of strong states to intervene in conflicts over territoriality, even where only norm enforcement is the goal, it can hardly be said with confidence that territorial rivalry has ceased to be a fundamental source of war.

My end note is thus cautionary rather than pessimistic. It is too simple and too stark merely to see the 'last age of empire' giving way to a 'new age of violence', in which territoriality and ethnicity merge as major sources of war.[42] We must expect wars — wars of all kinds. But wars and their consequences can be mitigated, and we can and should prepare for them. The experience of some parts of the world does suggest that territorial and resource rivalries can be channelled and tamed: by shared norms and values, and by peoples and states working together for common causes and in common institutions.

In conclusion, it is hard to disagree with Vasquez: 'Territory, given the nature of the animal we are, will probably always be the subject of disagreement', but, he continues, 'that disagreement need not always be resolved by war'.[43] Holding on to this idea helps make sense of the changing patterns of 20th century war and suggests some patterns for the future. In this century we have witnessed the obsolescence of some war types and the emergence, or re-emergence of others. Some states have put aside military and territorial ambitions and transferred those ambitions elsewhere. But other states remain highly vulnerable. 'If "war"', writes Jeremy Black, 'is considered to

---

[42]For this view see for example, Michael Ignatieff, *Blood and Belonging* (London: Vintage, 1994), p. 2.
[43]Vasquez, *War Puzzle*, p. 151.

include civil conflict and quasi-international wars then it can be seen as normative in many regions, indeed possibly the normal state of human society'.[44] Territorial rivalry and resource gain remain intrinsic to the ambitions of lesser states and groups which compete for statehood and political control, and here we need only remind ourselves of events in Kosovo, Bosnia, Kuwait, Kashmir, or Rwanda, but also Colombia, Kurdistan or Afghanistan. Effectively a zone of peace coexists with a zone of war, with the zones overlapping in critical areas. The dominant dialogues on war must shift from the peace zones to the war zones and employ both the language of the weak, as well as the strong state.[45] Only then can the continuing salience of territorial and resource rivalry be fully perceived, understood, and hopefully addressed.

---

[44] Jeremy Black, *War*, p. 2.

[45] I pursue this idea further in 'Conclusion: Wither the Third World', in Louise Fawcett and Yezid Sayigh, (eds.), *The Third World Beyond the Cold War* (Oxford: Oxford University Press, 2000) pp 234-246.

Akira Iriye

Misperception, Mistrust, Fear

Introduction

Misperception, mistrust, fear — there is little new about such feelings. The history of the world is distressingly filled with instances of international, inter-religious, intercultural, and inter-ethnic tensions born of lack of mutual trust and understanding, tensions that have too often resulted in brutal conflict.

The twentieth century was to have been different. Modern technological inventions, it was confidently asserted at the turn of the century, were narrowing distances among different parts of the globe, and cross-national economic activities were making the nations and peoples of the world more interdependent than ever before. Physical proximity and economic interconnectedness, many optimists believed, would be matched by the coming together of all people culturally and spiritually. They would even share certain mentalities and thereby develop a sense of global community.

In today's terminology, it may be said that what these observers were stressing was that globalization, that is, technological and economic interconnections across different parts of the world, was also producing an internalization of certain norms in all people. In other words, global forces did not remain a physical and material phenomenon but was also generating a psychology that would be conducive to peace. In the words of H. G. Wells, "a new kind of people" seemed to be emerging as a result of modern civilization, people whom he called "a floating population [with] customs and habits of its own, a morality of its own, a philosophy of its own".[1] Likewise, writing in 1906, J. A. Hobson noted that "great world forces" were "creating bonds of interests which band us together irrespective of the natural limits of the country to which we belong and in which we were born".[2] In such a situation, national boundaries appeared to be becoming less and less significant. Gustave Hervé, the French journalist, published a book entitled *Internationalism* in 1910 and asserted, "The nineteenth century was a century of nationalism, but the twentieth century will be a century of internationalism".[3] According to Norman Angell, the division of the world was becoming less between nations but between civilization and barbarism, the implication being that as more and more people achieved a level of civilization, conflict would become less frequent.[4]

Examples can be multiplied to demonstrate the widely shared optimism at the beginning of the twentieth century that modern civilization was rapidly integrating different parts of the world and that this phenomenon, in other words globalization, was synonymous with the emergence of a peaceful, interdependent world order. Some believed the emerging global community would be characterized by close interstate cooperation in preventing war, while others looked to the development of a universal language such as Esperanto that would be spoken and understood by all people, and still others dreamed of a truly ecumenical world in which religious faiths would come together and develop a sense of common humanity. All shared

---

[1] H. G. Wells, *An Englishman Looks at the World* (London, 1914), pp. 19-20.

[2] J. A. Hobson, "The Ethics of Internationalism", *International Journal of Ethics*, vol. 17, no. 1, pp. 19-21 (Oct. 1906).

[3] Quoted in Akira Iriye, *Cultural Internationalism and World Order* (Baltimore, 1997), p. 25.

[4] Quoted in Niall Ferguson, *The Pity of War* (New York, 1998), p. 21.

the view that modern civilization was producing a new identity, the identity of all individuals as members of an interdependent, integrated world. Material globalization and spiritual internalization would go hand in hand.

Globalization and Mistrust among Civilizations

If such visions had been fulfilled even partially, the twentieth century would have had a very remarkable history. Modern technology and international commerce would have integrated different regions of the world closely together, and individuals in all parts of the globe would have become interdependent not only physically but also spiritually.

We all know such was not the case, that, throughout the century, forces of globalization did not always lead to the establishment of a more peaceful world, and that, if anything, antagonisms among nations, cultures, and individuals grew intensified, often resulting in violent clashes in which weapons of mass destruction, themselves products of modern technology, were employed relentlessly. The persistent, even increasing, gap between material modernization and mental traditionalism (one could even call it tribalism) has been a central characteristic of recent history, and any inquiry into the question of peace in the twentieth century would have to start by understanding this gap.

In this short essay, I cannot attempt even to scratch the surface of this important problem. What follows is a rather impressionistic survey of certain developments in twentieth-century history that provide instances of misperception, mistrust, and fear in relations among states, cultures, and races even as they became enveloped in the drama of globalization — and, at the same time, an examination of some impressive instances where individuals and organizations sought heroically to generate a sense of common humanity and spiritual interdependence across nations and cultures.

There were different kinds of fear at the turn of the twentieth century as humankind was developing a new "culture of time and space", a technological civilization that was bringing different parts of the world closer together. For one thing, since this new culture was of modern Western origin and was being disseminated by Europeans and Americans throughout the globe, there was fear on the part of the non-Western parts of the world that they were increasingly being subjected to Western domination. As typically expressed by a Vietnamese poet toward the end of the nineteenth century, "Why do they [the West] rule the world, While we bow our heads as slaves"?[5] Some states, such as Turkey and Japan, sought to respond to this situation by avidly transforming themselves by copying from the West, but, as I shall note shortly, that did not erase the feeling of distance between West and non-West. And those countries that were less successful in this endeavor developed a sense of inferiority that the West (as well as some non-Western countries that were more effectively modernizing themselves) looked down upon more traditional parts of the world.

And those countries (in Europe and North America) that were most successful in undertaking technological and economic transformation did indeed despite or scorn those that remained unchanged, frequently referring to them as "barbarians" and "semi-barbarians". Modern biology, genetics, and anthropology appeared to give scientific legitimacy to the idea of fundamental differences among races and civilizations. Rather than stopping there, however, some of the self-consciously more "advanced" peoples believed it was their mission to "civilize" the rest of the world by establishing a system of imperialistic control. Such control was almost always sustained by a sense of superiority, indicating that the process of globalization was giving rise to an enhanced awareness of racial and cultural differences among peoples of the world. There is little doubt that this kind of inter-cultural distrust, derived from an image of a racial hierarchy, produced fears and misperceptions on a global scale.

---

[5]Quoted in Mark Bradley, *Imagining Vietnam and America: The Making of Postcolonial Vietnam, 1919-1950* (Chapel Hill, 2000), p. 16.

But that was not all. The very sense of superiority on the part of the West sometimes also produced fear, a fear of uncivilized barbarians rising up against the more civilized. As expressed typically by Charles Eliot Norton in 1896, "we are brought face to face with the grave problem which the next century is to solve, — whether our civilization can maintain itself, and make advance, against the pressure of ignorant and barbaric multitudes".[6] There were many more "ignorant and barbaric" people in the world than the "civilized". How could the latter defend themselves against the former? What would happen if those that lagged behind in the process of modern transformation and were believed to be still in a pre-modern and therefore more primitive, warlike state should rise up against the more civilized peoples? Would the latter be ready to fight back? Had they not become too soft, enjoying the comfort of a modern civilized living? Such fears induced thinkers to urge that the martial spirit be reintroduced to modern societies. Only through "great armies" and "blind outward impulses", Alfred Thayer Mahan argued time and again, would modern civilization be able to preserve itself.[7] That was why there was so much stress on manliness in the United States and elsewhere before the Great War.[8] The objects of such fears — people in Asia, Africa, and Latin America — might have been confused that the allegedly most advanced countries in the world seemed to be stressing some primitive virtues. It was as if globalization depended, for its survival, on the use of pre-modern means of destruction.

These were not the only instances of a mental clash between West and non-West in the age of globalization. Even more serious was the psychology of confrontation that accompanied the spread

---

[6]Quoted in Akira Iriye, *Pacific Estrangement: Japanese and American Expansion, 1897–1911* (Cambridge, Mass., 1972), p. 28.

[7]Quoted in Akira Iriye, *Across the Pacific: An Inner History of American-East Asian Relations* (New York, 1967), p. 61.

[8]See Kristin L. Hoganson, *Fighting for American Manhood: How Gender Politics Provoked the Spanish-American and Philippine-American Wars* (New Haven, 1998).

of globalization to more and more regions of the world. Whether
through imperialism, through multinational enterprises that were
making their appearance at this time, through trans-national migration,
or through their own initiatives, many countries outside Europe
and North America began to transform themselves and in the process
to integrate themselves into the globalizing world. An increasing
number of people from such countries started coming to Europe
and North America as laborers, merchants, and visitors. Physical
distances among peoples were becoming narrower, and there was a
large-scale intermingling of people of diverse backgrounds, even
leading to interracial marriages. This process was one of the most
significant developments of the twentieth century, and it produced
a myriad of responses on the part both of the modern West and of
the rest. Fear was one of them.

First of all, there was fear among Westerners that the non-West
was incorporating the technical aspects of modern civilization
without thereby becoming Westernized but remaining fundamentally
incompatible with, or hostile to, the West. Charles H. Pearson, an
Englishman of long residence in Australia, was one of the earliest and
most articulate writers on this subject. By its very global expansion,
he noted in 1893, the West was modernizing the rest of the world
to such an extent that the latter would emerge, in the not too distant
future, as a serious competitor, even a challenge, to the former. "The
day will come", he observed, "when the European observer will look
round to see the globe girdled with a continuous zone of the black
and yellow races, no longer too weak for aggression or under tutelage,
but independent, or practically so, in government, monopolizing the
trade of their own regions, and circumscribing the industry of the
European". Such a day would mark the beginning of the end of
Western expansion and therefore of Western civilization.[9]

The non-Western countries whose transformation was giving
rise to such fears among observers in the West had their own fear
and mistrust of the latter. To them the more modernized people of

---

[9]Quoted in Iriye, *Pacific Estrangement*, p. 29.

Europe, North America, and Oceania still remained the most powerful in the world who did not seem willing to accept the others, however modernized, as equals. The concept of the "yellow peril" that was quite popular in the West at the turn of the century seemed to suggest that, whenever a non-Western country succeeded in transforming itself, it was viewed as a menace to the West. If non-Western peoples were feared by the West because they were modernizing themselves, but if, at the same time, they were also feared if they remained in a state of pre-modern barbarism, what could they really do? Some thinkers in Asia responded to the question by conjuring up their own image of the menace of the West and began advocating a pan-Asianist response, the idea that non-Western peoples of the world, especially in Asia, should stick together to confront the West.

Some feared for their civilizational survival. The more the world appeared to be transformed under modern technological influence, the greater grew the apprehension on the part of some, in the West as well as elsewhere, that their traditional faiths and ways of life appeared to be in danger of being irrevocably lost and being supplanted by something uncertain and undesirable. The famous observation by Virginia Woolf that "on or around December, 1910, human character changed", and that the "sound of breaking and falling, crashing and destruction" was everywhere, attested to the fear of the unknown.[10] What she meant by "human character", and whether she had in mind not just Europeans but also people all over the world, cannot be determined, but the sense of the passing of a familiar universe was widely shared and gave rise to the phenomenon known as fundamentalism, whether Christian, Islamic, or of any other religion. Islamic fundamentalism was by no means alone in such a response, but it was perhaps the most influential and enduring. While Islamic "modernists" believed that their religion and modern civilization were compatible and, therefore, that Moslems

---

[10]Quoted in Stephen Kern, *The Culture of Time and Space, 1880–1918* (Cambridge, Mass., 1983), p. 183.

must endeavor to change their laws and social practices while remaining true to the teaching of Muhammad, fundamentalists argued that the doctrines of Islam must continue to remain the basis of all Moslem organizations, including states. To hold on to one's true faith amidst the changing "culture of time and space" was not easy, and for this very reason a conscious effort must be made to remain true to the fundamental laws of Islam.[11] Resentment and fear of the West's influence in the modern world undoubtedly underlay the development of Islamic fundamentalism, but the same thing could be said of Christian, Buddhist, and other sects that were opposed to the cultural and social implications of globalization.

The Development of Cross-cultural Dialogue

None of these intercultural, interracial fears proved critical when the European powers went to war against one another in 1914. Judging from all the utterances that had been expressed about the fundamental conflict between Western and non-Western civilizations, it might have been thought that future wars might be more like the Russo-Turkish War (1878) or the Russo-Japanese War (1904–05) than like the Franco-Prussian War (1870–71), in other words a conflict between civilizations and races. In reality, the Great War started out as a European civil war, dividing the allegedly most modernized of nations in the West into two camps. Far from being a struggle between the white and colored races, the war involved the latter as partners of the respective coalitions; Britain and its allies were joined by Japan and China, and Germany by Turkey, and both sides employed colonial troops recruited from Africa and Asia.

Not a few non-Westerners, indeed, marveled that material globalization did not seem to have produced among the European countries a habit of mind that would peacefully accommodate differences and promote international cooperation rather than

---

[11]Albert Hourani, *A History of the Arab Peoples* (Cambridge, Mass., 1991), pp. 307, 348.

confrontation. On the contrary, presumably the most advanced nations of the world had apparently remained mentally and psychologically pre-modern, driven by tribal instincts. Similar thoughts occurred to many in Europe, where there was a sudden loss of confidence. Anatole France remarked when the fighting finally stopped, "Europe is sick, perhaps dying", and Thomas Hardy even felt as if another Dark Ages was descending upon Europe.[12]

Such developments may have served to narrow mental and psychological distances between West and non-West, for they were equally dismayed and intrigued by the failure of modern civilization to have prevented the unprecedented mass slaughter. Perhaps all people in the world could now cooperate in understanding how such a disaster could have come about and in seeking to prevent similar tragedies in the future. To be sure, interracial and inter-civilizational antagonisms did not disappear during the European war. In the Middle East, Turks and Armenians clashed, resulting in a huge number of casualties among the latter, and in the European theater tens of thousands of laborers recruited and sent from China were forbidden to join British and French forces in combat, for fear that it might arouse interracial clashes. Some in Europe and the United States responded to the West's horrible fratricide and the consequent diminution of its prestige and power in the world area by stridently reconfirming white supremacy. Books like Madison Grant's *The Passing of the Great Race, or the Racial Base of European History*, published in 1916, expressed the fear that the non-Western countries and non-white races would take advantage of Europe's distress and begin to assert themselves. For this and other authors writing in a similar vein, there was a real danger that the non-white majority of the world would not only lose their awe of the West but that they would increasingly come to intermarry with Europeans, giving rise to a world consisting of mixed races. The only way to preserve Western supremacy was to maintain racial purity through prohibiting the immigration of, and intermarriages with, colored races. Not

---

[12]Quoted in Iriye, *Across the Pacific*, p. 145.

surprisingly, eugenics as a science came to be taken even more seriously than ever before.

However, in the aftermath of the war such voices were countered by those that were far more optimistic about the future relationship among civilizations and races. They pointed out, for one thing, that the war had not forever disrupted the process of globalization. As soon as peace was restored, international commercial transactions were resumed, and new technological innovations such as the automobile, the radio, and the movies seemed to re-connect distant parts of the globe. Many observers confidently talked of the emergence of "a single world community". As Manly O. Hudson, a Harvard Law School professor, stated, "all the people of the world have been drawn into a single world community which bears little resemblance to the world of separate and self-contained states upon which the nineteenth century dawned".[13] He must have been aware of the fact that there were many more states in the world during the 1920s than ever before; the peace settlement had created or reconstructed many of them, including several Islamic states such as Afghanistan, Saudi Arabia, Egypt, and Iraq. They all became members of the League of Nations, a fact that suggested that the international arena was now an even more diverse place than before. Hudson's optimism reflected confidence that, while more and more independent states were coming into existence, national sovereignty would become less exclusionary than earlier, thanks to the establishment of the League and other international institutions. Moreover, as the process of economic and technological re-globalization interconnected diverse peoples and civilizations everywhere, it seemed possible that there might at last emerge a culturally homogenous world. Robert Park, the University of Chicago sociologist, asserted that "an international society and an international political order" were on the verge of emerging. According to him, the nations and races of the world were coming into closer proximity with one another than ever before,

---

[13] Quoted in Iriye, *Cultural Internationalism*, p. 89.

but that would eventually prove to be a blessing, providing an opportunity for the development of a global melting pot.[14]

The Cultural Significance of the Second World War

If postwar globalization appeared to justify such optimism, in contrast to prewar globalization that had given rise to international, interracial, and intercultural fears, these fears returned with renewed intensity during the 1930s. Globalization was once again set back because of the Depression and international conflicts, and the world became divided into political groupings and economic blocs. Racism returned as a powerful force in many countries, and the world appeared to be witnessing the emergence of "the dangerous excesses and warped mentality that are born of hatred," in the words of a report written by the Paris Institute for Intellectual Cooperation in the mid-1930s.[15]

We know the story only too well. In a melancholy and catastrophic reversal of the hopeful beginning of the postwar years, nations, peoples, and cultures once again engaged themselves in collective hatred, aggression, and mutual destruction. It was as if mistrust and fear were proving to be far more enduring forces than trust and understanding in international and intercultural relations. And there is little doubt that during the 1930s those countries that consciously turned against the spirit of internationalism and based their foreign policies on a self-righteous rejection of "the other" — Germany, Japan, the Soviet Union, and many others — came close to destroying the world community, both as a vision and in reality. In a curious way, however, the very disasters of the 1930s and the 1940s may be said to have served to keep alive that vision.

That was the cultural significance of the Second World War. We may understand this significance if we recall that, even more than the First World War, the conflicts that comprised the Second World War were truly global, involving many states and regions of the world

---

[14] *Ibid.*, p. 83.
[15] *Ibid.*, p. 105.

in their racial and cultural diversity. Whereas the Great War had at least started out as a civil war among European states, the Second World War began, for all intents and purposes, when two Asian neighbors, Japan and China, collided and when Italy, a European state, attacked Ethiopia, an African nation. A global conflagration became all but inevitable when Japan and Italy entered into an alliance with Germany. Nazi Germany's hostility to all "non-Aryans", especially to Jews and Romas who were despised because they were "floating" people without their own states (the kind of people that H. G. Wells had seen as forerunners of a global community), did not prevent the country from forming an alliance with Japan. The latter, on its part, developed a fatalistic conception of a worldwide struggle between white and colored peoples, but the Japanese treatment of other Asians belied any protestation of pan-Asian solidarity. What united Germany and Japan, despite their obvious racial and cultural differences, against Britain, the United States, and their allies was their shared hostility to the international order that had developed under the influence of the modern West. Germans, Italians, and Japanese shared their abhorrence of liberalism, capitalism, and democracy and defined their objective as the "overcoming of modernity". In the context of our discussion, these nations were revolting against the globalizing trends of modern times, whereas the United States and its allies were seeking to re-globalize the world after the Depression had fragmented it. But the United Nations coalition included the Soviet Union, China, and many others whose commitment to globalization was less than total.

Because the Second World War was thus far more multicultural and multiracial than the First, it is not surprising that the victorious powers, in particular the United States, became keenly aware of the need to go beyond earlier definitions of a peaceful world order. Wartime American leaders sought to persuade their allies to accept a redefined conception of a more truly global order as their collective agenda. The agenda, best promulgated in the Atlantic Charter but also embodied in such other wartime documents as the draft charter of the United Nations Organization and the convention establishing war crimes tribunals, was to re-connect different parts of the world economically, politically, and, more important, morally. Technological and economic globalization would have to be resumed after victory, but there was recognition that this was not enough. If the disasters of the 1930s and the 1940s were not to be repeated, it seemed imperative to ensure that politically and morally, too, the whole globe would be much more fully integrated than before the war.

These ideas were nowhere more ardently and eloquently expressed than in the deliberations preceding the adoption, by the United Nations, of the Universal Declaration on Human Rights in 1948. What stands out in these deliberations is the universalism of the ideas that went into them. Expressions of this faith in the universal applicability of certain concepts and values were everywhere: "man is a citizen both of his State and of the world"; "Everyone has the right to personal liberty"; "Every person shall be free to receive and disseminate information of all kinds"; "All persons shall be free to constitute associations…for the promotion and protection of their legitimate interests and of any other lawful object"; "All men, being members of one family, are free, possess equal dignity and rights, and shall regard each other as brothers".[16] These expressions are evidence that there was emerging a worldwide faith right after the Second World War that certain values and principles would permeate all countries and unite them in their pursuit of shared goals.

Sharing (and Dividing) the Planet

Sharing thus seems to have been a guiding principle of international affairs at that time: not simply sharing in the material benefits of civilization but also in the same rights, the same aspirations, and the same commitment to universal justice. Resumed globalization would serve to internalize the sense of common humanity. Precisely because the war had involved all civilizations and all races, postwar

---

[16]United Nations, *Yearbook on Human Rights for 1947* (New York, 1949), pp. 484, 491, 495.

globalization would have to be a spiritual as well as a physical development. A world of diversity would have to exist on the basis of a shared commitment to intercultural, inter-faith, and inter-racial understanding.

The reality, once again, proved to be rather different. Material globalization resumed its pace and achieved phenomenal successes during the second half of the twentieth century. But it was not accompanied by a concurrent spiritual, moral, or psychological globalization. This gap could be seen in various contexts. The most evident was the Cold War that signaled the failure of the victorious powers to cooperate together in bringing about the kind of world envisioned by the United Nations. The Cold War globalized weapons of mass destruction, placing the whole of humanity at the mercy of nuclear arms. An atmosphere of mutual fear, suspicion, and mistrust prevailed in international affairs at the very moment when the world economy was slowly but steadily recovering from the devastation brought about by war and began to grow on an unprecedented scale. This "East-West" tension was matched by an increasingly serious "North-South" crisis in which many newly de-colonized states (the South) sought to develop their identity apart from the industrialized nations (the North), accusing the latter of having dominated the world economy and international politics for centuries and demanding that there be a more equitable distribution of resources and opportunities. But the de-colonized states consisted of diverse cultures and ethnic groups, and some of them began fighting each other almost as soon as they achieved statehood. Mistrust between Hindus and Moslems led to clashes between India and Pakistan, and mutual suspicion between Jews and Arabs created a condition of endemic antagonism in Palestine.

Clearly, postwar material globalization was not engendering a corresponding mentality of international and cross-civilizational understanding, what would come to be called the "culture of peace" at the end of the twentieth century, a state of mind conducive to a world free from fear and misunderstanding. Instead, local loyalties and identities often seemed opposed as much to spiritual as to material globalization. What some termed "globality", produced by the movement of capital, goods, technology, information, and ideas across national and cultural boundaries, was provoking fierce resistance and antagonism on the part of the forces of "particularity". That is why, at the turn of the twenty-first century, there was so much discussion of the clash of civilizations, so much literature on "Jihad" on one hand and "McWorld" on the other.[17] The terrorist attacks on U.S. targets on September 11, 2001, were only the most dramatic demonstration of the failure of a globalizing world to develop a parallel spirituality uniting all humanity. One could view the horrible tragedy as a culmination of the long history of mistrust and fear among different peoples and cultures, as proof that, despite talk of spiritual globalization, the realities were far uglier.

Cultural Internationalism

That, however, would be to be cynical about all the serious and sustained efforts that have been made to generate a sense of humankind's shared destiny. Because material globalization has not produced an internal globalization, it is too easy to be fatalistic and to say that people of the world can never be united spiritually or morally. But that would be a wrong conclusion. If nothing else, the September 11 attack would seem to have demonstrated that there did indeed exist a sense of common humanity. The virtually universal expression of outrage at the terrorist acts revealed that there was a shared sensibility, a mentality, a vocabulary that united all nations and peoples.

The existence of such a sensibility was no accident. It had been a product of patient efforts by individuals and organizations throughout the twentieth century to develop a global morality for the globalizing age. The century that witnessed barbaric wars, genocide, and terrorist acts was also the century when serious attempts were made to interconnect different peoples and cultures

---

[17]Samuel P. Huntington, *The Clash of Civilizations and the Remaking of World Order* (New York, 1996); Benjamin R. Barber, *Jihad Vs. McWorld* (New York, 1995).

in order to overcome mistrust and fear among them. What I have called "cultural internationalism" was one such attempt. Beginning in the late nineteenth century, but particularly after the Great War, artists, educators, and intellectuals in all parts of the world dedicated themselves to organizing conferences, exhibits, and exchange programs in order to promote cross-national interchange and cooperation. The spirit of cultural internationalism was best expressed by a group of European and American intellectuals who issued a manifesto on intellectual freedom in 1919. They would honor only one truth, the manifesto declared, "free, without frontiers, without limits, without prejudices of race or caste". Such a cosmopolitan vision, the manifesto's signers believed, was needed so as not to revert to the kind of nationalistic emotions that had been so rampant during the war. They wanted to unite, not divide, the world, and programs of cultural internationalism on the solid foundation of intellectual freedom seemed to be the answer.[18] Lest such a vision should seem too elitist, one should note that the League of Nations undertook many programs, through its Committee on Intellectual Cooperation, that encouraged exchange programs at the mass level. The idea behind these activities was always the same, that through them individuals from various parts of the world would come into peaceful contact with one another and develop a sense of shared civilization and a commitment to an interdependent world.

The vision survived the catastrophic decade of the 1930s and the Second World War, and it underlay the founding of UNESCO. Under its auspices, cultural internationalism became even more extensively promoted than before the war. UNESCO's fundamental commitment was and remains to the maintenance of dialogue among nations and among civilizations. The dialogue has continued through the decades, even during the height of the Cold War, and, if pessimists and cynics maintain that there is precious little to show for such efforts, we should remind them that there would be even less to show without these efforts. The fact that more people in the world

---

[18]See Iriye, *Cultural Internationalism*, Chap. 2.

today seem to support an ongoing dialogue among civilizations than believing in an inevitable clash of civilizations indicates that the cultural internationalist movement has indeed affected the hearts and minds of people. To the extent that cross-civilizational dialogue is accepted as a necessary condition for a peaceful world, even if such dialogue has not always prevented clashes, globalization may be said to have been provided with some spiritual underpinnings.

The Role of International Organizations

Besides cultural internationalism, in the recent decades many other movements have served to generate a sense of common humanity. Good examples are humanitarian relief, developmental assistance, and environmentalism. They are all issues whose importance transcends national and cultural boundaries, and for this reason they have been conducive to international cooperation and transnational movements. Many of these movements have been discussed by other papers at this conference, so I shall not dwell on their very important roles in developing a vision of global community, except to note that dealing with such transnational issues has provided one way of integrating postcolonial states into the world community. So many new states were created out of former empires after the Second World War that from the beginning there was an immense psychological distance between them and the more well established nations. George Kennan was by no means exceptional when he bluntly stated in 1949 that many non-Western governments represented "states with colored populations [who were] unsteadied by tradition…neurotic products of exotic backgrounds and…racially and socially embittered against the West".[19] This sort of mutual suspiciousness did not bode well for the stability of the postwar world order. How was the international community going to accommodate culturally heterogeneous states with very diverse histories? It is in the context

---

[19] Quoted in Bradley, *Imagining Vietnam and America*, p. 175.

of such a serious situation that the emergence of transnational issues that concerned all nations served to bring them together.

In this connection, I would like to stress the important role played by international organizations, especially of the non-governmental variety, for they took it upon themselves to respond to these global issues without being overly hampered by considerations of individual national interests.[20]

The growth in number and variety of international non-governmental organizations has been among the most impressive developments in the history of the latter half of the twentieth century. A conservative estimate at the end of the century put the figure at over 30,000, a spectacular expansion from what appears to have been the situation a hundred years earlier, where there were only about one hundred of them throughout the world. Although there is debate concerning the roles played by non-governmental organizations in world affairs — and here, I must make it clear that I am not including terrorist groups that clearly do not belong anywhere in the network of peaceful, voluntary associations — at least it seems possible to say that most of them have sought to generate a sense of international solidarity and morality. They have spoken as consciences of humankind in a century when there have been so much fear and misapprehension across and within national boundaries.

In 1897 H. G. Wells called for the establishment of an international code of conduct, arguing that "we [are] at the present time on a level of intellectual and moral attainment sufficiently high to permit of the formulation of a moral code...on which educational people can agree".[21] The moral code he was talking about included, but also went much beyond, the system of international laws and agreements that had been in existence for centuries in the West and

---

[20] For a fuller study, see Akira Iriye, *Global Community: The Role of International Organizations in the Making of the Contemporary World* (Berkeley, 2002).

[21] Quoted in Margaret E. Keck and Kathryn Sikkink, *Activists beyond Borders: Advocacy Networks in International Politics* (Ithaca, 1998), p. 83.

that had, in the second half of the nineteenth century, begun to embrace non-Western countries as well. Wells was more ambitious and was envisioning the development of ethical codes that would bind not just sovereign states but on which all "educational people" could agree. As education spread, and he was confident that it would steadily do so, there would in time emerge an international morality as the foundation of the global community.

It would not be too far-fetched to say that throughout the twentieth century, while states, tribes, and other groups fought against one another, international non-governmental organizations provided the institutional framework where "educational people" from all countries came together to promote the cause of international morality. In human rights, in environmental protection, and in many other ways, non-governmental organizations functioned as voices of reason, as consciences of humanity. And nowhere were their activities more persistent than in the search for peace. From the very beginning, peace-oriented international non-governmental organizations pitted themselves against war, armaments, and violence. Although they were powerless to prevent the coming of war either in 1914 or 1939, they were not discouraged but redoubled their efforts even during the world wars to prepare for a just and lasting peace. The role played by such organizations in the founding of the League of Nations and of the United Nations is very well recognized. During the long Cold War and in its immediate aftermath, many non-governmental organizations sought to steer the world away from military confrontation toward a peaceful accommodation. Their activities ranged from the Pugwash Conferences' call for nuclear disarmament, or the International Campaign To Ban Landmines' movement to remove these destructive weapons, to the people-to-people exchange programs undertaken by the American Friends Service Committee across the Iron Curtain, from Amnesty International's advocacy of the rights of prison inmates to Doctors Without Borders' humanitarian endeavors for victims of war, famine, and natural disasters. And it is a genuine pleasure to recognize the important contributions that these organizations, all recipients of the Nobel Peace Prize, have made toward developing global community, a community of shared interests and standards. Have they not contributed to the development of the international morality that Wells had called for?

Non-governmental organizations are by definition non-state actors, consisting of individuals who voluntarily come together to carry out common enterprises, whether they are humanitarian relief, cultural exchange, disarmament, or environmental protection. The fact that millions of individuals worldwide have joined them as officers, staff, or donors suggests that there is indeed a shared conscience, an international morality. We need to look no further for evidence of internalized common norms that provide spiritual underpinnings for globalization.

In the middle of the Vietnam War, a small number of non-governmental organizations, from Europe, North America, and Japan, were involved in relief work in the war-devastated country. Among the most conspicuous was Church World Service, the philanthropic organ of the Protestant denominations in the United States, that took the initiative to establish a separate Vietnam Christian Service to help Vietnamese refugees who numbered over a million by the mid-1960s. The leaders of this organization pointed out that the war in Vietnam "symbolizes the military mentality and the military dominance in our world. The resulting forces of hate and fear are real in the lives of the people here". It was all the more important, therefore, to "remind the nations that there is another kind of power, another way for men to relate to each other, another kingdom which transcends national and racial lines".[22] This was exactly the language of international morality and cross-national understanding that was combating international and interracial fears.

Conclusions

I have suggested that the twentieth century was a century of increasing globalization but that material globalization was not always

---

[22]Alice and Winifred Beechy, *Vietnam: Who Cares?* (Scottdale, Penn., 1968), pp. 19–20.

accompanied by spiritual globalization. The gap between the physical and mental aspects of a technologically interconnected world was often extremely huge, giving rise to misunderstanding and fear among different nations, cultures, and peoples. At the same time, serious efforts were made, by individuals and organizations of all countries and regions of the world, to fill the gap and to generate a sense of common humanity. It is to these individuals and organizations that we need to pay tribute even as we recount innumerable instances of misunderstanding and hostility among nations and people. For ultimately it is the individual heart that counts. Today there are six billion hearts that are beating, and if some hearts are filled with hatred and animosity, many more are yearning for peace and understanding.

How can we encourage these hearts and link them together in the spirit of common humanity? Can the world's religions help? Of course, they can, but so can the universities, schools, civic associations, and local communities. Will they be able to develop a common vocabulary, a shared memory, to humanize the process of globalization so that the world will become spiritually as well as physically interconnected? A conference such as this one provides an excellent opportunity to consider this, one of the most urgent questions facing the world today.

Geir Lundestad

The Nobel Peace Prize in Its Next Century: Old and New Dimensions

The Past and the Future

It is impossible to predict the course of the Nobel Peace Prize in the next 100 years. The records of even the most prominent historians in making predictions about the future are not very good. We historians should probably stick to what we do best, making predictions about the past. Yet, for what it is worth, here are some tentative remarks about the future, remarks that may have some relevance for the near-term future, much less for the longer term.

Since the first Nobel Peace Prize was awarded exactly 100 years ago, the world has undergone tremendous change. Still, most of the challenges that have faced the Nobel Peace Prize in its first 100 years, remain. Wars between states have become less frequent in recent decades. So, hopefully, at least a global war of the First World War, Second World War, and even a conflict of the Cold War type may have become obsolescent. Yet, the danger of war involving at least some major powers is probably not over; wars within states are still frequent on several continents. Arms control and disarmament may have made temporary progress throughout the 20th century, but with weapons of mass destruction still proliferating and arms reductions in some parts of the world being complemented with

build-ups in other parts, the basic challenge remains. In spurts
democracy has spread to ever new parts of the globe, but even today
almost half the world's population does not experience its benefits.
The economic growth of the 20th century has been truly spectacular
and ever new parts of the world have been able to lead a substantially
better material life, but with the world's population growing rapidly
the number of poor people has also grown correspondingly.

Thus, in my somewhat unimaginative opinion, while the technical-
economic world is likely to change beyond recognition in the coming
decades, not to mention the next century, the moral-political problems
which the Nobel Peace Prize has been grappling with for 100 years,
are likely to remain with us.

Then, there are the many new dimensions that the Peace Prize
will also have to address in some form or other: the environmental
challenge, the role of media and communications, the "fragmegration"
of the world, i.e. the curious combination of globalization in the
form of a rapidly shrinking world and fragmentation in the form of
an equally rapid increase in the number of state and non-state actors
on the world stage.

A Better Organized and More Peaceful World

If there is one thing the Norwegian Nobel Committee has tried to
achieve in the preceding 100 years, this must be what we might
call a better organized world. The Nobel Committee's ideals have
been those of Western liberal internationalism in the form of effective
global institutions with universal, and preferably democratic
representation. This international impulse was strengthened by the
Norwegian and Scandinavian faith in organizing one's way out of
conflict and by the Nobel Committee's obvious interest in anything
that could produce a more peaceful world. (It was hampered by the
remnants of a Norwegian isolationism which had striking similarities
with the American version. Norway, like the United States, was to
stay out of Great Power conflicts to protect its sovereignty and its
uniqueness.) While superficially the realist argument that international
cooperation can be no more than the sum of various national

interests has been accepted, in reality there has been considerable confidence that international cooperation will indeed temper and modify this national interest.

In the years before the First World War almost all the Nobel peace prizes went to persons and organizations associated with the Interparliamentary Union, the International Peace Bureau or with the promotion of international law. (The only two exceptions were the humanitarian prize to Henry Dunant in 1901 and the Realpolitik prize to Theodore Roosevelt in 1906.) This was the "holding and promotion of peace congresses" referred to in Alfred Nobel's will as one of the three criteria for awarding the prize. In the more pluralistic inter-war period many prizes went to persons and organizations associated with the League of Nations while in the even more pluralist years after the Second World War the emphasis on persons and organizations working for and with the United Nations has been quite pronounced. Thus, most appropriately, in 2001, in the very year of its centennial, the Nobel Peace Prize was finally awarded to the United Nations as such and to its Secretary-General Kofi Annan.

In the 20th century the world advanced from the rather ineffective state of the Interparliamentary Union and the loosely organized peace groups in North America and Western Europe to a potentially very powerful United Nations with government representation from 189 countries. After the end of the Cold War the UN is at long last beginning to realize some of its potential. Global interdependence will require stronger global institutions. In the next century the question of how to achieve this better organized and more peaceful world will again come up in many different versions. I would venture the guess that even in the new century the desire to strengthen this process will be the single most important line of development for the Norwegian Nobel Committee.

One set of questions will deal with the organization of the United Nations. The domination of the Security Council by the Great Powers will again be debated, but it seems doubtful that these powers will agree to any substantial diminution of their domination, or sovereignty for that matter. There is an obvious need to look again at who the permanent members of the Security Council are, but will a widened membership make it more or less difficult for the Council to act? And who does the UN really represent? If the UN were to be dominated by authoritarian governments, democracies would rapidly lose interest in its strengthening. This logic will of course work the other way as well.

What would actually constitute a more democratic system at the global level? It is difficult to imagine that the UN, or any other global organization, would move very far down the road towards one person one vote. At the world level that could easily mean the domination of China, India, and a few other very populous countries. In stable democracies the minority is willing to accept the decisions of the majority, but this implies a common frame of loyalty that clearly does not yet exist at the global level. In the EU we see how difficult the transition from national to regional is. We can only imagine how much more difficult it will be to the global level.

Very difficult is also the role of International Non-Governmental Organizations (INGOs). They represent some form of global consciousness or civil society that most of us will consider positive. The Nobel Committee has already given prizes to groups such as Amnesty and the International Campaign to Ban Landmines (ICBL). But who elected the INGOs? Who are they accountable to? What should be the balance between the United Nations, regional and national governments, and INGOs?

Just raising such questions illustrates how far we have to go in the debate on how to develop a more effective form of global governance than we have today. Michael Doyle has argued, in terms of democratic evolution on the global level, that the situation today "represents much less than a modern equivalent of the English barons at Runnymede in 1215, a cautious consultation far short of accountability". That seems to me too pessimistic. Much has actually been achieved. More needs to be done, however, much more. The Norwegian Nobel Committee will undoubtedly want to promote the emergence of a global consciousness and of effective global institutions.

After the Second World War the United Nations was generally built on the principles of state sovereignty and non-intervention, although there was an obvious tension between this and the Universal Declaration of Human Rights which the members had to declare their support for. The inaction of the UN in the terrible killings in Rwanda in 1994–95 illustrates the price that can sometimes be paid for *not* intervening in a country's internal affairs. "Humanitarian intervention" is a controversial concept. To the extent that it represents an extension of the centuries-old discussion of "just war", it may not be very revolutionary in theory, but it certainly is in practice. While there will inevitably be support for intervening against regimes killing substantial numbers of their own population, much will depend on who will do the intervening and what resistance they are going to meet. Obviously, the wider the mandate and the smaller the resistance the greater the support for such intervention.

Most of us tend to agree that non-intervention was a mistake in Rwanda. Yet, interventions quickly become quite controversial, and not only the unilateral interventions of the Great Powers. No one can be sure what the costs of intervention would have been in Rwanda. The failed UN intervention in Somalia immediately before Rwanda provides an explanation for the lack of action in Rwanda and illustrates how quickly interventions with even the best of motives can go sour. The lessons of NATO's bombing against Serbia in the spring of 1999 and the US-UK bombing of Afghanistan in the fall of 2001, both of them initially meeting with broad international sympathy, but neither explicitly mandated by the UN, are mixed and the final verdict will do much to shape our attitudes to this kind of more forceful intervention. Yet, again, while shying away from such controversial interventions, on the over-all point the Norwegian Nobel Committee will most likely want to strengthen the emerging emphasis on "human security", the protection of people, rather than the political and territorial integrity of states.

One main dimension in this respect will be the legal one. The UN tribunals for the former Yugoslavia and for Rwanda have represented early, but only partly successful efforts to strengthen international law. Soon the UN will move from this ad hoc basis and to a more general and permanent arrangement. When this happens, in the form of the International Criminal Court, this too is bound to attract the sympathetic interest of the Norwegian Nobel Committee.

So far the increased contact across national borders has led to a strengthening primarily of regional organizations and only secondarily of global ones. The emphasis will probably continue for some time to be on the regional level. Regional cooperation may supplement the global effort, but it may also lead to conflict among regions in the form of trade and monetary strife. In most countries there is likely to be more support for intervention from regional neighbors and than from traditional Great Powers. Yet, there is a downside to this regional emphasis. Thus, "African solutions for African problems" can easily lead to the developed world washing its hands entirely of Africa's many very substantial problems.

The Norwegian Nobel Committee has clearly favored global over regional cooperation. In fact, while in the inter-war years the Committee gave several awards to persons working for French-German reconciliation, no award has been given related to European integration after the Second World War. (With a partial exception for the prize to Willy Brandt, although that was given primarily for his *Ostpolitik*.) It is rather obvious that European integration has promoted peace among the members, particularly between Germany and France. The lack of a Peace Prize in this case is explained in part by the lack of a definite person or institution to give the award to, but primarily by the division inside Norway on the question of membership in the European Union. While Norwegian values have in most cases been very beneficial in a prize-awarding context, it would seem rather obvious that they have been negative in the case of giving the European Union its due. It is to be hoped that this kind of Norwegian provincialism will play less of a role in the future.

Human Rights in a New Century

More and more the Norwegian Nobel Committee has come to believe that a democratic world is a more peaceful world. This was the basis for the Committee's rapidly increasing number of human rights awards since the 1960s. The peace of authoritarian suppression can only be temporary. A truly peaceful world has to be a democratic one.

Democracy has made great strides in the previous century. From the mid-19th century until the First World War democracy was established in North America and in Western Europe. In the inter-war period fascism and communism threatened to reverse what had been achieved. In 1942 only 12 countries in the world had democratic governments. The second wave of democracy then took place in the years from 1945 to the 1960s. In this period the colonial empires were dismantled and in some of the new countries democracy was established, most spectacularly in India. In the late 1970s and particularly after the end of the Cold War and the fall of the Soviet Union, various forms of more or less democratic rule was established in Russia, Eastern and Central Europe, in Latin America, important parts of Asia, and even in certain countries in Africa.

Since still almost half the world's population is living under more or less authoritarian rule, the Committee will undoubtedly continue to focus on democracy and human rights. China will be the most burning question, since it alone has almost half of the population under such rule. The Nobel Committee prides itself on speaking out against Hitler through the Ossietzky award and against the Soviet Union through the Sakharov and Walesa awards. Sooner rather than later the Committee should speak out also against the regime in Beijing, despite the improvements that have been made in recent decades. The 1989 award to the Dalai Lama did of course have something to do with China after Tienanmen, but it also had other dimensions. In China it is very difficult for dissidents to become known; once they are expelled to the West, they tend to lose support even inside the dissident community. The award in 2000 to Kim Dae-jung represented the Committee's rejection of the Asian values argument, in the sense that it sees human rights as truly global and not as something reserved for the Western world. While democracy comes in many shapes and forms and always has to be adapted to local cultures, the Asian rulers who most strongly proclaim "Asian values" rarely consult their people on how they see the question.

(And Asia is of course much too large and diverse for one common set of such values to make much sense anyway.)

During the Cold War the Western countries emphasized political and civil rights, the Communist side economic and social ones. Now, after the Cold War, Western human rights organizations are broadening their focus more and more to take in also the latter. This raises difficult questions about what governments can do and not do. Obviously it is much simpler to refrain from torture than it is to provide a meal and a job for everybody. The Norwegian Nobel Committee will also have to deal with these difficult issues. Yet, this is probably going to be among the easier debates in that the Committee has already included economic and social rights within its definition of peace. The prizes to Jouhaux and ILO are the most clear-cut examples.

In this age of globalization there are also strong forces of fragmentation. Many feel a need to define their identity anew; nationalist, ethnic, and religious messages are easily spread in this new age, and the international economy makes geographical size largely irrelevant for a country's degree of development. Thus, it is probably no coincidence that religious fundamentalism has been on the rise within virtually all major religions and that ethnic conflict has also become more pronounced in recent decades. On the latter point, however, ethnic-national conflict is nothing new. It was just labeled differently during the Cold War. Cp. the national conflicts in Korea, Vietnam, and Cambodia, ethnic conflicts in Angola and Afghanistan in addition to in Nigeria, Sudan, Pakistan/Bangladesh. Evidence actually indicates a slight falling off in ethnic conflict from mid 1990s.

Religious fundamentalism has been strong recently, but probably does not lead to more or less permanent "clashes of civilization". For that developments across civilizations, on the one hand, and divisions within civilizations, on the other, are too pronounced. The "war against terrorism" is not a war against Islam, but against certain groups within Islam. If it does become the former, it will probably be lost already. The Norwegian Nobel Committee has already honored religious leaders of ecumenical and moderate persuasions (Søderblom,

Mott, the Dalai Lama), and it will probably continue to look for religious and other moderate leaders, in fact anyone that can serve to break up the stereotyping of other religions. Obviously there is a particular need to look for such voices within Islam where an image of extremism has been spreading in developed countries. Unfortunately, there is also an element of reality to go with such images. Within Islam there is yet no full-fledged democracy. The Nobel Committee will most likely want to encourage dialogue across religious divisions and to promote the democratic experiments that we see in certain countries where Islam dominates (Turkey, Jordan, Indonesia, Bahrain, etc.).

On the ethnic-national side, however, with ever new "nations" wanting their own states, it seems likely that such conflict will continue. In 1945 the UN had 51 members, today it has 189. It has been estimated that there are 3 500 "nations" in the world — the number seems rather on the low side. In only about half of the world's states does a single ethnic group comprise at least 75% of the population. If most of these nations are to have their own state, then the process has just started.

While the Nobel Committee has strongly promoted reconciliation between conflicting parties (in the Middle East, in South Africa, in Northern Ireland), it has also sided with ethnic minorities in their claims for autonomy or even independence (Tibet, East Timor.) Many such questions are likely to come before the Nobel Committee in future years, and the balance between promoting reconciliation and simply supporting one side in a conflict will probably become even more difficult than it has already been.

The Humanitarian Challenge

From its very first award in 1901 to Henry Dunant, the Norwegian Nobel Committee has made the humanitarian challenge part of its struggle for peace. A long series of humanitarian individuals and organizations have received the prize. One might argue that the relationship between humanitarianism and peace is far from clear. Even at the first award to Dunant some asked what humanitarians did to avert wars as opposed to alleviating the effects of war once it had broken out. Obviously the Committee has seen this differently. When despair is near, as during a war or when starvation threatens, the simple humanitarian act may show that there is hope, that a brotherhood of men based on certain minimum standards of decency still exists. This must indeed be "the fraternity between nations" Nobel referred to in his will.

The humanitarian challenge will be even larger in the years ahead than it has been in the past. While ever new countries are experiencing economic growth and the percentage of the world's population that is poor may actually be falling, the absolute number of poor people may be increasing. This is in great part due to the rapid increase in population in the poorest countries of the world. *The Human Development Report 2001* informs us that around 1.2 billion people live on less than one dollar a day and 2.8 billion on less than two dollars a day (based on purchasing power parity), although in percentage terms this represents a reduction from 29% of the world's population in 1990 to 24% in 1998. While a child can expect to live eight years longer than 30 years ago, many more people can read and write, and the share of families with access to safe drinking water has grown dramatically, of the 4.6 billion people in developing countries, more than 850 million are still illiterate and nearly a billion lack access to improved water resources. East Asia and the Pacific have made dramatic progress in most areas, but South Asia and Sub-Saharan Africa lag far behind other regions. The adult literacy rate in South Asia is still only 55% and in Sub-Saharan Africa 60%, well below the developing country average of 73%.

Discrimination against women is still prevalent. In many developing countries, particularly in India, male literacy rates are at least 15 percentage points higher than female rates. Female mortality rates are also much higher that male rates. In fact, although slightly more females are born and women in most parts of the world tend to live longer, there are still more men than women in the world. The discrepancy is explained by the treatment of girls and women particularly in India and China.

Among the new challenges in this very old picture of poverty, the spread of HIV/AIDS is most dramatic. At the end of 2000 about 36 million people were living with the disease — 95% of them in developing countries and 70% in Sub-Saharan Africa.

On this basis it seems rather obvious that the Nobel Committee will continue to award prizes to humanitarian persons and organizations. Despite the controversies of modern biotechnology, it might even continue to honor the scientists who work to reduce poverty in the world, in the tradition of Boyd Orr and Borlaug. It will also keep looking for women candidates, so that the Committee's not very distinguished record of 10 women among 109 laureates may be improved. (20 of the 109 are organizations.) I would guess that at least some of these women will be found in those parts of the world where women are particularly exploited.

It is more difficult to know what the Committee will do about globalization. On the one hand, the free trade leading to peace argument is an old one and it definitely seems to be strengthened by the findings of modern political science. There also seems to be little doubt that globalization has indeed improved the living standards of most of the world's population. That is why more and more developing countries are so eager to participate in the World Trade Organization and other globalist institutions. An award along these lines would not be without precedent, as the prize to Norman Angell in 1933 and perhaps also to Cordell Hull in 1945 illustrate. On the other hand, globalization is increasingly controversial in many developed countries and it does seem to widen many inequalities in the global economy. Some benefit much more from globalization than others. Some even suffer from the process. I would not be surprised if the Committee will honor even this side of the globalization argument.

"Reduction of Standing Armies"

While the point in Alfred Nobel's will about awarding the prize to those who have worked for "fraternity between nations" has remained rather vague and the one about the "holding of peace congresses" has become rather dated, the third one, about honoring those who work for "the reduction of standing armies", still has a rather obvious relevance. In this, and in his basic decision to include the peace prize among his prizes, Nobel actually went against other beliefs he held, for instance his expectation that his own invention of dynamite might do more to prevent war than would his friend Bertha von Suttner's work for disarmament and peace. In repeatedly honoring the champions of disarmament, the Norwegian Nobel Committee has been loyal to Nobel's will. It has rarely, if ever, honored the champions of Nobel's more private deterrence ideas.

After the end of the Cold War many expected the work for arms control and disarmament to speed up considerably. In some respects it has. START I and II will bring the number of strategic nuclear weapons down. There is even tentative agreement between the United States and Russia to bring this number down to 2,500 on each side by 2007. Ukraine, Belarus, and Kazakhstan have actually given up the nuclear weapons they inherited as part of the Soviet legacy, and South Africa has also closed down its nuclear option. Defense budgets in Western and Eastern Europe in particular have declined considerably. The Warsaw pact has been abolished while NATO's functions have been modified.

On the other hand, the total number of nuclear weapons in the world is still shockingly high, about 30,000. India and Pakistan have become new members of the nuclear club. The United States is planning to develop a missile defense that may destroy one of the cornerstones of modern arms control diplomacy, the ABM treaty of 1972. Other kinds of weapons of mass destruction are being developed by an increasing number of countries. The defense budget is rising again in the United States. Especially the countries of the Middle East and East Asia are once again buying large quantities of new weapons. The fight against international terrorism will certainly increase defense spending in many countries.

The Nobel Committee has repeatedly returned to the theme of reducing the importance of nuclear weapons in international relations (the awards to Noel Baker, Pauling, Sato, Myrdal/Robles, International

Physicians for the Prevention of Nuclear War (IPPNW), Rotblat/ Pugwash). The need to return to this theme so often underlines the limited success both the champions of disarmament and the Nobel Committee have had through these awards, even after the end of the Cold War, when the hopes have been so much higher than before. This, however, gives no reason to believe that the Committee will not continue to stress the work for disarmament. But perhaps the 1997 award to Jody Williams and ICBL will start a trend towards focusing also on other weapons than simply nuclear ones. On the arms side, the threats to the citizens of the world are indeed many and varied.

New Dimensions to the Peace Prize

What then of entirely new dimensions of the Nobel Peace Prize? Within the Nobel family there is agreement that no new Nobel prizes should be added to the existing ones. Some even feel that the addition of the memorial prize in economics in 1969 was a mistake. One should remain true to the will of Alfred Nobel and make no effort to cover all fields of possible interest. Other prizes will have to do that. On the other hand, this conclusion will undoubtedly strengthen the desire to see what can be done to address new concerns through the existing Nobel prizes.

The environment is clearly the most obvious new field of interest in this context. It is not as evident as many seem to think that there is a close connection between the state of the environment and peace. After all, the developed states have experienced polluted air and rivers without this having had any striking effects on social conflict, let alone relations between countries. The quality of the air and the rivers was also repaired surprisingly quickly once the decision was made to do so. Global warming may be an important phenomenon, but generally the effects would appear to be so slow in developing and so multi-faceted that it is not obvious that this will lead to international conflict. Even international environmental problems may be remedied, as the 1987 Montreal Protocol on ozone-depleting substances shows. It must also be added that some of the

effects predicted by environmentalists have not developed at all, at
least not yet. One thinks of all the warnings from Thomas Malthus
in 1798 about population outrunning food supplies to the Club
of Rome's *Limits to Growth* in 1972 that saw the world as running
out of many of its basic resources, particularly energy. Had this
happened, the price of food, oil, and raw materials in general would
have increased sharply. Disappointingly for many developing countries
in particular, this has not happened. As late as in the 1970s there
was even a lot of talk about global *cooling*.

Yet, links do exist between the environment and peace. It can
safely be predicted that it is only a question of time before the first
Nobel Peace Prize having to do with the environment will be
awarded. The world's demography is crucial in this context. World
population reached 1 billion in 1825, doubled to 2 billion in 1925,
to 4 billion in 1975, and in 2000 passed 6 billion. Guesstimates
suggest that it will reach 8 billion in 2025 and might then stabilize
only after having reached 9–10 billion; 95% of the growth is likely
to be in the poor countries of the South. This increase is bound to
strain basic resources, sooner or later. Of all basic necessities, water
is the one most likely to be affected by population growth. Some
crucial water systems are found in arid or semi-arid countries and
are shared by two or more countries. These would include large
river systems such as the Nile (shared by Egypt, Ethiopia, and Sudan,
among others), the Jordan (shared by Israel, Jordan, Lebanon, and
Syria), the Tigris and Euphrates (shared by Iran, Iraq, Syria, and Turkey),
the Indus (shared by Afghanistan, India, and Pakistan), and the Amu
Darya (shared by Tajikistan, Turkmenistan, and Uzbekistan).

Four-fifths of the world's known petroleum reserves are located
in politically unstable and contested areas, such as the Persian Gulf,
the Caspian Sea basin, and the South China Sea, along with Algeria,
Angola, Chad, Colombia, Indonesia, Nigeria, Sudan, and even Venezuela.
The lack of delimitation of territorial waters, for instance in the
South China Sea with seven states claiming all or part of the area, is
a source of great concern. Norwegians remember disputes over
fishing rights. More and more of the wars of Africa seem to be related
to rival groups' claims to local gems and minerals.

The consensus among scientists is now firmly on the side of global warming actually taking place. Leading experts have estimated that the global average temperature would increase by 1.5 to 6 degrees Celsius in this century, significantly more than the 1 to 3 degrees estimated only five years ago. At the local level, destabilization could quickly follow in the wake of a flooding that would affect millions of people, for instance of substantial parts of Bangladesh. Local ecocides, due to deforestation or desertification, would have similar effects.

The importance of the media would also seem to be of relevance to the Nobel Committee. In fact, two authors (Bertha von Suttner and Elie Wiesel) and two journalists (Alfred Fried and Angell) have already been honored with the Peace Prize. This was, however, primarily for their messages, not for their jobs as such. Similar awards could of course take place in the future as well, but may be even accuracy in reporting should be recognized. No one would dispute the importance of factual reports as opposed to the exaggerations and bias that so often encourage conflict and even war. In the past BBC would have been an obvious candidate in this field. Now there are many, but less obvious candidates.

Scientists dealing with the world's food situation have already been recognized through the Peace Prize. What about even other types of scientists? Many scientists have been honored, but in most cases not primarily for their contributions as scientists, but for other things: Physicians (Schweitzer, IPPNW, MSF), physicists (Sakharov and Rotblat), historians (Quidde received the prize in 1927), theologians (Schweitzer belongs even here), philosophers (in the past one would be thinking of Kant), possibly even political scientists (Kissinger) have already demonstrated their relevance. Other fields may well be added. The importance of science can only be growing.

What about peace researchers? No one should be excluded, but its relevance for peace has not been as striking as one could have hoped. At the moment the field is in considerable disarray, with the focus being more on specific disciplines than on peace research as such. A most central insight, i.e. that democracies tend to be more peaceful than dictatorships, especially towards other democracies, has been more or less assumed by most Western politicians long before this became the consensus among political scientists. (One thinks of how disputed such a finding was among scholars in the polarized atmosphere of the Cold War.)

In fact, only the imagination sets limits to the kind of peace laureates one could imagine in the future. Pop stars would not appear to be a very likely category. Nevertheless, pop stars may have great powers of persuasion and some of them have already used these powers in support of peace-relevant causes (Geldoff, Bono, Sting). If the Nobel Committee became more concerned about the criticism that it honors only white (less and less true), old (there have been at least four laureates in their mid-30s), males (also less true than it used to be), then it could perhaps be persuaded to enter the world of pop politics, although the three names mentioned would not appear to add that much in these three respects. It would introduce the Nobel Peace Prize to groups that so far have been only marginally interested in the work for peace. If the Nobel Committee really wants to go this route, may be even this could be seen as falling under Nobel's rubric of promoting "fraternity between nations".

Conclusions

In its first 100 years the Nobel Peace Prize reflected the ideas of western liberal internationalism, as perceived by five Norwegian committee members. Norway's foreign policy orientation combined realism and idealism. These elements are not easily combined in a country's foreign policy. Hard-headed security concerns may easily conflict with the desire to bring about a more just world. In that respect it was easier for the Norwegian Nobel Committee. It stressed the idealist side over the realist one. This was probably the way Nobel wanted it, despite his differences with the contemporary peace movement. Some of the Nobel Committee's forays into realism (Theodore Roosevelt, Kissinger/Le Duc Tho, Sadat/Begin, Arafat/Peres/ Rabin) have been very controversial and led to a lot of criticism of the committee. There is much to be said for the utopians of the world. So often it has even turned out that the utopians were the realists. Realism often becomes cynicism.

Yet, realists of the kind mentioned have also attempted to move the world forward by supporting peace agreements of a more hard-headed kind. Their deals may sometimes bring peace to war-torn regions of the world. They, more than the idealists, sometimes put their political, and even their personal lives on the line. What the role of realism will be in the next century will to some extent depend on the political balance on the Nobel committee. Those on the left have more sympathy for liberalism and justice, those on the right for realism and stability. In the 21st century we will undoubtedly want both stability and justice. In the turbulence of the new century it is far from clear that we can have both.

One may safely conclude that in the next 100 years the Nobel Peace Prize will be even more pluralist in its orientation than it was in its first 100 years. It took much too long for the prize to become truly global, but there can be no doubt that in the next century it will increase its geographical diversity even more. Other kinds of diversity will surely also increase, as I have suggested in this essay. Our imaginations are just too limited to predict what the world will really be like in the next 100 years. The safest prediction is probably that we will be in for many surprises in the next century of Nobel peace prizes.

Index